More praise for
The Civil War Notebooks of Daniel Chisholm

The Civil War Notebook of Daniel Chisholm

A Chronicle of Daily Life in the Union Army 1864–1865

Edited by
W. Springer Menge and J. August Shimrak

Ballantine Books • New York

Library of Congress Catalog Card Number: 89-92610

ISBN: 0-345-36571-2

This edition published by arrangement with Orion Books,
a member of The Crown Publishing Group.
Cover design by William Geller
The Battle of Cold Harbor, Virginia, 1-12 June 1864.
Lithograph, 1888 by Kurz and Allison (The Granger Collection)

Manufactured in the United States of America

First Ballantine Books Edition: September 1990

10 9 8 7 6 5 4 3

Contents

★ EDITORS' NOTE ★

Daniel Chisholm, upon returning to his family home in Uniontown, Pennsylvania, after his service in the Army of the Potomac, had the foresight to preserve a personal chronicle of the Civil War.

Chisholm enlisted in the Union Army in February 1864 along with several young men from Uniontown, many of whom served in the same company, including his brother Alex and also Samuel A. Clear. After the war ended, Chisholm transcribed Samuel Clear's diary into a notebook. He also collected and transcribed his own letters home, along with several excerpts from brother Alex's letters. In the back of the notebook, Chisholm transcribed and compiled various lists pertaining to his company and a section of the diary of a prisoner of war. Either Daniel Chisholm or someone else made entries and comments into the diary into the early twentieth century (Daniel Chisholm died in 1914).

We do not know why, or under what circumstances, Daniel Chisholm came to transcribe Samuel Clear's diary. Since there is no one still alive to ask, we must take the notebook at face value. One possible consideration is that Chisholm was wounded in June 1864 and spent more than six months in various hospitals, and even after he was released from the hospital he was not fit for frontline duty. Clear's diary maintains the company's narrative during this time.

Readers will find inconsistencies in the diary. For example, some of the lists at the back have contradictory or incomplete information. Once again, since there is no one to query, we present the material as Daniel Chisholm wrote it.

Chisholm transcribed the diary onto the left-hand pages of his notebook and his letters onto the right-hand pages, but there was not a precise matchup of the dates. For the sake of readability, we have chosen to present the diary first, followed by the letters. The various lists and other material that Chisholm placed at the back of the notebook are here also included at the end as an appendix.

In his transcription, Chisholm used an eccentric punctuation style. Specifically, he wrote very long run-on sentences punctuated by commas. These run-on sentences contained many independent, and often unrelated, phrases. These sentences can be rather confusing. For the sake of readability and clarity, we have separated these sentences with periods and also started the new sentences with capital letters.

Chisholm's grammar and spelling have been left alone. The words are presented here as he wrote them down. Luckily, Daniel Chisholm's handwriting is consistently legible and there were only a few instances of having to guess at what he wrote, although we did also occasionally have to guess at what he meant. We have used brackets to indicate those words that were not legible or where we suggest a guess at his meaning, or any other editorial intrusion.

We would especially like to thank and acknowledge the contributions of the following individuals: Sarah Chisholm Springer, whose love and devotion to family made this all possible; Peter Miller, for his knowledge and persistence; Peter E. Shimrak, for his genuine interest and support; and, of course, Johnny Lyons.

⋆ *INTRODUCTION* ⋆

I

It was the custom and it was the rule. When the men of the 116th Pennsylvania rose in the morning, they were assembled for roll call. In Company K, the chore of shouting out the names of the soldiers present for duty often fell to Sergeant Samuel Clear.

On Friday morning, December 16, 1864, behind the cold, wet Union siege trenches surrounding Petersburg, Virginia, the men of Company K woke expecting to follow their daily routine. But after roll call and breakfast, officers called them together to perform an unusual duty. On this day they would not take a turn in the "ditches," sniping at Confederates across the way. They would not go on picket, probing enemy fronts and flanks. They would not go on fatigue, cleaning up their camp, building defenses, chopping wood.

On this day — while their wives and sisters at home baked breads and cakes, while their children practiced singing Christmas carols, while their faraway friends stood in warm taverns drinking toasts to the holiday season — the men of Company K would be marched off through the raw December breeze to witness a hanging.

Sergeant Clear described this day in his diary: the half-mile hike to the gallows; troops jeering the three deserters who were about to die; how the executioner bungled his job. Then he concluded his diary entry with this remark: "And off we go, I think no more of it until we get our dinners, as that is the next thing on the program."

The sergeant's words were hard, disinterested. They made him appear unmoved by tragedy. He reread them in the postwar years and perhaps reconsidered them. In the end, however, he allowed them to go unchanged. On that day, in that diary entry, he had chosen his words for coolness and impact, and to record a subtle message: In his ten months of army service he had already seen thousands of dead men. He was no brute. But the Civil War had changed him. It changed everyone who survived it.

Clear's diary and the letters of two men in his outfit, the brothers Alexander and Daniel Chisholm, make up this work. From three different viewpoints, they provide readers with a capsule history of the last fifteen months of the American Civil War in Virginia. They also describe what it was that changed the men of Company K: the incessant marching, the frequent combat, the homesickness, the constant struggles with hunger and disease, and the pursuit of an enemy for whom they bore a grudging respect — the common Confederate soldier.

The men of the company — Captain John Weltner, Lieutenant Zadoc Springer, Sergeant Clear, the Chisholm brothers and their messmates James Collins, Richard McClean, and Tom Williams — were all from Uniontown, a community about 35 miles southeast of Pittsburgh, Pennsylvania. Before setting off for the war, they had farmed or had worked in small mills and other business enterprises. Their lives had revolved around their families and, in a world that ran on steam engines and sweat, just the hard daily business of earning money and getting by.

In late February 1864, these same men all took the step that would either transform their lives forever or end them. A veteran Union officer, Lieutenant Colonel Richard C. Dale, came to western Pennsylvania to recruit three infantry companies for the Army of the Potomac. Dale and his subordinates persuaded several of the hardiest fellows in Uniontown to come into the army, to volunteer for service with the 116th Pennsylvania Regiment.

The reason each man set aside civilian concerns and took up the rough life of a Union infantryman was his own. A few undoubtedly signed on with the 116th out of the purest patriotic motives. Others volunteered for the regiment because the federal and state governments were offering "bounties," payments of hundreds of dollars to any individual who would enlist in the army. Others may have joined to avoid the draft and all the stigmas and embarrassments that came with it (such as convincing other townsmen that it was not cowardly to wait until your country literally called upon you and demanded your services).

In 1861, the war's first year, many Uniontown citizens joined the 85th Pennsylvania Infantry. It was an outfit that saw hard service in Virginia and along the coasts of the Carolinas. These neighbors had already experienced more adventure and hardship than anyone ever could living in a small western Pennsylvania town. This fact may have induced others to join up with the 116th. When moved by strong curiosity, or by envy or guilt or other strong emotions, common men can be compelled to try the extraordinary.

And still others probably joined the 116th because they sensed that the war was near its climax. They wanted to be in on it, to see the finale. They did not want to grow old and explain to their grandchildren that they had willingly passed by an opportunity to witness history and to make it.

Judging from their letters home, Alexander and Daniel Chisholm signed up for the army because of the bounty money. The tone of Samuel Clear's diary suggests he may have gone off to the war for adventure. But none of their writings gives modern readers reason to believe they completely understood the risks they were about to take, or that they knew the 116th Pennsylvania was recruiting new companies because it, and the brigade and corps it belonged to, had already suffered staggering casualties.

The regiment was organized in Philadelphia during the summer of 1862. Between the time of its first muster and the end of the war, 1,661 officers and enlisted men appeared on its rolls. Of that number, 528 were killed or wounded, 61 died of disease, and another 28 died in Confederate prisoner-of-war camps.

The brigade to which the regiment belonged was the most famous in the Union's Army of the Potomac, the Irish Brigade. Membership in that hard-fighting fraternity guaranteed a high casualty rate. At war's end in 1865, brigade records listed 4,000 of its men and officers as killed or wounded. That number was in itself incredible. According to Lieutenant Colonel William F. Fox, a nineteenth-century authority on the records of the Civil War armies, there were never 4,000 soldiers in the entire brigade at any one time. The killed and wounded were replaced by new men, new companies, units like Company K and its troops from Uniontown.

Five regiments made up the Irish Brigade: the 116th Pennsylvania, the 28th Massachusetts, the 88th New York, the 63rd New York, and the "Fighting 69th" New York. Each carried a green Irish battle flag and marched in the 2d Division of the Union army's II Corps. For the first two years of the war, their corps was considered the most reliable in battle. Despite its consistent high losses in combat, commanders believed that its surviving troops were the toughest and most seasoned available. They called on them repeatedly to settle the issue on battlefield after battlefield.

Because of this reputation, as several historians have pointed out, by late 1863 the II Corps was badly used up. But the generals who led the army refused to recognize this fact. When the enlistments of a number of its regiments expired in that year, many of their men were persuaded to reenlist. Replacement troops recruited that winter, strategists believed, would mold themselves around these tough veterans of earlier campaigns and would prove themselves and the II Corps to be just as resilient as ever.

The difference between what the generals expected and what they received was significant. In 1864, they discovered that they were not fielding a hardy corps of savvy combat soldiers. Instead of the old II Corps they had come to rely on, what they had was a small core group of jaded veterans with finely honed survival skills and thousands of "greenhorns." The new men were either reluctant draftees who had to be carefully watched, or they were volunteers like those in the 116th Pennsylvania's Company K, men who had enlisted for a variety of motives and had marched south expecting a completely different sort of war than the one that confronted them.

In 1864, none of the greenhorns was completely naive. Before they were drafted or had enlisted, fellows like Daniel Chisholm or Samuel Clear talked to men who had experienced combat. But neither the veteran soldiers they spoke to nor the officers who led them had had much of an opportunity to stand back and look at how they had come by their combat skills. And few of them could know how much the Civil War would change in its last months.

The recruits of Company K were to experience the warfare of the future, not the conflict the veterans were familiar with. In the recruits' war the body count would serve as a scorecard. Combat would be made all the more miserable because it would be relentless; the troops would come into contact with the enemy nearly every day and never let him go. But they would not march across fields, their banners flapping in the wind, and meet the foe head-on; they would fight it out from behind rocks and trees and breastworks and trenches and wire entanglements and wooden obstructions. In Virginia, they would fight the sort of war the great armies of Europe would come to know in 1914.

II

Most modern readers are familiar with what the Civil War was like at its outset. In July 1861, thousands of patriotic Union and Confederate volunteers, wearing brightly colored parade ground uniforms, met on fields near Manassas, Virginia. There, in what is today suburban Washington, D.C., the soldiers of each army confidently expected to trounce the other.

The war, many believed, would be won for their side in that one battle. Throughout the struggle bands would play sprightly marches. All wounds would be superficial. Every man would conduct himself as a hero should and there would be plenty of glory to go around.

Instead, what the eager Northern and Southern patriots discovered was that this war would be ugly, painful, corrupt, and, for some, even embarrassing.

Confederates would call the July 1861 fight the Battle of Manassas and remember it as a bloody and confusing victory, won only in its last hours when Southern railroads helped deliver reinforcements in a timely fashion. Union soldiers would call it the Battle of Bull Run and remember it as something worse than a defeat.

On this battlefield, the bands did play, for a while. But the wounds were not superficial. Infantry armed with muzzle-loading rifles that fired soft lead Minie bullets discovered that they could inflict horrible damage to a man at a great distance. Gunners found out that their artillery could be used for more than just firing solid iron cannonballs at advancing lines of enemy troops; with crude time fuses, they could lob hollow shells filled with explosives on top of their foes; by loading up their guns with tin cans filled with lead slugs and sawdust they could convert them into enormous shotguns, killing dozens of soldiers with every blast.

Union and Confederate generals, many of them trained at West Point, also quickly came to the realization that each soldier was not conducting himself like a hero on this battlefield. It would take them several months, however, to deduce why.

The officers who led the armies in 1861 had been taught the tactics of Napoleon: Iron-straight lines of stouthearted infantrymen were to advance on the enemy, fire one volley (using inaccurate smooth-bore muskets) into the opposing ranks to disperse them, then carry the field with the bayonet. They failed to understand that advances in nineteenth-century death technology made this approach impractical: At Bull Run, infantrymen could fire an average of three shots per minute with their "modern" rifles and actually hit what they were aiming at; sophisticated artillery could break up attacking formations at a great distance; heavy volumes of black-powder smoke could blanket the battleground, making it more than difficult to see and direct attacks.

When the Southerners' reinforcements arrived at Manassas, inexperienced Union troops had already participated in a full day of uncoordinated attacks and been subjected to a steady rain of Confederate Minie bullets and artillery shells. In very un-Napoleonic fashion, they threw down their gear and ran away.

Union President Abraham Lincoln's administration was mortified by what happened at Bull Run. The Northern public was outraged. But the men who survived this baptism by fire came to understand something of the rhythms of this war and what it would take to survive.

As the war dragged on, they found that very little fighting would take place in winter. But over the next two years, each spring and summer, battles larger and more dogged than Bull Run would take place. Fights called Shiloh, Antietam, Fredericksburg, Chancellorsville, Gettysburg, Vicksburg, Chickamauga, and Chattanooga would be numbered among them. Waged on large open fields, in thick woods, or, more ominously, from behind hastily built breastworks, each would be the culmination of a campaign of feint and maneuver by large armies.

Soldiers in the battle-hardened II Corps proved themselves to be among the best students of the war's harsh practical lessons. For instance, in the December 1862 Battle of Fredericksburg in Virginia, they learned it was always folly to charge uphill against an entrenched enemy. (There the 116th Pennsylvania lost so many men that it had to be reorganized into a battalion-sized group of four companies.) At Gettysburg, Pennsylvania, on July 3, 1863, when the corps helped shoot apart a 13,000-man Confederate onslaught called Pickett's Charge, they learned it was always easier to fight from a defensive position. And, between summer 1861 and summer 1863, they learned they could always rely on President Lincoln to fire their army's commander after they met with a major defeat: four different major generals led them over two years' time.

Then, between November 1863 and May 1864, much of what the Union soldiers had learned and had come to expect changed.

In the war's last months, an individual's combat skills would still be important. But, if he was a raw recruit, he would have no time to learn them — he would survive on instinct or not at all.

The seasons would mean nothing — fighting would be continuous, on all fronts, all the year long.

And a Union soldier could no longer expect routine changes in command. One man, and one man alone would dictate the moves of all Union troops on all fronts for the remainder of the war. He was the man responsible for all the other changes — Lieutenant General Ulysses S. Grant.

For 50 years after the Civil War, the details of Grant's life story were religiously taught to every American schoolchild. The biographies all began by explaining that Grant, a West Point graduate and a veteran of Mexican War combat in the 1840s, had never intended on making the military his career. His father had encouraged him to pursue it for the free educational opportunities it presented.

In peacetime, this native of Galena, Illinois, quickly became disenchanted with army life. Like many frustrated young officers in the 1850s, he indulged in a period during which he drank a bit too much, reevaluated his life, then resigned his commission. Instead of wasting away his prime at some desolate post out west, he decided he would devote himself to establishing a stable family and business life.

Grant's decision to become a civilian was a poor one. He had no acumen for commerce or farming. Despite all his protests to the contrary, he possessed great military talents, and the outbreak of civil war in the United States proved to be his salvation. Within a year of securing an appointment as a colonel of Illinois volunteers, he rose to the rank of major general and won two decisive victories in Tennessee: the February 1862 capitulations of Confederate forts Henry and Donelson and the April 1862 Battle of Shiloh.

Though some officials in the U.S. War Department were unsure of Grant's abilities, he did make important friendships that helped him both on the battlefield and in Washington, D.C., Assistant Secretary of War Charles Dana became one of his intimates and Major General William T. Sherman was his partner in campaigns in Tennessee and Mississippi. His responsibilities increased and he was assigned the task of taking Vicksburg, Mississippi, a Confederate stronghold that bristled with artillery — guns that denied Union vessels use of the Mississippi River. Through trial and error, a successful land campaign east of the town, some frontal assaults on Vicksburg's elaborate defenses, and a 48-day siege, he succeeded.

Vicksburg's Confederate garrison surrendered on July 4, 1863, one day after Union troops won a great victory at Gettysburg, Pennsylvania. These back-to-back Federal successes signaled a turning point in the Civil War and prompted President Abraham Lincoln to study his roster of major generals and look for a man who could take firm command of all Union military operations.

Weeks passed. One of Lincoln's major generals, William S. Rosecrans, thrust his troops into battle with a Confederate army led by General Braxton Bragg and suffered a stunning defeat at the Battle of Chickamauga, Georgia, in September 1863. The beaten Federals ran several miles north across the Tennessee state line and took refuge at Chattanooga. Bragg's army followed slowly, positioned itself on heights surrounding the city, and effectively besieged Chattanooga.

Having lost confidence in Rosecrans, Lincoln appointed Grant commander of an army department called the Military Division of the Mississippi, and ordered him to go to Chattanooga and assess the situation. Grant arrived in the surrounded city in late October 1863, relieved Rosecrans, opened a supply line for the hungry Union troops there, and in late November directed a series of attacks on the Confederates around him, driving them south into Georgia.

This last victory provided Lincoln with the sign he had been looking for. In February 1864 Congress revived the rank of lieutenant general, U.S. Army (previously, only George Washington and Mexican War—victor Winfield Scott had held this rank), and in March, at Lincoln's urging, gave it to Grant. Immediately afterward, the president appointed him commander of the armies of the United States and directed him to conduct the war as he saw fit.

What Grant did see fit to do was to assign his old friend Sherman command of troops in the western theater, operating in Tennessee and Georgia, and direct him to take Atlanta. He, meanwhile, would travel east and make his headquarters with Union Major General George Meade's Army of the Potomac in Virginia and personally oversee its coming campaign against the largest Rebel force in the state, Confederate General Robert E. Lee's Army of Northern Virginia.

The strategy Grant adopted for the spring 1864 offensive was one that would finally break the back of the veteran II Corps and stagger the usually composed Confederate General Lee. On May 4, the Army of the Potomac battled Confederates in a heavily wooded area called "The Wilderness," just a few miles west of Fredericksburg, Virginia. Whipping each other to a standstill the armies then broke off the fight and raced one another to a crucial crossroads north of Richmond, the Confederate capital. The juncture took its name from a nearby village, Spotsylvania Court House.

Confederates reached Spotsylvania just shortly before the first Federal troops did on May 7. They began digging in even as the first shots of this next battle were being fired, and kept building breastworks and falling back on them for the next several days.

As they did so, Grant had General Meade throw assault columns at them repeatedly from May 8 through the 12th. And during this struggle, the Union lieutenant general made a remark in an official dispatch that would distill his tenacious personality down to a few words: "I propose to fight it out on this line, if it takes all summer." Many of his troops and many Northern civilians would, however, interpret these words differently and mutter that Grant was "a butcher." His opponent, Lee, would be nearly dumbstruck. All other Federal generals had fought setpiece battles, lost or won, and then pulled away. This one was different. Grant knew that no matter how many men he lost in any action, he had more to replace them, while Lee, with limited troops available, would have to keep up the fight with ever-diminishing numbers. The pattern for the remaining months of the war in Virginia was established. It would be a war of attrition.

III

In 1864, the Uniontown recruits for the 116th Pennyslvania regiment were sworn into Federal service in Pittsburgh on a day that comes just once every four winters, February 29. Shipped to Braddock, a river town a few miles outside the city, they waited in snow and cold to become soldiers. Then they discovered they would have to wait a little longer.

It was not until the men of the 116th's Company K found themselves outside Washington, D.C., in mid-March, that any real training began. There they were first issued weapons and given drill instruction. Meanwhile, they acquired other pieces of gear, uniform and accoutrements.

The company's unofficial chroniclers, the Chisholm brothers and Samuel Clear, never noted how much equipment they were given. But it can be deduced from what they wrote that, in its hurry to field large numbers of fresh troops, the government issued these men smoothbore muskets, not the accurate rifled weapons carried by veteran troops. To compensate them for this battlefield handicap, they were also issued "buck and ball" loads for their pieces — paper cartridges filled with gunpowder, an oldfashioned musket ball, and three large buckshot. The government's reasoning was that, the scattershot loads that left the muzzles of Company K's muskets, though not accurate, were bound to hit something in heated, close combat.

In their early letters, the Chisholm boys did complain about uncomfortable government-issue clothing and shoes that quickly went to pieces. And they did as many new recruits did throughout the war: they ordered substitutes from hometown tradesmen. But the practice of mail-ordering substitute clothing and shoes, or buying these same items from a sutler (a licensed peddler who followed each regiment or brigade) was usually the sign of a greenhorn. Veterans on campaign got their shoes and clothing where and when they could — from the wash lines of unhappy housewives or from the bodies of very recently deceased comrades. Each man concluded that if the government, as it regularly demonstrated, was naive enough to buy its infantry enormous lots of shoddy shoes from corrupt contractors and sometimes purchase blind or spavined horses for the cavalry, then each man would have to look out for himself.

A Union veteran of western campaigns named Henry Dwight kept a diary in which he recorded what he carried on the march when he was a new recruit. The diary, edited by historian Albert Castel, cited that while moving to attack Confederate fort Donelson in 1862, Dwight's load was:

1 Knapsack	weighing 30 lbs.	
1 Haversack with rations	" 4 "	
1 Canteen with water	" 1 "	
1 Rifled musket	" 10 "	
1 set of accoutrements & 40 rounds of cartridges	" 4 "	
1 Sergeant's sword	" ½ "	
TOTAL	50½ lbs.	

By the time Company K took the field, the average veteran's load was reduced to his weapon, his haversack, his canteen and cartridges, and whatever he chose to stuff into a blanket roll that he carried draped across his left shoulder. And much else was reduced; by 1864 the practical combat training new soldiers received was next to nonexistent.

A little more than six weeks after they were issued their muskets, the men of Company K were involved in Grant's first full-scale eastern battle, The Wilderness. There they followed orders blindly and hoped for victory. Daniel Chisholm had the bill of his uniform cap shot off. The first man in his company was killed. And every survivor, veteran and greenhorn, was stunned and agitated by what he had seen.

Any Irish Brigade veterans who had fought at Bull Run in 1861 could easily have told the new men of the 116th's Company K how horribly different the conflict had suddenly become. The war's first battle cost the Union anywhere between 2,600 and 3,300 casualties. In The Wilderness, Grant lost approximately 17,660 troops.

The killing would go on. Samuel Clear and his comrades in the 116th would fight at Spotsylvania, in the June 3rd Battle of Cold Harbor; in the first assault on Petersburg on June 16th, at a place called Williams Farm, along the Weldon Railroad on June 22nd; at Deep Bottom on July 27 and again on August 14; at Ream's Station on August 25th; through the autumn in the Petersburg trenches, in a December 9th fight at Hatcher's Run; in the April 1, 1865, Battle of Five Forks; at the fight for Sutherland Station along the South Side Railroad on April 2—the day the Confederates' Petersburg defenses collapsed, and along through the pursuit of Lee's decaying army until its surrender at Appomattox Court House on April 9.

Modern book-length accounts of many of these battles can be found by serious students of Civil War history. They are able to provide a clear overview of events and explain much that would have been bewildering, or at least unclear, to a common Union soldier involved in fighting on "foreign soil" and writing about what he saw. For instance, these works spell out the geography of Virginia clearly. Unlike Clear's diary or the Chisholm brothers' letters, they point out that the significant rivers in that part of the state are the Pamunkey, Rapidan, North Anna, South Anna, Appomattox, James, Rappahannock, and Po. They point out that the chief railways supplying Confederates at Petersburg, the objects of several small battles, were the South Side Railroad and the Weldon Railroad. And, where the men of Company K occasionally misidentified a general or a unit (i.e., Clear writes of a general named "Burney" — actually Major General David Bell Birney), these works properly identify commanding officers and army organizations.

But what some of these same modern histories do not provide is relative perspective. For example, readers of this work will easily notice how much space Sergeant Clear's diary gives to a description of the Battle of Ream's Station, a fight almost completely forgotten in the late twentieth century. This soldier fought in larger, more historically significant struggles, but for him this battle had the most serious impact. Why?

The Battle of Ream's Station virtually emasculated the Army of the Potomac's II Corps. These Federals had been tearing up the Weldon Railroad's tracks south of Petersburg when they were overrun by a corps of Lee's army. Approximately 2,000 of them were captured or were listed as missing. Only about 370 were recorded as killed or wounded. In Bull Run style, most of the rest had simply run away.

Their corps commander, Union Major General Winfield Scott Hancock, was deeply chagrined. He and other apologists claimed that this was not the work of the redoubtable II Corps of old. And it was not the corps veterans, they said, who had brought this shame on the army. It was, they accused, the draftees and "bounty men," the greenhorns — men like those of the 116th's Company K — who had fled.

A reading of Sergeant Clear's account of Ream's Station and the diary entries that follow it do not give any hint of shame on his part. Instead, they distinctly communicate fear.

This man, and the others in his company, had already stood up on several battlefields and taken the worst the enemy could give out. They had just done it too often, in too short a time.

The men of the corps were demoralized. At last, their officers conceded that they were badly war-worn. For the rest of the conflict on that front, they would relegate them to supporting roles. They would no longer spearhead assaults. The war had changed and so had they.

IV

On December 16, 1864, the men of Company K, 116th Pennsylvania — a group that was now composed of fewer than 20 soldiers — spent their morning watching the execution of three deserters behind the Petersburg siege lines, and then they marched off to have their dinner.

As these men walked on through the December cold, to the north, in Washington, D.C., their Constitutional commander-in-chief, Abraham Lincoln, was dispatching a telegram to Union Major General George H. Thomas in Tennessee. It was a message congratulating Thomas and his men for whipping the army of Confederate General John Bell Hood at Nashville. The last Confederate offensive of the war had been crushed.

Fighting began outside the Tennessee state capital on December 15th. But by late morning, December 16th, the battle had turned into an unqualified disaster for the Confederates. The final shots were fired, and Hood's men, the once mighty Army of Tennessee, retreated south out of the state.

Over the next few weeks, many of these Southerners would be sent to backwater posts in the Deep South where they would quietly wait out the rest of the war, or where they would take part in a few last futile engagements with superior numbers of Northern soldiers. The rest would be sent staggering after Union Major General William T. Sherman's forces, troops that had already taken Atlanta, laid waste to most of the state of Georgia, and were preparing to march north, looting and burning, into the Carolinas.

This was as Lieutenant General Ulysses S. Grant had planned it. On all fronts, his war of attrition — of laying waste to both the enemy and the enemy's country — was bringing the foe to its knees. Grant's subordinate commanders sensed the end was near. His infantrymen in the west and south and in the siege trenches around Petersburg all smelled victory in the wind. They all reduced it to a debate about time, to a question of just when the Confederates would finally collapse.

In the 116th Pennsylvania's ranks, though, there was little time for debate. For those who may have enlisted because they did not want to miss the war's dramatic conclusion, these became fulfilling days.

The April 1, 1865, Battle of Five Forks saw the regiment's Company K in the thick of the action, absorbing four casualties. The following day its men, along with other now-veteran members of the II Corps. faced the troops of a once powerful Confederate lieutenant general named A. P. Hill and crushed them. Then the race was on. Robert E. Lee's remaining troops abandoned Petersburg, Confederate government officials fled Richmond 25 miles to the north, and all armed parties moved north of the Appomattox River.

Lee's forlorn hope was to gather his men at Amelia Court House, a village 40 miles west of Petersburg, then veer south. His ultimate goal would be to elude Grant's pursuing army and join what remained of the Army of Tennessee in North Carolina, footsore troops who were then parrying with the van of Sherman's force. Perhaps, united, these Southerners could turn on one or the other of the two main Union hosts and defeat it. After that, perhaps, they could pursue a course of evasion and maneuver. But what could be done after that, no one could be sure.

It was all over within a week. As Sergeant Clear recorded in his diary, Lee littered the roads behind him with abandoned cannons and heartbroken Confederates, men who just could not run or fight one more day. Alex Chisholm wrote home there was still danger to face; on April 7 he lost a friend to a desperate Rebel's bullet and his own shoulder was grazed by a shot. But Confederate surrender was taking on the shape of the inevitable.

On April 9, 1865, far in front of Sergeant Clear's position, Lee gave up his army. He surrendered out of sight of his own dejected troops and away from curious Union infantrymen, inside the McClean House at Appomattox Court House. There would be no more war for him or others. But a few more emotional peaks and valleys would be traveled over the next several weeks.

Word of President Lincoln's assassination on April 14 reached the men of the 116th in the field on occupation duty, and it left them somber. To their south, the news turned many of Sherman's still campaigning troops into mobs, men willing to burn Confederate towns to the ground out of their own anger — not on the orders of others.

Twelve days later, the last Confederates facing Sherman, troops led by Confederate General Joseph E. Johnston, surrendered. The war was over for good and all. Within weeks, Sherman's army and the Army of the Potomac would be disbanded and the Uniontown volunteers of Company K would be returned to their families, to work again, to nurture or forget their memories of combat. Just one more great chore remained.

The men of the 116th Pennsylvania's Company K took part in a gargantuan parade down Pennsylvania Avenue in Washington, D.C. It would be remembered in history as "The Grand Revue." Over two days, May

23 and 24, every man to be spared in both the Army of the Potomac and in Sherman's force would march through the capital.

Once honored, once shamed, and finally rehabilitated, Clear and the Chisholms' II Corps was given a respected place in the march of the 23rd. As one writer noted: "Last came the II Corps, led by Major General A. A. Humphrey and his staff, all mounted on matching white horses. In its 1st Division marched the remnants of [the] Irish Brigade . . . every man sporting a sprig of evergreen in his cap."

After this last march, there was little left to do. With enlistments still in force, the men of Company K endured dull garrison duties around the nation's capital until mid-July, then were paid and mustered out. They arrived in Uniontown without fanfare and, if Samuel Clear's diary account described the typical experience, did little more than get a good night's sleep before walking into fields or mills and picking up their work where they had left it in February of 1864.

This, at least, was the routine for those who came through the fighting relatively unharmed. Daniel Chisholm, injured early in his enlistment, found himself still in a government hospital in autumn 1865. Like many other unlucky soldiers in many wars to come, it would be his lot to be left to make his own peace with the government and his own way in the world. But like his own brother, like his sergeant Sam Clear, he had survived the Civil War. It had undoubtedly changed him and all the others. Yet he had survived it.

For men who had been forced to look into the nightmare face of the next great war to come, for men who had endured the pain of sicknesses for which there were not yet cures, for these men, perhaps, to have survived was testimonial enough.

John E. Stanchak
Editor, *Civil War Times Illustrated*
Harrisburg, Pennsylvania

Diary

Thursday, Feb'y 25th, 1864 — Brownsville

I give up my job at John D. Pringles & went home (at Dawson Ferry) for I have made up my mind to go to the army. I did not feel that I was doing my duty to stay at home when nearly all my comrades and friends was leaving for the seat of war.

I went home and told them I was going to the army and was going to Uniontown tomorrow (February 26th 1864) to see what chance I could get.

Friday, Feb'y 26th — Uniontown

I started for Uniontown and arrived there at 12 O'clock, and at one P.M. started with Captain John R. Weltner's Company for Pittsburgh. This was a new Company raised at and about Uniontown, it was composed of as good boys as ever wore the blue with very few exceptions. We arrived at Pittsburgh at 6 O'Clock and went to the Hare Hotel on Water Street. That night went to Ben Trimbles and had a jolly good time in general.

Saturday, Feb'y 27th — Pittsburgh

Have not enlisted yet, Capt Weltner wants me to enlist in his company. I have not concluded what I will do yet, I have some notion of going to Co I 85th Reg P.V. where Brother Ed is. We put in the time running around in squads seeing the sights of the city, &c &c.

Sunday, Feb'y 28th

I have made up my mind to go with Capt Weltner. A lot of us got on the Street cars and went out to the arsenal, and seen Baily and Aaron Johnson. We had a very nice trip and plenty of fun.

Monday, Feb'y 29th

I went up to the guard house and was sworn into the U.S. Service for three years or during the war, and put on the Army Blue for the first time and feel first rate. My clothes fit me well.

Tuesday, March 1st — Camp Copeland

We sent our clothes home. The Boys bought me a violin, and we have a high old time in the Girard House where we are quartered.

Wednesday, March 2nd — Braddock

This morning very blustery, snowing and blowing, stayed indoors most of the day. In the evening we got on the cars and run up to Camp

Copeland at Braddock. The camp is on a hill close by the Rail Road and we found it covered with four or five inches of snow and a very cold place. When we arrived there the officers was having a good time so we had to stand in line out in the snow and wait until they got done eating and drinking. After a while the boys teeth commenced to chatter together and all kinds of oaths came out, easy at first, but finally they came out with such force that it would lift them off the snow some inches. I took out my violin and commenced to scrape Old Dan Tucker on it, and such a time they all had (180 of them). They shouted and danced and made such a noise they soon brought out the officers. They made us unsling our knapsacks and examined them to see that we hadn't any citizens clothes stowed away in them, when through they marched us to a small church to spend the balance of the night as best we could. It was very cold there being but one stove in the building. There was but very little sleeping done that night.

Thursday, March 3rd — Braddock, Camp Copeland

After passing a restless night we arose early and went up to camp. It was a regular hog wallow, for it was covered with six or eight inches of mud of about the consistency of a thin mortar. We go in the new Barracks just finished and they are very nice, good bunks and a good stove. I. L. Ervin and I are bunking together, we have lots of fun, the violin is on the go all the time.

Friday, March 4th

We was out in the camp getting our knapsacks lettered this morning and everything quick. All at once I seen a man run out of the Commissary with a big cheese knife in his hand and run up and threw down a man who was standing by a tent & stab him seven times with the knife in the breast. I learned afterward the man with the knife had been quarreling with another man who ran past this one by the tent and he thought it was the same man he had been quarreling with. The man he stabbed was standing looking at some distant object, not thinking of such rough treatment. Poor fellow I could hear the knife cut the bones where I stood, at least twenty paces away. The Soldiers was going to mob the fellow but they got him away and I never seen him or the wounded man afterwards. I heard afterward that the wounded man recovered.

Saturday, March 5th

It is raining and spitting snow this morning, and is very disagreeable weather. We have plenty to eat such as it is, if we do not get enough at the Infantry cook house we borrow a cavalry or artillery jacket and get more.

Sunday, March 6th

Preaching all over Camp to day, but I am afraid not much good done, for Cards and Sermons don't mix well, and we have both. The boys are very wild as a general thing, they feel like young Colts or at least they act so.

Monday, March 7th

At 2 O'clock this morning our barracks caught fire from the Stove pipe. We had quite a lively time for a little while, but no great damage done. Nothing else worthy of note.

Tuesday, March 8th — Harrisburgh

Held an election for Co officers today. John R. Weltner was elected Capt. Hezekiah Dean and I ran for 2nd Lieut for fun, he beat me 4 votes. We made a start east by Penna Rail Road leaving Camp Copeland at 3 O'clock P.M., arrived at Harrisburgh without accident. We cheered and was cheered all the way. We eat our suppers and laid down to sleep in the Soldiers Rest, slept soundly. We had a happy time.

Wednesday, March 9 — Washington City

We left Harrisburgh at 7 A.M, passed through Little York at 9 O'clock. This is a beautiful little clean shady town, one of the nicest places I have seen. The station and platform was filled with ladies of all ages with everything in the eating line from peanuts to roast ox. We arrived at Baltimore at half past one O'clock P.M., left at 8 P.M. arrived at Washington City at 12 O'clock at night. Went to the Soldiers Rest, eat our supper and laid down and slept soundly for we was *very very* tired.

Thursday, March 10th — Alexandria

We got up at 6 A.M. Eat a hearty breakfast of cold ham, bread, butter & coffee. Started through the city to the wharf, got on a transport and run down to the quaint old city of Alexandria, passed through to the soldiers rest and when we arrived there we needed just such a place for we were as usual tired.

Friday, March 11th

This beautiful morning finds us in nice clean quarters and plenty to eat. We put in the time looking at the troops coming and going, writing letters, &c.

Saturday, March 12th

Still in same place — eat, sleep & write letters.

March 13th, 14th, 15th & 16th

The same as on the 12th.

Thursday, March 17th — Camp Briggs

We left the Soldiers Rest this morning, 49 men of us and pitched our tents on the grassy banks of the Potomac. We call our Camp "Briggs." We receive recruits for our Regt, The 116th Penna Vol's. We lay at the edge of Alexandria near the old canal, we have a nice view of Washington City. In short it is the most beautiful place I most ever seen.

Friday, March 18th

Capt. David W. McGraw has charge of the camp and he appointed me commissary. My duty is to go to Alexandria and draw rations every two days. We drew our arms to day (Muskets) and we have to drill four hours each day.

Saturday, March 19th

I drew rations for 72 men to day, as some more of our men arrived last night. Sent some of the men to the front at Brandy Station. Drill the same as yesterday, regular routine of camp life.

Sunday, March 20th

We got up at 6 O'clock for roll call, had inspection at 2 O'clock P.M. Capt gave me a pass until further orders, and I come and go when I please. I am in the city more than half of my time, I have a hunky time. The coming and going of soldiers make the place very lively.

Monday, March 21st

Last night was very cold in our tents. We have been very busy building fire places in our tents. We dig a small place four feet long and two feet wide, half in and half out of the tents, put a flat stone over the ditch and have barrels outside for chimneys. If we have plenty of wood we can keep warm and nice, but we have to carry wood half a mile and we make little do us. Sent 2 men to the hospital.

Tuesday, March 22nd

No drill to day, cold and windy. Haynan went to the hospital with the meazles. An old woman brought us a good mess of apple dumplings, we went in kind of loose.

Wednesday, March 23rd

It snowed and blowed all last night. This morning the snow was four or five inches deep. Went to the city and drew two days rations. Twenty of the boys went to Brandy Station. It is getting pretty airish on the Potomac Bank. I have a good fire in my tent and feel O.K.

Thursday, March 24th

We received our commissary tent this morning. The company has wedge tents. I have not had time to build my fire place and it is pretty cold.

Friday, March 25th

I built my fire place this morning, went up to the 8th Penna Reserves and seen many old friends and passed the day very pleasantly there. We have a cold rain this evening. I have a good fire and feel all hunky.

Saturday, March 26th

Fifteen new men came to day, S. W. Bolen, Simon Sampsel and Blinkey Bill was in the squad. Very windy and cold, the boys have to stand around the cook fire to keep warm. By the looks of some of them I think if they had it to do over again they would be by the parental hearth stove.

Sunday, March 27th

This beautiful Easter Sunday finds us all O.K. for it is a pretty and warm day, but we have no eggs. We could have them at 40¢ per doz but I guess we will do without this time.

Monday, March 28th — Alexandria

We drew rations, are ordered to the front, struck tents, went to the soldiers rest, put away our accoutrements and then for a last big time, I went to the Theatre. The play was Cricket on the Hearth. I found Yauger and Bolen and others there. It was a splendid play, I enjoyed it very much. We run around nearly all night and had a gay time.

Tuesday, March 29th — Brandy Station

We got up early and left Alexandria at 7 A.M. on top of the cars. We had a bad ride in the rain, reached Brandy Station at 4 P.M., got off, marched five miles in the rain and mud up to our knees, reached the camp of the 116th Regt at 6 P.M. We was halted among a lot of Stumps and puddles of water, without any shelter or any way of making any, wet and hungry. I went down to the Priest's tent and got permission to sleep in the cathedral, an old log building with a tent covering, both ends being open. We threw ourselves down and slept in the mud and water, we had had all our white bread.

Marched 5 Miles from the above place near Stevensburgh.

Wednesday, March 30th

This morning disagreeable and muddy, wind cold and raw. Nine of us fixed up an old tent and have a good fire and feel very comfortable to what we did yesterday and last night. We drew our days rations.

Thursday, March 31st, 1864 — Brandy Station

The weather fine, we moved our tent fifty yards and built it up again, built a chimney, made new bunks &c. In short we are all O.K. and very comfortable indeed to what we have been.

Friday, April 1st — Brandy Station

While everybody is moving in civilized life we are taking things easy, we have plenty to eat, wear and have a good warm place to sit and write to our friends. While I write the rain is pattering down on our canvass roof, which is water proof and answers for windows at the same time.

Saturday, April 2nd

Regimental orderly been running all day in the mud and rain to Division Head Quarters, Brigade Pioneer &c. My jaws are swelled up like a lager beer Dutchmans, I cannot eat with any comfort at all. This has been a very bad day, snow and slush over the shoe mouth. I am afraid I will get cold.

Sunday, April 3rd

My jowls are very sore. This morning I went over to the Surgeons he examined my jaws and pronounced my ailment the mumps, and excused me from all duty. The boys came back off of Picket, they enjoyed themselves in the best manner.

Monday, April 4th

It is raining again and our camp is awful. My jaws are bad, I have an old stocking tied around my neck. I am running around all the time. I went over to the 140th P.V. Bert Beeson belongs to it. It is still raining.

Tuesday, April 5th

Still raining and mud. "Oh Jeaminee." My jaws are still bad, swelled out even with my face. I am still off of duty, and yet it rains.

Wednesday, April 6th

My jaws are still sore. Lieut James D. Cope and 1st Sergt James E. Jolliff came last night. Still raining at intervals, camp is more than muddy.

Thursday, April 7th

We have been very busy building Jolliffe and I a new tent. Am still on the sick list. I have been appointed Commissary Pro tem. Mumps are better, can eat very well and have plenty to eat.

Friday, April 8th

Our Brigade had drill for the first time to day, that is since we arrived. Our Brigade is composed of the 88th N.Y., the glorious 69th N.Y., 28th Mass, 63rd N.Y. and 116th P.V. our Regt. It is the Irish Brigade. I did not drill to day. A man shot himself to day through the bowels by accident.

Saturday, April 9th

Raining again. My Jaws are still swelled, but not painful. No drill to day.

Sunday, April 10th

This is a beautiful sabbath morning. Lieut Jas D. Cope went with 24 of the men out on picket. My Jaws are a little better. It is raining again.

Monday, April 11th — Brandy Station

This is a beautiful day, mumps about the same. We had our first dress parade at 5 O'Clock P.M.

Tuesday, April 12th

This was a nice day. Capt Jno R. Weltner and Lt Zadoc B. Springer (2nd Lieut) came to day. Our Co has not been lettered or organized yet.

Wednesday, April 13th

We built the capt's quarters to day. Our Co has been lettered "K" and our Commissioned officers are as follows, Capt Jno R. Weltner, 1st Lieut Jas D. Cope, 2nd Lieut Zadoc B. Springer. Non Commissioned officers as follows, 1st or orderly Sergt James E. Jolliffe, 2nd Sergt Warren S. Kilgore, 3rd Sergt Edward Pence, 4th William H. Sembower, 5th Aaron S. Watson, 1st Corporal James Collins, 2nd Stephen S. Beckett, 3rd Daniel Crawford, 4th Hezekiah Dean, 5th Robt Brownfield, 6th Samuel A. Clear, 7th George I. Cruse, 8th Richard A. McClean. We had dress parade to day, our Regt looks fine.

Thursday, April 14th

My jaws are better, I have taken the stocking off. They are beginning to trot us through. We had inspection, Brigade Drill, and Dress parade, wore our knapsacks to day for the first time, they feel a little awkward. Our boys returned from picket.

Friday, April 15th

We were on Division Review to day. Genl Barlow our Division commander reviewed us, our division looks real nice. Charles Yauger was tied up for lip to the capt.

Saturday, April 16

I had a bad head ache to day, laid in my tent nearly all day, as it rains nearly all the time.

Sunday, April 17th

We had Brigade inspection after which we laid in our tents all day.

Monday, April 18th

This was a beautiful day. We had Brigade Drill.

Tuesday, April 19th

This was a fine morning, we fell in and marched three miles and was reviewed by our Corps Commander Gen Winfield S. Hancock, and Genl Frances Barlow Divn Commander. To day I seen Hancock for the first time.

Wednesday, April 20th

We sent our Overcoats to the rear. That means something. Had Brigade Drill to day. Lt Col Richard C. Dale came to us to day. We had Dress Parade this evening.

Thursday, April 21st

I left camp this morning for my first picket duty. We are five miles from camp. I have charge of posts 7 & 8.

Friday, April 22nd

Was relieved at Midnight and came back to the reserve, have lots of fun, no enemy near.

Saturday, April 23rd

Still on Picket.

Sunday, April 24th

Still on Picket.

Monday, April 25th — Brandy Station

Came back to camp last evening, had Brigade Drill. I feel first rate, and my mumps are entirely gone.

Tuesday, April 26th

Had Division Drill to day, and had a sham bayonet charge. The old Irish Brigade made a tremendous noise.

Wednesday, April 27th

I was detailed for Color Guard to day, had Brigade Drill, I like the change. Sergt Sloan Co E. ("Timothy A. Sloan") Sergt Co B. ("Jacob W. Adams") Quinter Co G. ("Henry R. Quinter") Clear Co K. ("Samuel A. Clear") Carrigan Co. C., Diffendaffer Co I., McElroy Co A, Barker Col H. ("Wm H. Barker").

Thursday, April 28th

Drill, Dress parade, &c.

Friday, April 29th

Drill, Dress parade &c. Jacob Allamon came to us to day, getting pay rolls ready.

Saturday, April 30th

Was mustered for March and April pay to day, raining a little, &c.

Sunday, May 1st

We had Sunday morning inspection, went to church, sit on the ground, most of the boys played Mumly Meg instead of listening to the sermon. This was my first church going in the army.

Monday, May 2nd

We tore down our tents to our log. Instead of light, it made me feel sad to see the whole division at work at one time tearing down and spoiling our nice camp.

Tuesday, May 3rd

We struck tents and packed up at Ten O'Clock to night and started on the march to where we do not know.

Wednesday, May 4th — Chancellorsville

On the march. Our first march and we do not know where we are going, or what we are going to do. The road was strewn with Blankets, operplus [sic] Clothing, Boots, shoes, well I might say everything moveable. We never halted except when the rebels had cut trees and piled logs across the road. We found this done in many places, but our pioneers soon removed them, and on we would go again, and at last arrived at the Old Battlefield of Chancellorsville, and rested in line of battle.

Thursday, May 5th — Wilderness

We got into line this morning, crossed the Rapidan and went 3 or 4 miles as near as I can tell. The last mile we went we could see the Johnnies dodge in and out of the woods on the left flank. As we went the thicket got more dense, and the road less travel worn. We finally halted, everything was as still as the grave, we could almost hear one anothers heart beats. All at once a small volley was discharged and then another and another and soon it [was] one continual roar, away to the right in the 5th Corps, then nearer and nearer until it was almost on a line with us. We could hear but could not see one hundred yards either way while we stood there as quiet as mice. A staff officer dashed down the road in our front and gave Genl Barlow some orders, who galloped to our front and shouted attention, by the left flank march. We pitched into the dark scrubby pines, grape vines, over old logs, ravines, tree tops, and everything else that went to make up a wilderness. It was a very irregular line of battle but it was the best we could do. The time was between three and four O'clock. We just got there in time as the Johnnies was trying to turn our left flank. Fire at will was the command, and we did fire. I wont pretend to describe my feelings, it was my first battle, but I did better than I ever thought I could. Our boys fell very fast wounded and killed, we was pressed back about fifty yards, but we regained the ground again and held it until 9 O'Clock P.M. The leaves and dry brush caught fire and we had to drag our wounded and killed back to keep them from being burned up. Two of the color guard killed and three wounded at one time. I held the colors alone as the rest of the guard and Sergts was carrying back our wounded comrades. Co F had thirty five killed and wounded, Co K nine and the other Co's more or less. At nine O'Clock we fell back to the road (100 yards) and commenced to pile up old rotten logs, dry brush, &c. We had no shovels and we had to dig with our bayonets and throw up dirt with our hands. We could do but little good, but we expected to be attacked in the morning and we worked all night, and then our works was poor.

Friday, May 6th — *Wilderness*

This beautiful morning we made coffee and eat our breakfast early. Everything very quiet after the storm, we lay around fixing our old rotten logs a little. At 5 O'Clock P.M. (our Corps Hancocks the 2nd, held the left) Sedgwicks 6 Corps held the right. Both corps advanced over the ground of yesterday. We found the rebs a little beyond. The old rebs let fly but we pressed them back and for hours the battle raged. Our Division (for I could not see the other troops) fell back to the old logs at the road. The rebs followed they thought we were whipped, I found out afterwards it was done to draw them on. On they came with a womanlike scream then we let them have the buck and Ball from behind the old logs and brush. The burning paper fell into our old logs and they took fire and as far as I could see it was one vast logheap on fire. We had taken off our knapsacks and laid them against the works in the excitement many of them was burnt up. The heat was so intense we had to fall back over the road at the very hottest of the fight. It was now dusk, the rebs fell back but left hundreds piled up in our front. We also lost heavily, we built new works, laid all night, slept soundly for we were very tired.

Saturday, May 7th — *Wilderness to Spottsylvania*

This is a fine morning, I went over to our front they had piled the Rebs in holes during the night, but the old hats of every kind, shape, color and make laid around by the hundreds. The day was past in skirmishing along the whole line, by taking turns we got some risk but not much. At 10 O'Clock P.M. we were ordered into line, and we moved off in the darkness. We could see nothing but the scrubby pines and occasionally a fire to guide us. We halted and drew rations, moved on again, we could hear heavy skirmishing away off in our front, but we moved on through the gloom.

Sunday, May 8th

We halted at 4 O'clock this morning and commenced to throw up works. Very heavy fighting by fifth corps, we expected to move every minute, but lay until 4 O'clock in the afternoon. We advanced over the works and moved on through the underbrush, at 300 yds we ran against the Rebs. We drove them back after half an hours fight, we seen them skeedaddle into the darkness. We followed on a short distance and halted and lay down, all was quiet, we laid half an hour or more and moved again, but we could not tell which way we come or the way we were going. We struck a hill about half way between the top and the bottom. All at once a voice was shouted lay down. We fell down on our faces, and it was well we did so, for we hardly got down until the top of the hill was raked with solid shot, shell and grape and canister. We were going directly into a rebel battery and being too close they shot over us. We had lost our way. There was a good many killed and wounded, but they over shot us and that was all that saved us. We fell out of there in a hurry when ordered and got back to the works with our shins and faces dreadfully skinned and scratched up.

Monday, May 9th, 1864 — near Po River

Moved this morning by the left flank 2½ miles formed in line of battle, halted. Threw up works, just got them finished and Fall in was the word. We moved out through the woods, It seemed to me four miles and struck the Rebs again, a small body of them, made them skeedaddle. We the 116th Regt went on picket, color guard stayed at Brigade Head Quarters. We had crossed the Po River.

Tuesday, May 10th

Went to the Regiment this morning, laid in the works until 2 O'clock. We advanced again, but got drove back across a large field and over the Po River, with heavy loss. The shot and shell we got was awful, they more than give us thunder. When we got into the woods they fell back, Into the woods they had driven us out of. We lost heavy I cannot tell how Co K fared and I was with the colors.

Wednesday, May 11th

We spent this day skirmishing by turns all along the line, but neither made or lost anything. Commenced to rain in the afternoon, not hard but drizzled. At dusk we started on the march — our Corps — (the 2nd). On we went through the rain and mud up to our knees, over mud holes swollen creeks and runs. Sometimes we had to creep through the wet underbrush. We were a sorry looking lot of boys, judging by the way we felt. It was so dark and foggy we could not see one another. I cannot describe the suffering of this night. It was the worst march we had to endure up to this time. We went as hard as we could go until 3 O'clock.

Thursday, May 12th — Spottsylvania

At 3 O'Clock we halted with orders in whispers to lie down on our arms, after loading and fixing bayonets. It is still raining and very foggy, between four and five O'Clock, still dark, wet and gloomy. Attention was whispered and silence was enjoined. Then again forward was whispered and away we went falling over stumps, old logs, brush and into gullies, it was still not light enough to see well. The ground we were passing over had been washed by the recent rains and was full of ditches. Just as we were crossing a ditch the rebel Pickets commenced to fire. Then such a yell as only the Old Irish Brigade can give, and in we went, like as if the devil had broke loose, over the works in among the Johnnies, and many of them lost their lives by the bayonet. We captured and sent to the rear hundreds of prisoners, I said to a lot of them how is now Johnnies. A big orderly sargeant sang out Clubs is trump by god. They belonged to Johnsons Rebel Division. Here I picked up a Flag, I thought it was our Regimental Flag but I found it belonged to the 61st P.V. In the works when we got over we captured a Battery. It was partly and some of the guns already hitched up as if they had just moved or was getting ready to move. We killed the horses and turned the guns on the retreating enemy. We drove them back over the inner works but here they rallied and a long and bloody fight took place. They threw Ewell, Hill, and Longstreets Corps against us, they charged us five times, *but the old 2nd was there and they could not drive us out* — Column after column charged up to the works and while our colors was sticking on our side they planted theirs on the other, but we would mow them down and they would fall back and make room for others to meet the same fate. Our artillery made gaps in their lines from dawn until after dark, the roar of the guns was ceaseless. A tempest of shells shrieked through the forests and plowed through the fields; I went over the works and seen the Johnnies laying in piles, the dead laying on the wounded holding them tight, and hundreds torn into pieces by shells after they was dead. It was an awful sight, and our boys, they laid dead and wounded by the hundreds and our division was relieved at 10 P.M. I took the flag and started for Brigade Head Quarters. Through the darkness I went stumbling into Gen Barlows Head Quarters, he was alone, helloa Corporal which way. I told him I was directed there for 2nd Brigade Head Quarters — He pointed about Two Hundred yards away. I struck out through the rain over logs, brush piles &c. I found three or four staff officers around a handful of fire. They pointed to a tree, I threw myself down, tired, wet and hungry and was soon in the land of nod.

Friday, May 13th

At daylight this morning I woke up stiff, sore and hungry. I gave the Colors to a Corpl of the 61st Regt P.V. who came after them. He thanked me for taking such good care of them, he said their Color Sargeant was killed dead. I went over to my Regiment, they were still in the works. I found the boys what was left of them in good spirits, cooking and eating and laughing over yesterdays work. I went over in front to see what I could see. The Dead had been buried and the wounded taken to the Hospital, but there was everything scattered over the field. We cleaned up our guns and it took us most of the day.

Saturday, May 14th

It rained all of last night, and all day to day. We are still in the same place.

Sunday, May 15th

We were relieved at daylight, and moved back one mile and camped in a cornfield, corn is 4 inches high, still raining, awful place here.

Monday, May 16th

It is very muddy this morning but nice overhead. We are busy fixing and cleaning up as we have marching orders. We had inspection, we got some of the mud off of our clothes, and they look blue again. We lay, where the Pike leads from Richmond to Fredericksburgh.

Tuesday, May 17th

Cold and Cloudy this morning, we lay quiet all day, but are still under marching orders. Got on the march at 8 O'Clock P.M. and away we go on about such a march as on the 11th, at twelve we are still a going.

Wednesday, May 18th

We halted at 2 O'Clock this morning, laid down and slept, was wakened up at daylight with orders to load, fix bayonets and be very quiet. Then forward march was given, but the Rebs was not asleep this time. We did not advance fifty yards until They poured the Minie Balls into us mighty thick, but on we went and was within twelve feet of the works when I was struck and knocked senseless. When I came to one of the color guard Corpl McElroy was holding me up. The troops had taken the works and I could hear them giving the Johnnies thunder, like they always do. I examined and found that a minie ball had struck me in the side on the belt plate. (I have it now in my trunk.) On the march my belt plate had worked around. In my blouse I had a big knife, with a spoon and fork, also Ten rounds of cartridges. The ball passed through the cartridges, struck the knife and then struck the belt plate with such force that it nearly sent it through me. When I first looked at the place it was as black as the hide of the darkest african. It felt like a square scantling had been punched through me. I do not think I ever felt so sick, I threw everything that was in my stomach and I came near throwing it and all my insides with it. I laid for about two hours and then dragged myself back to the troops supporting us. (The 2nd Heavy Artillery) and found some of the boys from Brownsville that I was acquainted with. The fight went on, the shells bursting all around us, scattering their fragments like hail stones. There was a great many killed and wounded. I laid here all day with the troops. After dark I went to my Regt and found its ranks fearfully thinned. I turned H and was ordered to the Hospital but could not see it. We rested until 10 O'Clock, fell in and marched again through the darkness, every false step I made it seemed as if there was a knife running through me. My suffering I could not describe.

Thursday, May 19th

This morning we found ourselves in a nice clean place. At One O'Clock the Division fell in and doublequicked away and left me and some others. The Reb Gorillas had captured part of our train. They recaptured it and returned at dusk nearly tired to death.

Friday, May 20th — near Spottsylvania

This is a most beautiful morning, we laid out streets and fixed up nice. Seen a man shot for desertion. About the time we got fixed up and feeling comfortable we got orders to be ready to march at a moments notice. I went to the surgeon and had my side dressed. He ordered me to go to the Hospital. I told him I would not go and he gave me a cursing. I had made up my mind to never be taken prisoner or go to the hospital if I could possibly avoid it. At 11 O'Clock we struck tents again and off we went through the gloom and darkness. At midnight we were still going, faint and weary. I was very nearly played out.

Saturday, May 21st

All night we trudged along. This morning we passed nice residences, trod over beautiful wheat fields, ready to cut in several weeks, through corn fields knee high. Passed through the village of Bowling Green at 10 A.M. It is a beautiful little place. The Rebel young ladies peeped at us through the palings and windows, some of them were hansome. The boys would sing out we are going to take Richmond. They would stick out their pretty mouths and say we have a Lee that will attend to you. We marched in good order, no one was allowed to leave the ranks without permission of his Capt. We passed Milford Station at 2 O'clock, and a short way the other side encountered the Po River which we waded. It was up to our arms and a good many went in over their heads. After we got out we shook ourselves like water dogs. Marched one mile into a wheat field and threw up breastworks. The Troops, Horses and Cattle soon had the wheat all down like it had been rolled with a roller. The sun was hot and our clothes soon dried. We cut up wheat with our Pen Knives and made bed, laid down and slept soundly.

Sunday, May 22nd — Near Milford Station

This is a beautiful Sabbath. We are still in the same place. We expected to be attacked but we lay all day unmolested and had a nice rest. This Evening have marching orders. We threw ourselves down on our soft wheat beds, with the expectation of having our sweet and peaceful slumbers interrupted.

Monday, May 23rd — North Anna

The 2nd and 5th Corps all busy getting breakfast this morning, at 8 O'Clock A.M. we filed out of the wheat field and away we go again in a hurry. We arrived at the North Anna River at 3 P.M. The 5th Corps had the lead and had to fight its way up above the Rail Road Bridge at Jerico Ford after it crossed. They pitched into the Johnnies and gave them the very devil. While Warren was fighting the 5th on the South Side Bank our Corps, The 2nd, was giving them thunder on the North Side. They were trying to keep us from crossing but old Hancock always crossed when he wanted to, so General Burneys Division the 3rd led the Charge, while Barlows — ours the 1st divn advanced on the left. We charged the Rebs and took the Bridge and held it. The Johnnies set it on fire and run. We are entrenching and so are the enemy.

Tuesday, May 24th — North Anna

This morning our Regiment the 116th crossed over and went back and commenced to tear up the Rail Road. We worked hard all day and tore up miles of the road. We went into camp at night and are going at it again in the morning.

Wednesday, May 25th — North Anna

Raining this morning, we are busy tearing up the Railroad, worked all day in the rain. We could hear heavy Shelling and Skirmishing at the river. Worked until noon and then returned to the corps. Took us nearly all afternoon to get there. We have played The devil with their Rail Road. Recrossed at dark (whole corps) went one mile or so, laid down and slept soundly.

Friday, May 27th

We started on the march at 11 O'clock. Travelled through a pretty country, beautiful scenery. Marched all day and until midnight. We had a fast but rather pleasant march. We bivouacked and slept soundly.

Saturday, May 28th — Near Pamunkey River

Started again this morning, arrived at the Pamunkey river and crossed over at One O'clock, went one mile, threw up works, finished them and lay down to rest. I have a carbine and I carry my cartridges in my blouse Pocket, my side is still too sore to wear my cartridge box.

Sunday, May 29th

We advanced over the works this morning two miles. While in line of battle Lt James D. Cope sent for me to come to Co "K". I had been with the colors so long that I hardly knew how Co "K" was standing the hardships she had been called upon to go through. I reported to the Lt, he told me he wanted me in the Co as he had appointed me 5th Sergt, I told the Lt I would rather be a Color Corporal than a Sergt with my Co, I hated to leave the color guard. The Rebel shells were bursting over and around us continually. Just three months in The service of Uncle Sam. We moved again and threw up new works, finished late in the night.

Monday, May 30th

Laid all day, then moved half a mile and threw up new works, drew rations. Very heavy Picket firing in front, shells are bursting all the time.

Tuesday, May 31st

We are in the same place. This morning at 10 O'Clock we made a short advance, under a heavy fire, threw up new works. Very heavy artillery fighting all day also Picket firing. Sent 8 men on Picket from Co "K" 5 of them were wounded, we captured a few Rebs.

Wednesday, June 1st

Very heavy skirmishing to day, things very lively. At 10 O'Clock P.M. we started on a forced march. Marched all night, had but little rest.

Thursday, June 2nd

Halted at Gaines Mill, threw up breastworks, heavy firing on our left and skirmishing in front.

Friday, June 3rd — Cold Harbor

The position of the Army to day is as follows. The 9th Corps (Burnsides) on the right, The 5th Corps Warrens next, The 18th Smiths next. The 6th Wrights next. The 2nd Hancocks (ours) on the left. At Sunrise our Division Barlows advanced on the enemies works. Charged them, captured 3 cannons and several hundred prisoners. Our second line failed to come up soon enough and the Rebels rallied and forced us back, but not to the old lines, only a few yards and they could not get us any farther. We lay about forty yards apart. If they showed themselves we let them have it and they returned the compliment when they had the chance. The McKean Brigade was within fifteen yards of the rebels, we had to hold our position, there was no chance for any retreating, as to expose ones person was sure death. So we had to lay, the fighting going on continuously. They were using solid shot, shell, grape and canister and small arms. At nine O'clock our Regiment went on picket we had to fight our way to the Picket line. Both armies was like hornets. We dug holes with our bayonets to protect ourselves and more than one poor fellow was shot before his little dugout would protect him. We lay there expecting every minute to be gobbled up and sent south.

Saturday, June 4th

This morning still finds us on Picket, and the shells passing over us both ways. Some of them fall short of going where they were started for and burst over our heads. We make ourselves in as small bulk as possible. Time goes slowly. This is a very dangerous position, but we have to take our chances and trust to providence.

Sunday, June 5th — Cold Harbor

We were relieved at 2 O'clock A.M., came back to main line which was only a few steps. All day long we have to huddle close to the breastworks, as the Reb sharpshooters are very watchful and a great many are shot in our own works. They have flank fire in places. At Seven O'clock P.M. everything became as quiet as the grave, we felt it was a calm before the storm. We fixed ourselves as well as possible to be ready for what was coming. And at 8 O'clock P.M. it came. The Johnnies charged our works. The charge did not last long but it was the fiercest one we ever checked, but we checked them and gave hundreds of them their last check.

Monday, June 6th — Cold Harbor

This place should be called *Hot Harbor*. This morning we moved to the right, near where we first halted on the 2nd. We lay all day comparatively quiet, but we were still in Hot Harbor, for at 9 O'clock P.M. the Johnnies tried again to break our line, but the Old 2nd was there. At 11 O'Clock P.M. they tried it again but they found us still there. These was long and fierce charges — they came right up to the works but they could not effect a lodgement. We did not pretend to sleep and was watching at midnight for another break.

Tuesday, June 7th — Cold Harbor

At 2 O'clock this morning they made a long determined charge, but the boys never wavered. We could hear the Reb officers shouting forward, forward. On they came but it was only to be mowed down by the Thousand. We never thought of getting drove out, I rather enjoyed it and I believe the rest of the boys did also. At daylight this morning all was quiet. The enemy advanced a white Flag, asking permission to bury their dead, which was granted. We had an armistice of two hours. The quietness was really oppressive, It positively made us feel lonesome, after a continual racket day and night for so long. We sit on the works and let our legs dangle over on the front and watch the Johnnies carry off their dead comrades in silence, but in a great hurry. Some of them lay dead within twenty feet of our works — the live Rebel looks bad enough in his old torn, ragged Butternut suit, but a dead Rebel looks horrible all swelled up and black in the face. After they were through there was nothing left but stains of Blood, broken and twisted guns, old hats, canteens, every one of them reminders of the death and carnage that reigned a few short hours before. When the 2 hours was up we got back in our holes and they did the same. A large gun at the fort gave one shot and both sides passed a few but no damage was done. Things quieted down except the continual crack of the Sharpshooters rifles. They are busy from daylight until dark, they hide in trees, behind stumps, along banks, or where ever they can protect themselves and see their enemies.

Wednesday, June 8th — Cold Harbor

All quiet but the Sharpshooters, they are cracking away. The Pickets are getting very friendly. They trade Tobacco for Coffee, also exchange papers, &c. The Pickets on both sides have agreed not to fire on each other. We have a duel with shells once in a while, we have to run the gauntlet for water, and some get shot but we must have water.

Thursday, June 9th — Cold Harbor

We are still in the same place and things remain about the same, sharp shooting and a shell now and then.

Friday, June 10th — Cold Harbor

Still no change — got leave of absence and went to the right through the 6th 18th & 10th Corps to find Bro Ed, he was left with a part of his corps that remained at Bermuda Hundred. I seen the Boys of the 112th Pa 2nd Heavy Artillery.

Saturday, June 11th — Cold Harbor

Very heavy fatigue duty now building forts, &c. Hezekiah Dean came up to day and was reduced to the ranks for bumming. Everything remains about the same.

Sunday, June 12th

This is a beautiful sabbath day, and quiet. Have Marching orders and we are laying around in the sun wondering where we go next. At 7 O'clock P.M. we quietly packed up and fell back without noise or confusion and struck out through the darkness, and left Cold Harbor behind. It had been a hot place for us as our thinned ranks show. At midnight we are trudging along.

Monday, June 13th

At Seven O'clock we halted and got breakfast, after breakfast on we went again. We crossed the Chickahoming river, two branches at 3 O'clock P.M. We were tramping down the beautiful clover, corn and wheat on the Rebel Brigadier General Wilcox farm. I must say I never seen a more beautiful place. This house was a large white frame with three porticos, the yard and garden enclosed with nice white palings, the chimneys was on the outside of the house. Our Right and Left rests on the James River, we expect to be attacked and we are all busy carrying Rails, boards, logs and everything that will stop a bullet, and are building breastworks. We are playing the devil with the farm. I took ten men and went back for beef. I had the headache all day and when I smelt the dead Beeves I got so blind that Andy Cease and Abe Hull had to carry me to my tent.

Tuesday, June 14th

We finished our works last night by the light of the moon. This is a fine morning, we lay by all day, I feel all O.K. The Cattle, Mules, and Horses have nearly destroyed all the meadow, wheat and corn. At 11 P.M. we packed up and left the farm with a fence around the outside which we made in one night that will take the farmers about ten years to fix as we found it. Any one to see that farm now would never think it had ever been under a state of cultivation. We marched to the James (one mile). The troops commenced to cross on transports going every way for they were maneuvering to blind the Johnnies. I tell you it was a grand sight.

Wednesday, June 15th

At break of day this morning the troops had all crossed and we marched up the sandy shore 2½ miles and rested. We hadn't any rations and the boys were nearly starved. We would dive in to our haversacks but would find nothing but crumbs of Hardtack and but few of them. We went back to the landing for rations but they had not come, I tell you by that time we were hungry indeed. We went back & reported, started on the march again, marched until midnight. Hunger began to tell on us by this time, we became very weak, and staggered along like drunken men. We were too hungry to sleep.

Thursday, June 16th, 1864 — In front of Petersburgh, Va

We got up early marched 2 miles and halted. I took a detail and went back after rations. Our rations had not come but we borrowed one days rations from Burnsides Corps in the evening late. At noon I had gave a teamster twenty five cents in silver for 5 hardtack, reported back to the

Division and soon got shut of our rations, fell into line and charged the rebel lines with Burnsides Corps. Carried their works, worked all night at entrenching.

Friday, June 17th

This morning our Division and Burnsides Corps charged the Rebels on the right and captured the redoubts and five hundred prisoners. I tell you we lost the Blue Coats fast for a while, but we worsted them a good deal. The rest of our Corps came up but we could do no good.

Saturday, June 18th

We packed up before daylight and moved to the left two miles and charged the Rebels again. Took two lines of works but could not go any farther, but held what we had taken. We laid there all day. In the evening I went on picket but returned.

Sunday, June 19th

It was quiet and we laid around all day. Went on picket at the brick Rail Road Bridge. The Reverend S. Wilson's son had command of the picket of the 140th P.V. We have little holes dug in the side of the Rail Road and the Johnnies have a flank fire on us. We have to stay in very close. It does not do to expose ourselves.

Monday, June 20

We are still on Picket. Alexander Chisholm and I were in one hole, he was asleep or at least his eyes were shut, a Reb minie ball struck him in the head and it waked him in short order. It was a spent ball having come through the clay flanks of our pit. He d ——— m'd a little and then got his gun and popped away all day at the reb who was behind sand bags up the railroad track. Alex was determined to kill the Son of a B ———.

Tuesday, June 21st

Came off of Picket at 3 O'Clock this morning. All right. At Eight O'Clock moved to the left for 6 hours, our Company "K" and Co H skirmished on the flank of the moving column. I shot at a reb cavalry man I thought I had killed him, I went down and found the Johnnie gone, but I found where he had been the most beautiful double barreled shot gun I ever seen. I kept it a while and then I had to lay it down in the woods and leave it lay. I would have given fifty dollars to of had it sent home. On we went, at the last we ran against a strong body of the enemy who gave us battle and we had to halt and build works. Moved out over the line of works and built a new one in advance of the other. About the time we finished the second line, we had to move to the left to make room for troops on the right. We were on the extreme left so we had to build another line in our front again. This made the third line of breastworks since noon, it took us working hard nearly all night to finish them.

Wednesday, June 22nd

This morning we find ourselves in good works and feel pretty comfortable. We drew rations, and lay in the works until 3 P.M. We then advanced over the works one and a half miles. The sixth Corps was on our left but did not connect by some three hundred yards. We lay down and we could hear the rebels coming forward. Our skirmish line fell back to us, attention: Forward, was the command, we moved out and met them, and then the woods resounded with the crashing volleys of musketry. We moved towards them slowly, our boys dropping wounded or killed at every step. All at once we became aware of a rear firing. The rebs had passed through the opening between us and the sixth Corps. The sixth Corps did not advance when we did, so the sneaking devils took advantage of the gap and came in on our rear, so we wheeled around and charged right through them. I reached our works in safety but a great [many] was taken prisoners, wounded and killed. Lt James D. Cope and three men were taken prisoners and two men killed of Co "K". Some of the other Companies of our Regt fared much worse. On came the rebels flushed with victory, but we were now in our works. (I think that they did not know we had built works.) And when they cam[e] close up we let them have a warm reception. It was fun to see them fall like gross, and the rest run like the devil was after them. We more than paid them up for the rear fire they gave us. I must now see how Co K is getting along as I am acting Orderly Sergeant. On Entering the battle of the Wilderness May 5th our Co "K" numbered Eighty seven men. To night I find but eight men left for duty, Capt Weltner away sick, Lt Cope captured to day, Lt Springer wounded, I have my hands full.

Thursday, June 23rd

We strengthened our works to day in the morning, everything being quiet in the afternoon we laid down, slept soundly, awakened rested and refreshed.

Friday, June 24th

We tore our new works down and moved to our old ones, we worked hard all day putting up Stockade, abattis &c. I went along the line of our old Irish Brigade. It made me sad to see how she had been cut to pieces, her thinned ranks tell the tale of her battles and hardships, that she has passed through on this campaign. The Glorious old 88th N.Y. and the gallant old 69th N.Y. the always ready 28th Massachusetts and the spoiling for a fight 63rd N.Y. and our own gallant 116th Pennsylvania comprise the Brigade. They all now present the appearance of Companies instead of Regiments. Our Regiments Ranks does not number One Hundred men. She numbered Eight Hundred and Sixty Seven when on the banks of the Rapidan May 5th. Co F of our Regiment numbered 107 men, now 41 reports at roll call. Co K draws 17 rations and has ten men for duty out of the 87 that we started with on this campaign.

Saturday, June 25th

We are still in the same place, are busy fixing up our works, making them strong, have made two rows of abbatoes in our front, and if the rebs would charge us they would find a hard place to run against. Fatigue duty is the watch word of the day & night.

Sunday, June 26th

It is very warm, indeed it has been all this month. They have broken up the "old Irish" Brigade, and distributed us into the other Brigades, our Regt the 116th Penna goes into the Fourth Brigade. It was awful to hear the men swear when they found the Regiments forming the Irish Brigade had to separate, some of the men swore they would never charge again.

Monday, June 27th, 1864

The Irish Brigade's Regiments separated this morning. Our regiment moved to the right, and we pitched our tents between the 53rd Penna and Seventh N.Y. We cleaned ourselves up nicely and feel very well, I think we will get a little rest. The old Irish Brigade is a thing of the past. There never was a better one pulled their triggers on the Johnnies.

Tuesday, June 28th

To day the officers are all busy making out pay rolls. The boys are cleaning up and improving their quarters. All quiet in front, and it looks as if we might have a short rest, I tell you we need it.

Wednesday, June 29th

We are still in the same place, all quiet in front, days are hot and nights are cool. We have marching orders. Our rations consist of soft Bread, pork, beans, Crout, Sugar, Dry Apples, Coffee and Whiskey. All hunkey.

Thursday, June 30th

This day was very pleasant, we gave our quarters a good cleaning, not forgetting ourselves, guns & accoutrements. We were mustered for pay, present in Co K 14 men — all quiet along the line.

Friday, July 1st

I am very unwell to day, nothing worthy of note transpiring, very warm.

Saturday, July 2nd

We moved our tents into better shape. The Sanitary Commission gave us Lemons, Tobacco and Canned Tomatoes. I am sick and can not go in for the good things. It is all quiet along the lines.

Sunday, July 3rd

I feel quite well this morning. We need rain very much. We can hardly stand the heat, we are laying around in camp and it is still quiet in front.

Monday, July 4th

This is a beautiful day. The Brass bands are playing all around us, we have had a very pleasant fourth. A little cooler would not have hurt us. It is quiet in front.

Tuesday, July 5th

To day the same old rigmarole, Picket. Fatigue, improving our camp, &c. I went on picket, have a charge of two posts, all quiet and lonesome here.

Wednesday, July 6th

I am still on Picket. It is exceedingly warm to day, we were relieved at 5 P.M. and came back to camp. I have a very bad head ache to night. All quiet in front.

Thursday, July 7th

Still in camp, things same as usual, I have had a bad head ache all day but feel better this evening. All quiet.

Friday, July 8, 1864

At 2 O'Clock this morning we were ordered out in a hurry. It was reported that the rebs were massing in our front, but it proved to be a false alarm, all quiet.

Saturday, July 9th

It is all quiet. The boys are busy digging a well. We only have to dig Eight feet, to get good cool water.

Sunday, July 10th

All quiet except artillery fighting, which is kept up most of the time.

Monday, July 11th

We have orders to be ready to move at a moments notice, James McCuen of the 85th came to see us. Ed and all the boys of the 85th are well.

Tuesday, July 12th

We tore our works down, and moved two miles to the left. We are doing some maneuvering, but I cannot tell what for. I am not very well.

Wednesday, July 13th

We packed up this morning our Corps (2nd) and moved about six miles to the right, we are now about four miles to the right of where we leveled our works. We are on the reserve, at least we are back from the front line. We have a nice camp, but water is at least a mile away. But if we stay any length of time we will have plenty in camp.

Thursday, July 14th

We got up early this morning, and went to tearing down some forts that we captured on the 3rd of June. Worked hard all day, and have to work to night. These forts are not in the right place.

Friday, July 15th

Still tearing down old Forts, worked all last night and are still at it to day at noon — *we are on reserve.*

Saturday, July 16th

We arrived in camp at 2 O'Clock A.M. and very tired boys are we about this time. My appetite is very bad, I had a chill, something like the ague. I am very unwell to night.

Sunday, July 17th

I feel better this morning. We are all taking a good rest to day. Raining a little this evening.

Monday, July 18th

At 3 O'Clock this morning we were called to arms, and stood so until daylight, but did not strike tents. We were dismissed at 7 O'Clock, and things are going on the same as before.

Tuesday, July 19th

It rained all night and all day. It cleared up nicely this evening. My health is not very good.

Wednesday, July 20th

Our corps is on fatigue duty to day, digging a trench for the artillery and ammunition wagons to get to the forts without getting shelled by the rebels. The trench is like a fence now and one mile long, twenty feet wide and fourteen feet deep. I tell you it is a big job. Returned to camp in the evening tired and hungry.

Thursday, July 21st

Resting to day. Same routine of camp life, Drill 2 hours, Dress parade, &c &c.

Friday, July 22nd

I am to day as yesterday. I am quartered with Lieut Springer, we have a good tent.

Saturday, July 23rd

Our whole division is at work on the trench again to day, returned to camp at 9 O'Clock P.M.

Sunday, July 24th

This is a day of rest for once with us. Mike Canan of the 85th was here to see us. Rain commenced falling after dinner and is still raining at roll call.

Monday, July 25th

We are again on fatigue at the same old place, two hours on and two off. Returned to camp at 9 O'Clock P.M.

Tuesday, July 26th

It is all bustle and confusion in camp this morning. Tents struck and are ready to move, we are not laying around kind of loose. At 4 O'Clock P.M. we started on the march. To the right, we crossed the Appomattox river at 11 O'Clock P.M. and on we go like mad.

Wednesday, July 27th — at Deep Bottom

We marched all night, crossed the James at Nine O'Clock. At 12 O'Clock our Division had captured one rebel battery of brass pieces and Two hundred and twenty prisoners. We lost pretty heavily in killed and wounded. We scoured the woods all day, at night our regiment went on picket.

Thursday, July 28th

We lay all day in line of battle 2½ miles from the James River at Turkey Bend. We threw up works in the evening.

Friday, July 29th

We worked all night at our breastworks and finished them this morning. Laid out streets, pitched our tents, then went to the river to bathe. We had any amount of fun in the river. One soldier of the 53rd P.V. was drowned. Got back to camp at 5 O'Clock P.M. struck tents at 9 O'Clock P.M. Recrossed the James at 10 O'Clock and on we go.

Saturday, July 30th

We marched all night and pitched our tents in front of Petersburgh at daylight this morning. In the rear of the Ninth Corps. We lay quiet until dark & then moved to our old camp in rear of 5th Corps, pitched tents in same place — all O.K.

Sunday, July 31st

This morning finds us in our old camp, our tents pitched on the same spot we left, and are feeling all right except a little sore.

Monday, August 1st

Still quiet in camp. We had marching orders, but they were counter-manded, and now we are ready for something else.

Tuesday, August 2nd — In front of Petersburg

We are still in our old camp, our suttler came up to day. We are now living on the fat of the land, and *dear fat at that*. The Molasses cakes has to fly now. We had inspection of arms and dress parade in the evening, so we are all hunkey.

Wednesday, August 3rd

I am still acting orderly sergeant, had Co Drill for 2 hours. I am helping make out pay rolls. Dress parade in the evening.

Thursday, August 4th

Fast day, we cleaned up in fine style to day. Finished the payrolls. Our whole Division went to church, formed a circle on the green sod, some playing mumble meg and very few listening to the sermon. The Pay master has come and they are thinking of greenbacks and suttlers wares instead of preaching.

Friday, August 5th

Had Inspection of arms, Collins reduced to ranks and Alexander Chisholm promoted to his place. The Rebels blew up one of our forts, we got into line in ten minutes and double quicked to the rear of the Ninth (9th) Corps. Turned and came back to camp, and went to bed damp with perspiration.

Saturday, August 6th

Still in camp, Drill, Dress Parade &c, nothing worthy of note transpiring. Only the Pickets firing day and night. The Colored troops started it. It is one continual Crack. Crack all the time.

Sunday, August 7th — Same Camp

We had our usual inspection of arms &c, went to church. Camp Robt J. Taggart of Co I preached. Capt Weltner came to us to day. The Capt looks very bad yet, he was very sick. We had dress parade in the evening.

Monday, August 8th

The same old thing, Dress Parade &c — John Nicholson came to see us to day.

Tuesday, August 9th

Ordered to pack up this morning. Afterwards countermanded, pitched our tents again, in the evening struck our tents again and moved to the left of Brigade.

Wednesday, August 10th

Changed places with The 7th N.Y. Heavy Arty, pitched our tents and fixed up in good order. Dress parade &c.

Thursday, August 11

Cleaning and fixing up camp all day. Drill & Dress parade, &c, &c.

Friday, August 12th

Orders to move, some say to Washington City but that is too good to be true. We packed up at 5 P.M. and moved to the right and halted within one mile of City Point, turned in and slept soundly.

Saturday, August 13th

In the same place this morning, drew clothing, went to the Point, raided sutler store with our cash and at 5 P.M. we got aboard of the transports, we was going to Washington City sure. I bet Capt Weltner Fifteen Dollars we would not go to Washington. We anchored until 10 O'Clock, we all felt good, the bands played and the colors were flung to the breeze.

Sunday, August 14th — Deep Bottom

This morning when I woke up the troops were disembarking at Deep Bottom. We soon landed. When we reached the bank we were greeted with a few rebel shells from the edge of the woods. We turned by the left flank and moved to the left then double quicked up and flanked the rebels. We took one line of works, moved two miles into a cornfield and was shelled terribly, many, many men were torn to pieces where we lay. I found a knapsack one Navy plug tobacco, a testament, a Box of salve, 2 dice, a looking glass, &c &c. Our regiment lost many. Moved back twenty yards, built works, and lay on our arms all night in the rain.

Monday, August 15th

We moved to the rear this morning, cleaned up and had inspection. I hear the 10th Corps is here. I seen troops passing, Ed Campbell was riding at the head of the column. I took after them they turned back. I seen Brother Ed for the first time since the 85th Penna left Uniontown; he and I had been in the same battle but we did not know it. I knew nearly all the men in his Co and shook hands with them. They had to pass on and I had to return to my Regt.

Tuesday, August 16th — Deep Bottom

Very heavy fighting in our front, a part of the Tenth (10th) Corps charged and took the rebels line of works with heavy loss. Our Second Division supported them but the rebs rallied and drove them back. We fell in in the evening and double quicked up to the right and was hotly engaged for some time. The Colored Division of the Tenth Corps relieved us, we laid down and they passed over us, and theirs was the best line of battle I ever seen go into action, it was perfect. When they came to us they swung around *like a gate,* and passed over us without a falter. Our Regiment fell in and was double quicked to the left to support the skirmish line which was hard pressed, we let a few volleys in to them and they fell back. We lay down but the bullets would fly all around us as though they came a long distance. While we lay here Brother Ed called up to me and wanted me to go back with him. I told him I could not leave our Company, he pointed to our four or five men and said they would never miss me. He coaxed a good deal but finally gave it up and went back to his regiment. We was relieved soon after and our regiment returned to our division.

Wednesday, August 17th

Cleaned up our guns this morning, I then went over to the 85th Regt P.V. and had a chat with my old friends. Ed gave me a loaf of soft Bread and half the money he had — 75¢. The Johnnies made another stir in front and I left for my regiment. Joe Johnson was there to see me.

Thursday, August 18th

We lay all day close to the 10th Corp, I spent two or three hours with Ed and the boys. We moved back to the road, rained like the devil, built new works and worked hard, still raining.

Friday, August 19th

Still behind works, have not heard of 8th to day. We can see the rebel pickets in their rifle pits, it is quiet but still. The rain falls increasingly and mud, Oh! Geminee.

Saturday, August 20th

Still in the same place, all quiet in front, still the rain comes. We packed up at 9 P.M. and moved to the rear and such a move was never moved before. It was as dark as a stack of black cats. We have to hollar at one another to keep in line, we fell in mud holes run over stumps and done most everything to make ourselves miserable. After we got out of the woods we could see a little, we reached the James river at Eleven O'Clock P.M. crossed and then away we went on a forced march.

Sunday, August 21st

Still on we go, crossed the Appomattox at 2 A.M. and reached our Old Camp at 6 O'Clock A.M. halted but did not pitch tents. At 10 A.M. we started again and halted in rear of the 5th Corps. A distance of six miles from our old camp, we bivouacked and slept soundly for we was more than tired.

Monday, August 22nd

We moved out to the left this morning and commenced to destroy the Weldon R.R. A detail went before and pulled out the spikes and then we march down parallel with the track, a whole Brigade at a time. The word is given — lay hold and they all stoop at once, then over goes three or four hundred yards at a time, then we move to the left again and repeat the same operation. Then a detail piles up the cross ties like a play house and lay the R.R. Iron across it, fill the inside with pieces of rails and brush and set it on fire. The ties burn and heats the iron in the middle and the weight of ends bends it down and makes it as crooked as a horse shoe. On we go making a clean sweep of the old road and the rain coming down the rear way all the time. Our Regiment went on Picket.

Tuesday, August 23rd

This morning the 16th Penna Cav passed us. Seen John Loomas and Ed Whetzel. We were relieved and went to the division. The Cavalry is raising the Johnnies by the way the carbines are cracking (at the station where Wilsons Cavalry had the fight sometime ago). Co K went on picket again or skirmish line.

Wednesday, August 24th

At daylight this morning we commenced skirmishing with the rebs, but neither advanced, we stood and popped away at each other, at noon we quit and called it a drawn game. I went back after rations, and when I got within one fourth mile of the skirmish line, they commenced again. I stopped at a house and commenced to cook and eat, roasting cans, young chickens, Pigs, also have plenty of Apples, Peaches, Pears, melons, &c. We are living very fat for the first time since leaving home. At dusk the boys were relieved and came back to get their rations, joined our Division. The 1st and 2nd is all that is here, the 3rd was left at Petersburgh. We worked all night building breastworks. The Pickets and Cavalry kept plugging away like thunder and we worked very hard.

Thursday, August 25th — Battle of Reams Station

This morning finds us behind good works, our line is the shape of a horse shoe as described on opposite page at the top. We now have the upper works. About One O'Clock P.M. the Pickets commenced to blaze away, both sides were like hornets, I never heard guns crack so. The Balls whistled by and seemed to say we will stop this raid or die in the attempt. They came closer and closer, and about the time we expected to fire Genl Hancock rode up to us and shouted right about face, double quick march. We left them works & down through the corn field we went like mad race horses, we halted in the old works of Wilsons cavalry (which they had made some months before while on a raid). They had settled down and was too low, they was very poor works. The skirmishers were now having a hot time and the 116th was orderd over the works to support them. We advanced over in a murderous fire. Just as we reached the skirmish line the rebels with two lines of battle emerged from the woods. We was then ordered back to the works, but we had lost twenty one killed and wounded in that half hour. Capt Nolen of Co B commanded the Regt, he went along the line and encouraged us to stand firm, and not to fire until he gave the word. As he spoke the last word a bullet from a sharpshooters rifle pierced his breast and he fell, his last and only words were tell Capt Taggart Co I to take command. Capt Taggart was going along the lines repeating the same orders given by Capt Nolen when he was shot through the heart, he never spoke again. There fell two of as brave Captain as ever drew swords. Capt Taggart was from Pittsburgh he was a pious, praying christian man, almost every night he had prayer in the street of his Co or in his tent. We would often attend for we knew he was a good man. Lieut price then took command, on came the Johnnies in grand style. There we sat with our guns many of them double charged with buck and Ball (we had the Old Fashioned Musket at that time). They had to advance 200 yards over a nice level sod, and when they got close enough they screamed that womanlike scream and with fixed bayonets on they came. Four of our batteries opened with us and we mowed them with grape and canister, Buck and Ball, but on they came within twenty paces of our line. But they recoiled fell back and left the sod covered with their dead and wounded. In half an hour they charged again and met with the same disaster, if *anything worse.*

They now opened on us with their batteries, but they done the 2nd division more harm than they did us. The shells passed over us and took the 2nd Division in the back. This lasted over a half hour, it seemed hours to us, all the time the sharpshooters were picking off our artillery horses. In one team they killed seven horses out of eight, in another five. Suddenly the firing ceased and with low yells and without firing a gun they sprang forward, hats pulled down over their eyes and guns on a trail. There was a narrow strip of woods on our right, in front of a new Regiment, the 7th N.Y. I. They had massed a whole Brigade and charged this Regiment out and that put them around on our flank and rear. We had no thought of giving away until we seen there was no chance and we fell back but not before we sent hundreds of them to their long homes. They came up in front of Co B. First Sergt Reber clubbed his musket and dashed the brains out of four of five of them before he fell back. (He was promoted to 1st Lieut afterwards.) We fell back to the 2nd division, who we found was all demoralized (Wade Hamptons dismounted Cavalry in front of them and the shells and musketing that over shot us took them in the back). I tell you it was enough to demoralize any troops.

This was the only fight that we could ever see after we had fired a few volleys, but this we *could see all,* the smoke would raise from the guns in an instant. When we had our guns cocked waiting for the word to fire, I picked out the very largest man I could see & took sight. When they would drop wounded they would haul out an old dirty Handkerchief and wave it while they lay on their backs. I am very much afraid their flags of distress was not regarded much. While we joined the 2nd Division pulled off our caissons and left the cannon and dead horses for the Johnnies. By this time it was dark and the rain was pouring down, as hard as ever I seen or felt it. The troops fell in promiscuously and off we went through the rain mud and darkness, leaving Thirty five hundred men and five guns in the hands of the enemy.

I am sure *we killed* as many of them as they killed, wounded and took prisoners of us. Now on we go, faint, hungry, and drenched to the skin. At 11 O'Clock I could go no farther, I fell out at a fire to rest. I had not been there long when Capt Weltner came. He had been away on the left on Picket, he was mud from head to foot and staggering as he walked. I called him & he was glad to find one of his own Company, he greeted me as if he had not seen me for years. I spread my Blanket and he lay down and slept like a log. I sit by the fire and watched him. In half an hour I woke him up and on we went arm in arm staggering into ruts and mudholes. Some Cavalry overtook us and he got on behind one of them and I seen him no more that night. On I went.

Friday, August 26th

At 3 O'Clock this morning I came up to the column, we kept on marching until daylight. Then we halted near where we started from in rear of the fifth (5th) Corps, and such a sight as we presented, we went to washing, cleaning our guns, and getting ourselves into a presentable shape again, instead of taking the rest we so much needed. After getting our clothes washed and dried, our guns cleaned and accoutrements shined up and resting until evening we felt like new men. At roll call 92 men answered to their names of the whole regiment, out of the almost Nine Hundred that we started on the campaign with on May 3rd when we left near Brandy Station.

Saturday, August 27th

We are still at the same place. Co "K" has one Sergt (myself) two Corporals and seven men. Weltner is Ir[?] Capt and has command of the Regiment, 1st Lieut Cope was captured June 22nd, Lt Springer captured the day before yesterday, I am in Command of the Co. I have the piles very bad and was ordered to the hospital but I will not go.

Sunday, August 28th

Packed up this morning and moved to the right a few rods. Near our old camp, we laid out streets, pitched our tents and polished up nice and clean and now we are ready for whatever duty comes next.

Monday, August 29th

I was very busy to day making out pay rolls, reports, &c. Bro Ed also Joe and Sam Johnson was over from the 85th. I have the piles very bad.

Tuesday, August 30th

To day busy cleaning and fixing up for muster, we were mustered for pay to day. I am still acting Orderly Sergeant, I am the only sergeant present. The Co now has 14 men present.

Wednesday, August 31st

I am still busy fixing up Co papers. Sent 1 corpl and seven men on forage. Old complaint no better.

Thursday, Sept 1st

To day no change from usual routine of camp life.

Friday, Sept 2nd

At 12 O'Clock to day our Division was called out to see a man shot for desertion, we formed as is usually done upon such occasions in a hollow square. His grave had been dug. They sit him on the end of his coffin, a file of Provo Guards (twelve men) with one of their 12 guns loaded with a blank cartridge let him have the other Eleven and soon fixed him.

Saturday, Sept 3rd

The Regiment all went out on Fatigue duty, I sent over to the 85th. Bro Ed had peas for dinner, we got to talking about old times, I eat all the peas and when I started home I could hardly get there, while we was eating a shell came over (a very common thing) and took a mans arm off. I got back to quarters safely.

Sunday, Sept 4th

We are still in the same place. Had the usual Co Inspection, laid around all day. Things quiet in front. At 12 O'Clock P.M. One Hundred guns was fired in honor of the fall of Atlanta, all the bands played and we had a nice time.

Monday, Sept 5th

Left camp this morning, went to the left to build forts, we worked all day and night.

Tuesday, Sept 6th

Came back to camp this morning and packed up, moved to the left and built breastworks and a fort, pitched tents. We have a cold rain to night.

Wednesday, Sept 7th

Moved to the left again, are behind good breastworks. Capt Weltner went to the Hospital, we lay quiet all day. No detail from the regiment which is an unusual thing for us.

Thursday, Sept 8th

We aroused at 3 A.M. Moved back to Corps Head Qrs and left a large detail, laid around loose all day.

Friday, Sept 9th

I took the Pay rolls back to Division Hospital to get them signed and examined. When I came back I found them moved and in Camp near Hancocks head Quarters. I am still acting Orderly Sergt.

Saturday, Sept 10th

Very heavy cannonading all last night, but quiet again to day.

Sunday, Sept 11th

All busy cleaning up for Sundays inspection, had inspection and put in the day writing letters.

Monday, Sept 12th

Very busy fixing up & getting ready for brigade inspection on the 14th.

Tuesday, Sept 13th

We had two hours drill. The boys went out on fatigue duty this afternoon, I am making out my tri monthly report. The boys got back at midnight.

Wednesday, Sept 14th

Had Brigade inspection to day, also 2 hours drill. Alex Chisholm and I went over to the 85th, spent the afternoon.

Thursday, Sept 15th

Had Brigade Drill to day. Orderly Sergt James E. Jolliffe came up. In the evening we went front into the trenches to support the red diamonds (our 3rd Divn). Very heavy Picket fighting all night. In fact picket firing day and night without ceasing.

Friday, Sept 16

Returned to Camp this morning, I gave the roll back to Jolliff, had Co Drill in forenoon and afternoon. Had Brigade Drill also — Regt went to the Flank works.

Saturday, Sept 17th

Came back at 1 A.M. all quiet in front except the pickets banging away at each other as usual.

Sunday, Sept 18th

This is a beautiful day. After our usual Co inspection we laid around and slept and wrote letters to our friends. Elliott Finley came over to us on a visit from the 85th Regt P.V.

Monday, Sept 19th

We had Co drill for 4 hours, nothing else worth mentioning going on to day.

Tuesday, Sept 20th

Regt went out and guarded the Rail Road Depot. I went over to the 85th and took dinner with the boys, had a very pleasant time. Returned to camp at dusk, found The Regt in its place.

Wednesday, Sept 21st

Orderly Sergeant was detailed for Quarter Masters Clerk, I am promoted to his place. I went over to the Hospital to see Capt Weltner found him very bad.

Thursday, Sept 22nd

Sergt James E. Jolliff took leave of the Company this morning and went to his new position, which a great many would be very glad to have. Sergt Hezekiah Dean came up to day and took his old position of 5th Sergt.

Friday, Sept 23rd

Everything quiet all along the line.

Saturday, Sept 24th

Struck tents moved to the right, and relieved a part of the 10th Corps, and went on picket.

Sunday, Sept 25th

Was relieved last night, moved to the right and relieved the 69th N.Y. and slept all day.

Monday, Sept 26th

At midnight we moved to the right, on the Picket line and under heavy fire, still in trenches, drew rations. We have been under heavy fire all day but no serious damage done.

Tuesday, Sept 27th

We was relieved at midnight and moved back to bombproofs. This morning we are all right, our baggage and tents came.

Wednesday, Sept 28th

We lay quiet all day. In the evening our Regiment went on fatigue duty, to work on forts. We had worked two hours when a Staff officer came up and ordered us out. We had just time to get out of the fort when the rebel artillery dropped shells in by the hundred. It has always been a mystery to me how they knew they were going to shell the fort. If we had stayed ten minutes longer they would have tore us to pieces.

They opened all along the line as far as you could see right and left. It was a grand and awful sight, and one to be seen, never forgotten. We reached camp at 12 P.M.

Thursday, Sept 29th

Got into line this morning and went to Division Head Qrs and was paid off, I received $69.75. Capt Mcgraw paid me $10.00 borrowed money. Returned to camp & turned in.

Friday, Sept 30th

The whole division was ordered out to see a man shot that belonged to the 63rd N.Y. Returned and went on Picket. The rebels came out over their works to charge us, but we made things too hot for them and they climbed back in a hurry. We kept watch all night, but they did not try that game again.

Saturday, Octr 1st

Was relieved this morning and came to our breastworks. Have had a long and heavy rain, it is very muddy and disagreeable, very heavy fighting on our left.

Sunday, Octr 2nd

This is a fine morning, cleaned up our rusty guns and have had a quiet rest.

Monday, Octr 3rd

Very heavy fighting on our right and left, but quiet in our front. We are still on reserve picket.

Tuesday, Octr 4th

We lay quiet all day. In the evening the Johnnies opened on our front with shells and musketry, but we soon dried them up.

Wednesday, Octr 5th

Moved back to Fort Steadman, pitched our tents on the left and fixed them up very nicely. A lot of us boys was sitting out talking. A shell came over and bursted and threw dirt all over us. Jim Collins run under his shelter tent for protection, we worried him a good deal about it.

Thursday, Octr 6th — Fort Steadman

This is a beautiful day. We have cleaned up and have arranged everything in our little village so that we are comfortable, we drew new clothing last evening. The boys have stopped the Knee and Elbow holes with new blouse and Pants. Moved out on Picket line at 9 P.M.

Friday, Octr 7th

We are still on the front line and are very well contented, for when in front we have no fatigue duty to do, in fact this is a lazy place. We lay around like treed fox hounds, all quiet in front.

Saturday, Octr 8th

This morning still finds us in front line, almost every evening the rebel Forts and ours open fire at each other, and such a throwing of shells was never seen, the air is full of them for an hour at a time. In the evening came to the Fort.

Sunday, Octr 9th

We was ordered at 3 A.M. this morning into the breastworks, they were expecting an attack. We had to stand in the works until after daylight. In the evening everything was quiet.

Monday, Octr 10th — Fort Steadman

Things quiet except a duel very evening with the mortars. Some of our Co "K" boys was playing with powder making squibs. I told them they had better not play with old cartridges, but they took no heed. After a while Albert Fraser got his eyes nearly burned out, he was totally blind and had to be led off to the hospital, I never seen a man in more misery than he was. The Johnnies are hollowing and cheering for the Copperheads this evening.

Tuesday, Octr 11th

This morning we are making arrangements for holding our election. About forty of us was collected down below the fort appointing Judges, &c. Some one was saying I move that Lt Vander — (meaning Lt S. G. Vanderheyden afterwards promoted to Capt of Co G.) but before he finished getting the name out *bang* came a rebel shell over within about two feet of our heads and bursted behind us. I do not think I ever seen polls closed as quick in my life. In three seconds there wasn't any of the party to be seen. So we all collected in the bomb proof and held our election amidst the thunder of our guns. I voted the way we was shooting for Old Abe and the Stars and Stripes. I knew I was right for the Johnnies would take off their hats by the hundreds and shout for McClellan. Our Regiments vote was very close, we only beat them three votes. There wasn't any electioneering going on and no whiskey to do it with if they had wanted to, so our Election ended without any trouble.

Wednesday, Octr 12th

To day we laid around until evening, then we struck our tents and went on Picket at the Rail Road Bridge where we was on the 19th of June. Lt Wilson and a lot of us liked to have been killed with our own batteries. They shot too low until they got the range, after that they passed over us into the Johnnies where we liked to see them go. This is the same place Alexander Chisholm got hit with a spent Ball. The Rebels shoot under the bridge at us as we pass.

Thursday, Octr 13th

I have charge of Eight posts, that is I have to see that the Corporals relieve the men on post every 2 hours. This morning just before daylight I went up to post No 7 and Johnnie Hayden and Abe Hull was eating breakfast. We are liable to eat at any hour when we have it to eat with us. I sit down with them and was helping to put the Hard tack and Coffee out of the way. All at once a Johnnie Jumped up and leveled his gun over the works and cried halt, I surrender. I surrender come out of the darkness, I am a Johnnie deserter and there is no one with me. I told him to come in and such a looking fellow, mud all over and trembling like a leaf. You wont hurt me will you, I told him no, we would not hurt him and to sit down and have some breakfast, he sit down. He was so scared that he could hardly eat any at first, but he soon came around all right and made the Hard tack and Coffee disappear like as if he had not had anything to eat for the last month. He said his officers told them if they came over — the Yanks would kill them like dogs, he said his brother and brother in law was coming over the next night. He also said if the Rebs knew how we treated them when they came over that half of their army would be over in a week. After he had eat a huge breakfast he took out a big plug of Old Virginia Tobacco and passed it around, we took a sailors cut [?], around we sit and talked until daylight and then I took him back to Brigade Head Quarters. He was a fair specimen of the Rebel Soldier. I came back to the Picket Line.

Friday, Octr 14th

We was relieved at 8 O'Clock last night and returned to the Bomb proffs, pitched our tents and cleaned our selves up this morning, and are spending the day resting.

Saturday, Octr 15th

Still laying around resting, all quiet along the lines, I am very tired of being Orderly Sergeant. I went to the Quarter Masters to day to try and get Orderly Sergt James E. Jolliff to come back and take his old position, as I would rather be duty Sergt than orderly. He said he thought he would as it was very lonesome back in the rear. Got back at dark, sent all the Co on fatigue duty.

Sunday, Octr 16th

This morning the whole regiment Orderly Sergeant and all went on fatigue, worked all day and returned to Camp at 4 O'Clock. The batteries had quite a duel to night, and it was a beautiful sight to see the shells bursting by the dozens.

Monday, Octr 17th

Had Brigade inspection this morning, lay around all day, in the evening sent all the Companies on fatigue. We are on picket or fatigue duty all the time. The boys would sooner be on Picket all the time than on fatigue half the time.

Tuesday, Octr 18th

Sent all the boys on fatigue again this morning. I washed my clothes. The boys returned this evening all O.K.

Wednesday, Octr 19th

The same as yesterday, learn to labor and to wait until you *get your eagle.*

Thursday, Octr 20th

This morning we had Regimental Inspection, we have Company inspection every evening. This evening the Johnnies got very wasteful, they sent over shells by the hundred, some came into our Camp and exploded. One struck the tent next to mine and tore it up as well as a blanket that was hung on it. Fortunately there was no one in it. Another tore up a gun in Co B. but our forts opened up and give them the very devil long after they had quit. I think they got enough to last them awhile.

Friday, Octr 21st

Drilled in forenoon and afternoon, at dark all the Regiment was ordered to tear down the front works, they were too close to the rebel works (30 yds). The officers told us the works *had to be down* and the *sooner the quicker.* And also to be quiet about it, for if the rebels would find out what we was doing and would open fire on us they would kill us all. So into it we went, and never was works torn down any faster for we was working to save *our hides,* and midnight we were half down.

Saturday, Octr 22nd

All night we toiled, and just at break of day we finished and moved back to the fort. Afterwards I went back to look at what we had been doing. It almost made the hair on my head raise to see what a place we had been in. While we had been tearing down another detail had been building new ones one Hundred yards back of us. If the Johnnies had of known what we was doing and opened fire on us (for we was in the range of two batteries) they could have killed every one of us, but good luck, Providence or something had saved us. I tell you if we had of been half an hour longer daylight would have shown us 30 yds from them and nothing to protect us. It was an awful place to be but a miss is as good as a mile.

Sunday, Octr 23rd

This morning I went out with a squad of fifty men from Regiment and found the same No from other Regts, we had at least 500 men and 50 wagons. We went to the woods to cut abattoes to put in front of the works to jab the Johnnies if they should want to pay us a night visit. We took things moderate & sent back several wagon loads of trees. It was laughable to see some of the men handling an ax that had never done the like before, they put me in mind of women cutting fire wood at home they was so awkward. We arrived in camp at dark without any serious accidents.

Monday, Octr 24th

We lay around all day until 6 P.M. We struck tents and moved to the left to Fort Morton. We pitched tents and sent out a detail for Pickets, and here we are at home again, we are getting used to this moving and take it all in good part without grumbling.

Tuesday, Octr 25th — Fort Morton

To day we laid out streets, cleaned up, drew rations, &c. The Regiment came back off of Picket all O.K. Co G was detached and sent to the left to another fort. All quiet.

Wednesday, Octr 26th

Nothing of importance transpired to day.

Thursday, Octr 27th

We moved this morning where the 85th P.V. lay, and the boys are pitching tent within fifty yards of Fort Morton. At 3 O'Clock P.M. we was ordered into line and under arms. It is reported that the Johnnies are massing in our front, our batteries all along the line opened and for three hours the very ground shook. I never heard much harder cannonading. At Nine O'Clock the 148th P.V. with seven shooters, led by 1st Lieut Henry D. Price of Co C. of our Regt by *his request* charged across and took a rebel Fort. It was a bold undertaking, but *they done it*. Lt Price was killed shot through the head inside of the Fort. We supported them, they did not hold the fort, they did not try to. I think it was only to try the rebel line. The survivors came back leaving many of their brave comrades dead in the fort and laying between the lines. This was all done in the rain and darkness. We passed a very disagreeable night.

Friday, Octr 28th

This is a fine morning, all quiet but the Pickets they blaze away day & night. As we go to bed the pickets is having a lively time.

Saturday, Octr 29th

All quiet in front to day.

Sunday, Octr 30th

This is another fine morning. Middle of the day very warm. Evening Cool. Last night the rebels came over and relieved about three hundred of our pickets and took them over prisoners. It was very dark, they captured two posts first without making any alarm, and then a large party came over and moved to the rear of our Pickets. Our Pickets thought it was their relief coming. So they got in back of them and drove them in to the rebel camp as prisoners. They belonged to the 6th Corps and joined us on the left. The Johnnies are a sneaking lot of devils.

Monday, Octr 31st

This morning packed up and moved to Smiths farm in the rear of Hancock Station, was mustered for Sept and Oct pay. Then moved to the left about the same distance from the station, only on the other side.

Tuesday, Novr 1st

Got up at daylight, policed up our Camp, Clean & Nice. Had inspection and battalion drill, took men this evening to work on a fort near Fort Morton, raining like blazes.

Wednesday, Novr 2nd

This is a fine morning, we had Company Inspection and battalion drill. We moved two (2) miles in the afternoon and had Division Inspection. We came back to camp at 7 P.M. very tired.

Thursday, Novr 3rd

A cold rain lasting all night and is still raining this morning, very raw and disagreeable indeed. We are trying to fix up warm quarters as we can feel that winter is coming with its cold rains and snows. I feel very tired for we worked hard.

Friday, Novr 4th

It is a little warmer this morning, had Co and Battalion drill in the afternoon, moved out and had Division Inspection again, did not get back to Camp until 8 O'Clock P.M.

Saturday, Novr 5th

Our whole Corps went out to the same place that we had Division Inspection and was reviewed by Genl Hancock. Returned to Camp and packed up at dusk and moved to our old place. (Fort Morton.) We got there just in time as the Rebels made a bold dash at our lines, after a hard struggle of half an hour what was left of them fell back. Our loss was very light, and as I go to bed I hear the Artillery & Pickets keeping up the same old time *Spit-Spit* boom.

Sunday, Novr 6th

All quiet this morning in front, Pickets always excepted.

Monday, Novr 7th

Our overcoats came up to day that we had left at Brandy Station April 20th. I went over and took charge of Co "K's" boxes. I opened them and took out 68 overcoats, some dress Coats, shirts, Drawers, &c, and we have only 17 men left here in Co K to take them and some of them did not send coats to the rear. 70 men killed, wounded, sick and missing since May 3rd. It makes me sad to read over the names & know so many of them will never say here or present again.

Tuesday, Novr 8th

Election again to day. Sergt Jolliffe took charge of the Co. to day. There was some flaw in his detachment papers and he returned to duty. Now I am Second Sargeant again and feel much better, as I think Orderly Sargeant is the meanest position in the Army. While we were holding our Election to day the Johnnies sent a flag of truce requesting permission to bury their dead that have been laying in front of our works since they charged on us on the night of the 5th of November, they were granted two hours, from 8 to 10 A.M. After the election I was sent as Sergeant of Brigade Guard for the first time. In the afternoon Lt Henry D. Price's remains was sent over by the Johnnies, he belonged to Co C and was killed on the night of the 27th of October when he led the 148th P.V. and captured the rebel fort and was killed Just within the gate. I put a guard over his remains which was sent home at 10 O'Clock P.M. And thus ended the life of one of the bravest officers of the old Irish Brigade. While the Armistice was on the Rebels cheered by the hundreds for McClelland and it hurt our friends of little Mac, as they called him, very much. Everything quiet in front except the pickets.

Wednesday, Novr 9th

I am still on Brigade Guard. Our Regt went four majority for little Mac. The bands are playing merry tunes to day. Our Company went for old Abe with a *tremendous* majority. We were relieved and sent to the regiment this evening.

Thursday, Novr 10th

I was ordered to report to the Col this morning and he put me in charge of Co C as that Co has no officers higher than Corporal. I tried to get off but it was no go, so I am in a worse fix than ever. I expect some of the Co will come up and relieve me. I think I will have some trouble as taking a man out of one Co and putting him over another is not a very good way, but I will soon see how things go. I went up this evening and reported to the Company and they said they was very glad as they had no one to see to their rights. I took them out on dress parade and had no trouble. They are very careless about their appearance but I think I can bring them around all right.

Friday, Novr 11th

I am getting along with my new duty very well, a good deal better than I expected. We are not doing any Picket or fatigue duty. John Lynn of the 85th was over to see me.

Saturday, Novr 12th

I heard to day that the Johnnies had a mine dug nearly over to Fort Hell. Our men dug down and came on to some of the rebel miners & captured them. We have a cold shower of rain this evening.

Sunday, Novr 13th

This is a fine day but cool. We had church at the 53rd P.V. to day. All very quiet in front, we are having quite a rest as there has not been any details for Picket or fatigue duty for some days. All quiet to night.

Monday, Novr 14th

I was over to the depot to day and got weighed and pulled down 187-½#, I am as fat as a pig, 167 is my usual weight. Had Co and Battalion Drill to day, all quiet. I am getting along fine with Co C.

Tuesday, Novr 15th

This is a fine day, we cleaned up nicely and had Brigade Inspection, all quiet along the line.

Wednesday, Novr 16th

This morning Co Drill and afternoon Battalion Drill. All quiet along the line.

Thursday, Novr 17th

We pulled up this morning and moved back in 2nd hollow between fort Morton and Rail Road Cut. We have our tents pitched and have a beautiful camp.

Friday, Novr 18th

This morning the whole regiment was put on fatigue duty, consisting of digging a cut to sink the track so the rebels cannot shell our cars. We have marching orders this evening.

Saturday, Novr 19th

It rained all night and is cold and raw to day. Are doing nothing but roasting our shins and cracking jokes.

Sunday, Novr 20th

Still raining this morning, *quietly* but all the time. It is a general rain.

Monday, Novr 21st

The cry is still it rains, and we are laying in our tents writing letters and punishing hard tack &c.

Tuesday, Novr 22nd

It has ceased raining this morning and is getting very cold. The officers are fixing up their quarters, I mean the boys are fixing them up for them. Very cold this evening.

Wednesday, Novr 23rd

Very cold last night, and clear and cold this morning. We are all very busy fixing up our quarters. I and chums built a new chimney to day. We had very heavy picket fighting in our front all last night.

Thursday, Novr 24th

All are busy this morning putting more logs on our tents to make them higher. We have to carry the logs about one mile. About noon we was putting on the last log. I had an old hatchet as dull as a hoe cutting a notch in a log so as to fit it down over another. The old hatchet slipped and I nearly tore the whole back off of my left hand. I had to go to the Surgeons and have seven stitches in it. It made the sweat stand out on me in big drops while he sewed it up. He is a very rough tailor and it hurt cruelly. My hand is very painful to night. We got our tents down and are very comfortable.

Friday, Novr 25th

To day the sanitary Committee sent us geese, chickens and apples. Jacob Allamon and I are bunking together, we got for our share a goose leg and a chicken leg, we cooked them in a quart tin cup and put in some drop dumpling, made the dumpling by mixing a little flour and water in a cup and dropped it in. I enjoyed that dinner as well as the good old home dinners. My hand is very sore.

Saturday, Novr 26th

A little more sanitary to day in the shape of a turkey leg. We went in on the drop dumplings again. My hand is perfectly stiff. It is very sore and I have to carry it in a sling.

Sunday, Novr 27th

This is a beautiful day, the nicest day we have had for some time. We are enjoying it by sitting out in squads talking and speculating who is to be our Corps Commander in the future, as the talk is that Genl Hancock is to take command of the 1st Vet Corps. The boys say if they take Hancock away from us they wont fight a bit, will run and let the Johnnies whip us. Before this they was always cursing him and saying he was always trying to get us into a fight when it was not our turn. Now if they take him they say they wont do anything for my part I hate the idea of losing our General. My hand is very sore.

Monday, Novr 28th

Genl Humphreys takes command of our Corps. We have not seen him yet, and of course we do not know whether we will like him or not. We are all very sorry to lose Genl Hancock. All quiet, my hand is about the same.

Tuesday, Novr 29th

Our Division struck tents last night, moved to the left near Yellow House and relieved the 9th Corps. I did not go this morning, I was sent to the Hospital. It was about to move and they had a squad of 115 men to go to our Corps. So I got in among them and was put in charge to take them to Corps Head Quarters. I started and got to the Regt at 9 O'Clock P.M. and left the men laying scattered along the road for 5 miles as I could not get them along. So I let them go and I went to the Regt. I found the boys in snug quarters that the Ninth Corps boys had just finished. The latter swore a good deal about having to change places when they had just got their quarters to suit them. My pards Sergt Wm Sembower and Jacob Allamon are all right. I turned in with them, and I am all right except my hand.

Wednesday, Novr 30th

We are all right up here except very lonesome, as everything is quiet. It is quite a contrast up here on extreme left and being in front of Petersburgh, there it is shoot all the time day and night. I am excused from duty but I must have something to do so I am running old Co C. as usual.

Thursday, Decr 1st

Very quiet up here we relieve pickets at 9 O'Clock in the morning. When we was on the right we could hardly get onto picket in the dark. The change suits us very well. My hand is a little better.

Friday, Decr 2nd

We had a dull day, all quiet, nothing of importance transpiring.

Saturday, Decr 3rd

Regular routine of camp life.

Sunday, Decr 4th

Had the usual inspection, Genl Miles and Staff rode past and halted a little, took a gaze at us but said nothing, my hand is better.

Monday, Decr 5th

Everything very quiet to day. Our Sutler came up and pitched his tent and the boys are patronizing him in fine style. He credits them to the amount of three dollars, and they pay him when they are paid off. Many of them may be dead by that time. In that case he would be the loser.

Tuesday, Decr 6th

This is a beautiful day, we are all busy washing and cleaning up our arms.

Wednesday, Decr 7th

Another beautiful day, we have marching orders, but we do not care for, that we are used to those little jobs. The 9th corp boys put their tents too close to the Breastworks, the first tent of each company is only twenty feet away. To night at 10 O'Clock we have orders to tear them all down and put them one hundred and twenty feet back. Now this is very easy for them to order, but for us after we got them fixed to our liking, chimneys built, and in as good order as we could possibly put them, then to have to tear them down and move them is a little too much, but at midnight we was working away singing and whistling.

Thursday, Decr 8th

We worked nearly all night. This morning we are daubing and building our chimneys, we will soon be fixed up and ready to move again as
that is sure to follow after getting fixed up good and comfortable. I have
a bad head ache this evening.

Friday, Decr 9th

At 1 A.M. we pack up and moved four miles to the left to Hatchers
Run. We maneuvered around first to the left and then to the right. All
this time the snow was falling fast and this being a very marshy place it
melted underfoot and made a thick slush over shoe mouth deep and our
feet was soaking wet before we had gone a mile. About four O'Clock
we advanced and found the enemy on the farther bank of the stream
(Hatchers Run), which was now very much swollen with the recent rains
and snow. We charged right through the stream and drove them back
capturing some prisoners. The water was deep. One Corporal and four
men was drowned. The rebs had dug deep holes in places and then built
a dam below and backed the water up so we could not see the pitfalls.
They fell down and the water being over their heads they soon drowned.
The water was so cold our clothes froze stiff in a few minutes. This was
the hardest trip yet. We recrossed lower down, and stacked arms and
commanded to build fires. The logs and brush are all wet and we have
one awful time shivering and blowing. In an hour or so our labor was
rewarded by having a big log heap burning, I do not think I ever felt
anything so nice to stand up and warm my back before the log heap. It
is snowing and has been all the time. At twelve we was still drying our
clothes and the snow wetting us as fast as the fire dried.

Saturday, Decr 10th

What a miserable night we had of it. The snow continued to fall all
night. I spread my blanket down and wrapped myself into it, put my gun
over the top and laid down about one O'Clock this morning, covered up
head and heels and was soon fast asleep. When I woke up this morning
I could hardly push off the load of snow that was on me. When I did
get out the smoke rolled out of my nest like as if something was on fire.
I went around kicking in the snow piles hunting for Co C boys — after
spending an hour I got them out for roll call. Of course the other Orderly Sergeants was enjoying the same business. We piled on fresh logs
and soon it looked like we was on a clearing expedition, and soon the
cooking, eating, laughing, talking and swearing was going on like there
was no better place than this to be found on earth. At 3 O'Clock P.M.

the rebs drove in our cavalry pickets. On they came in two lines of battle and we expected to have a warm time. We had orders to load and stand at *attention,* and about the time we thought we was to let them have it, we moved out by the left flank our whole brigade & went to the rear of the first and so on until we nearly reached camp and then we moved off to our old Camp and left the Johnnies pitching around hunting us in the mud and snow. We reached camp a little after dark and found our tents full of snow. We went to work and scraped the snow out, built a fire and at 10 O'Clock went to bed.

Sunday, Decr 11th

This morning finds us all right, our camp is covered with a snow 3 inches deep but not very cold to day. We stick to the fire and tents very close.

Monday, Decr 12th

The snow still lays on. I suppose the pickets have a hard time of it, I get off of that duty. I get along smoothly with Co C.

Tuesday, Decr 13th

The same old Camp duties, and it is very cold.

Wednesday, Decr 14th

Still cold. Sergt Sembower and myself carried mud, warmed water and made mortar and stopped all the air holes in our tent, and we feel very comfortable.

Thursday, Decr 15th

Still the same old thing, no change worthy of note.

Friday, Decr 16th

To day the whole division was ordered out to see the execution of three deserters. We moved about a half a mile to the rear of our camp and formed in hollow square. The men looked clean and nice, their guns glistened in the sun which shines nice, but the air is raw and cold. At half past eleven we heard the brass band strike up the dead march and move slowly from Division Head Quarters. The Gallows was already up and the graves dug and the men could look down in them as they was led up the steps of the Gallows, on they came and passed through a gap that was made through the Square. First came the band then the three poor devils and then a file of twelve men before and twelve behind —

They was led up one under each rope. Then the priest (for they were Catholics) went to them and pow wayed a while and then the ropes was tied around the neck and a white cap was then drawn down over the head to the shoulder, arms tied behind them and legs tied together. While this was going on you could hear the boys talking in this way, desert us will you, fight against us will you — Old Phil Sheridan happened to know you did he — a little bit sorry for what you have done ain't you. I will bet the little fellow dies game. I know by the way he stands, that big one says another is such a calf he can hardly stand. Some one cold and teeth chattering. I wish they would hurry and not keep us waiting here all day gaping at them Sons of B ——. Now a fellow stands under with a big-wooden mallet ready to Knock out the stanchion at 12 O'Clock, he gets the signal, out goes the prop and down goes three poor fellows about three feet but they stop suddenly and commence to struggle. It is an awful sight, I will stop here. — As the word is attention, right face — forward — file right — march. And off we go, I think no more of it until we get our dinners, as that is the next thing on the programme.

Saturday, Decr 17th

All busy cleaning up for inspection at 2 O'Clock. Inspection is over, Co C all O.K. Twelve sick men sent back out of our regiment. Capt Weltner came up.

Sunday, Decr 18th

We had the usual Co inspection, we got our dress coats this evening.

Monday, Decr 19th

We all got into line to receive Genl U. S. Grant and lady, but it was too cold for them and they did not make their appearance — very cold.

Tuesday, Decr 20th

Things look like a short stay, officers and men fixing up for the winter. I went over to Division Head Quarters to see the guard mount, all guards has to go there and be inspected, of the Whole Division.

Wednesday, Decr 21st

Very wet and muddy to day, rained all last night and until noon to day, we have a bad looking camp.

Thursday, Decr 22nd — Near Yellow house.

Cold this morning, the rain has stopped, the air is getting cold. All quiet in front, we have the regular old routine of camp life.

Friday, Decr 23rd

We drew new clothing to day and the boys all have a full suit, and we need them for it is a good deal like winter here.

Saturday, Decr 24th

Nothing worthy of note to day. The same old rigmarole of camp life.

Sunday, Decr 25th — Christmas

To day our Division was ordered out to see a man of the 5th New Hampshire Regt shot. He was shot at 12 O'Clock, the time they always

Monday, Decr 26th

All quiet here except great rejoicing for Shermans victories, the boys are shouting themselves hoarse to night.

Tuesday, Decr 27th

It is drizzling rain to day, we have to house up, all quiet in front.

Wednesday, Decr 28th

Nothing of importance to day or to night.

Thursday, Decr 29th

Same old rigmarole as usual.

Friday, Decr 30th

To day our Division was ordered out to see a man of the 5th New Hampshire Regt shot. He was shot at 12 O'Clock, the time they always shoot or hang them. While we was returning to camp the snow commenced to fall and is still falling like mad.

Saturday, Decr 31st

The weather very bad to day, the snow is 3 inches deep. We was mustered for pay to day for Nov & Dec. So the old year has gone out and left us in good Winter Quarters and in good health.

Sunday, Jany 1st, 1865

The New Year came in and found us near Yellow house Va. Our camp ground is covered with four inches of snow, we have warm quarters and are very comfortably situated. Orderly Sergeant James E. Jolliffe is now with our company. I have charge of Co "C." Our New Years dinner consists of hard tack and Salt Pork with a cup of very strong coffee. Abe Moore of 140th P. V. was here for tea.

Monday, Jany 2nd

It is cold and raw this morning, still snow enough for tracks. We have orders to be ready for review and we are very busy cleaning up for the same. All quiet in front.

Tuesday, Jany 3rd

All busy this morning getting ready for review, and we are ready. We left camp at 10 A.M. and moved to the rear one mile ("Whole Division") and was reviewed by General Humphreys, who now has command of 2nd Corps, Genl Hancock takes charge of the 1st Vet Res Corps. There was a good deal of dissatisfaction in our Corps at first, but Humpy, as the boys call him, got himself into the good graces of command and they like him pretty well. The old 1st Division 2nd A.C. looked splendid to day. The guns and accoutrements bright as new silver dollars, the uniforms nice and clean, the boys all fat and saucy. The Genl gave us a good deal of praise. This evening spitting snow again and is rather cool for white cotton gloves and paper collars. We returned to camp without accident and are feeling all right to night.

Wednesday, Jany 4th

Very cold this morning. The ground still white with snow. Went out and drilled 2 hours, and had a cool time of it. In the evening had dress parade. I paid a visit to the 145th P.V. and spent a very pleasant evening there, not so cold tonight. All right at roll call.

Thursday, Jany 5th

This is a beautiful day overhead. The snow is melting and is very bad underfoot. We had the usual Co Drill — Dress Parade, &c. All quiet in front.

Friday, Jany 6th

Drizzling rain this morning and more than muddy underfoot. Another deserter of the 5th New Hampshire shot at 12 O'Clock, and our Division had to go and see that it was done right. It causes us a good deal of trouble and the boys say a good deal of swear words. Quiet in front.

Saturday, Jany 7th

Still raining and so muddy we can hardly step out of our tents and keep our feet dry. Orderly Sergeant James E. Jolliffe is sick, one of Co C boys got a box from home with goodies and a great roll of N.Y. Ledgers. He and I are having a good time reading and we are enjoying ourselves *fine*. All quiet in front.

Sunday, Jany 8th

Sergeant Jolliff was so bad they had to send him to the Hospital this morning. Sergt Wm H. Sembower took my place in Co C. and I had to take charge of Co "K" as the boys wont let Sembower order them about. They more than go for him — he is sick a good deal and has to go to the hospital and they think he is a bummer.

Monday, Jany 9th

We are still at the same place, old Camp of the 9th Corps. The rain is falling nearly all the time, our camp is very muddy. Same old routine of Camp life. Nothing worthy of note to day.

Tuesday, Jany 10th

The cry is still it rains, rained all last night and is still raining to day. Major William A. West and Lt John R. West of the 16th Cavalry P.V. was here to see Capt Weltner to day. Major West just came on from Washington City. They left for their camp this evening. All quiet along the line.

Wednesday, Jany 11th

The sun came out nice and warm this morning and is drying up the mud very fast. I went over to Division Hospital to see sergeant Jolliff and found him very bad. I stayed and cheered him up all I could. He is *very* bad, poor fellow I am afraid he will not get well. I got back to camp and am very busy making out Co "K" pay rolls to night. All quiet along the line, the continual picket firing night and day excepted.

Thursday, Jany 12th

The weather is beautiful to day, as fine for the time of year as any one could wish. I am busy working on the company pay rolls yet, nothing worthy of note transpiring.

Friday, Jany 13th

Finished the Co rolls and sent them off to day. We have orders to be ready for a rigid inspection on the 15th. Had dress parade &c. All quiet in front.

Saturday, Jany 14

We have special orders for every non commissioned officer to have chevrons on their arms and stripes on their pants. The quarter master hasn't any, we have to take old blouses and make them ourselves. It is laughable to see the boys all at work with their needles. You may depend some of the stitches are long.

Sunday, Jany 15th

This is a beautiful sabbath morning. We had our usual Co Inspection. The boys looked real nice in their home made chevrons and stripes if they did have to make them out of old blouses. At 3 O'Clock P.M. we all went to church and heard a good sermon. Everything going along as usual to night.

Monday, Jany 16th

The weather still continues fine, at 11 O'Clock A.M. we was Inspected by the Brigade Inspector. Our Regiment was in good trim and no reprimands. In the afternoon the whole Division was in line at the works for the Corps Commander Genl Humphreys to look at. Had our usual dress parade in the Evening, &c. Albert W. Bolen promoted to Corporal by my recommendation. All quiet in front.

Tuesday, Jany 17th

The nice weather still continues. I paid another visit to sergeant Jolliffe and found him a little better. Everything same as usual, nothing worthy of note.

Wednesday, Jany 18th

Fine weather still continues, same old routine of camp life, drill, dress parade, &c, &c.

Thursday, Jany 19th

Old sol still shines down on us and makes us feel good. The boys are all in good condition. Corporal Daniel Chisholm returned to us to day, he was badly wounded on the shin June 16th 1864 but did not leave his company until he was forced to on June 19th, 3 days after he was wounded. His wound in all that time was not dressed or any care taken of it, not even washed off, and he was under fire all three days besides

running through the underbrush caused it to become very much inflamed and his limb swollen so that he could scarcely walk. He came very
near losing his leg on account of gangrene setting in. On the evening of
May 5th, 1864 in the first engagement that we participated in at the battle of the Wilderness, he had the front part of his cap pierced by a Minie
Ball — tearing the whole front part of it out, passing through his hair
above his forehead. It was a narrow escape for if it had of been one half
inch lower he would have been killed. While in the Hospital at City Point
one of the Christian Commission seen his cap and told him he would
attend to forwarding it home for him to his father, as it would be a great
curiosity and show how near he had come to being killed. He did so and
now it hangs in his room at his home. The same old routine of camp
duty.

Friday, Jany 20th

The Sun is still shedding his rays down on the heads of Uncle Sams
boys, they are very cheerful and seem to have no cares. I received a letter from Lt Zadoc B. Springer with the following modest request —please
send me a Knife and Fork also a spoon, four pounds cut and dried Tobacco, forty or fifty pounds Hard tack, one pipe, Four loaves of bread,
one blouse and one pair of Pants. He was captured at Reams Station Va
August 25th 1864 and is at Danville Va, a prisoner still. Now if we had
these things to send we could not send them, but we haven't them. I enclosed the letter to his father in Uniontown and he can send these things
if he chooses. He is no great favorite of Co "K" and the boys soon forgot his request.

Saturday, Jany 21st

It is raining and sleeting this morning. We are all housed up as we
cannot have our inspection to day. I spent the day writing letters to my
Northern friends and fixing up the Co Books, &c.

Sunday, Jany 22nd

The rain is still coming down, the weather is very disagreeable and
too bad for review. The boys have to go on wood fatigue, picket, &c just
the same as if the weather was good.

Monday, Jany 23rd

More rain more rest in civil life, but here it is go ahead rain or shine.
It is still too bad for review and we are not very sorry for we hate to go
out for a show. It is still raining to night.

Tuesday, Jany 24th

This morning it is beautiful overhead, underfoot bad. Still we fixed up and moved back to the old place and was inspected by Brevet Brig Genl Ramsey. He found the troops in good trim and had no fault to find, everything passed off nicely. To night the wind is whistling around our tents like mad.

Wednesday, Jany 25th

To day it is cool. We was ordered out for review, so we fixed up, put on Paper Collars &c. Moved out to Brigade Head Quarters, orders countermanded and we returned to camp with orders to be in good trim for tomorrow. So all this fixing and cleaning was for nothing and all has to be repeated over again. All quiet along the line except Picket firing.

Thursday, Jany 26th

Very cold but we had to turn out with our paper Collars on, our shoes blacked, with our old blouse stripes &c. We moved back to Division Head Quarters and was reviewed by Major Genl Humphreys. The Division is small but it looked splendid. Genl Miles always attends to that, he is the most particular commander in the service. We returned to camp without accident.

Friday, Jany 27th

Still very cold, and the same routine of camp life goes on. Wood fatigue duty is very heavy. Nothing of importance transpiring.

Saturday, Jany 28th

Very cold, about the coldest we have had it yet. All quiet in front, nothing worthy of note.

Sunday, Jany 29th

A little warmer to day. Had our usual Co inspection. The wood fatigue duty is a little lighter on the boys. Nothing of importance going on. All quiet along the lines.

Monday, Jany 30th

This is a fine day. Our co has been busy all day tearing down and rebuilding Capt Weltners quarters, we did it in fine style. We set a pattern for the other companies and they are acting on it. All quiet in front.

Tuesday, Jany 31st

This is the last day of January and finds us in good Quarters. The weather is raw but not so very cold. Our mates is to take things easy and let the wide world wag as she may. All quiet.

Wednesday, Feby 1

February came in with fine weather, and finds us in good health generally, and ready for anything that turns up. Five deserters came in this morning and passed through camp on their way back to Corps Head Quarters. They were fine tall fellows and looked as if they could stand a little more reb service.

Thursday, Feby 2nd

This is ground hog day and he can see his shadow without any trouble. We tore our chimney down and rebuilt it. When we finished it we found we had made quite an improvement. All quiet in front.

Friday, Feby 3rd

All busy fixing up our camp in fine style. We are giving the whole camp a general overhauling. It is a bad sign to fix up for we are most always sure of leaving soon. Fine weather.

Saturday, Feby 4th

Are still having nice weather. Capt G. W. Mcgraw of Co H received his commission as Major. He is not very well liked in the Regiment. All quiet in front.

Sunday, Feby 5th

We have marching orders. This morning at 3 O'Clock we fell in and moved to the left about four miles (we left our tents standing). and relieved the 3rd division. About the time we got fixed the Johnnies made a very fierce charge. We repulsed them handsomely. They repeated the charge twice again but was beat back with heavy loss and finally they gave it up as a bad job. We lay on our arms, things [quiet] in our front, except picket fighting. Very heavy fighting in front of the 5th Corps. Midnight finds us still awake and ready for a charge.

Monday, Feby 6th

Very heavy picket firing all night, and this morning finds us under arms, and have been all night. The Rebs pelted it into the 5th Corps all night. The rain is falling and it makes it very disagreeable without our tents. The boys are busy putting up abettoes in front, to night finds us a piteous plight, wet, no fire, no tents, still under arms.

Tuesday, Feby 7th

This morning finds us wet, cold and hungry and in the same place. The snow fell about two hours and then turned to rain. We are about as hard looking set of fellows as ever was seen and we do not deceive our looks very much, judging the way I feel. About One O'Clock P.M. our tents came up, we soon pitched them. This evening we have permission to build fires and the smoke is raising all along the line but the wood is in bad order and the fires hard to start. We have got dried off. The weather is cool, no rain or snow falling. All quiet in our front but on the left the Pickets are pelting away. We are still under arms.

Wednesday, Feby 8th

Cold and windy this morning, we cleaned our arms up and have inspection. We suffer dreadfully with the smoke, it blows along the works and nearly puts our eyes out. I never had my eyes in such a fix by smoke. We have to go it blind. The reception we gave the Johnnies has completely cowed them in our front, as we do not see anything of them, but it is a caution the way them and the 5th Corps are clipping away.

Thursday, Feby 9th

The weather is good. Our eyes look like pickled beets and feel miserable. We packed up and moved back to our old camp which we reached at 10 A.M. Halted a few minutes and then moved toward the place we had just come from. After going two miles we turned back again and pitched our tents in the old Camp. Everything is lovely to night and we feel very good indeed. After we advanced our lines with so small a loss our Regt and the 53rd P.V. lay in our old Camp, but the left all had to move forward, tear down their tents and rebuild them.

Friday, Feby 10th

Things going along in the old way, heavy Picket and Fatigue details, all is quiet in front.

Saturday, Feby 11th

The weather is good. Since the new line was established everything is quiet. We are on the right of our Corps and the 6th Corps Joins us on the right.

Sunday, Feby 12th

We have beautiful weather, we have our usual Co Inspection. Supts Grey of Co "H" Foster of Co "C" & Reber of Co "B" promoted to 2nd Lieutenants to fill vacancies. Quiet in front.

Monday, Feby 13th

Still fine weather. The same of Camp Life going on as usual. Nothing of importance transpiring.

Tuesday, Feby 14th

Another fine day. The boys are all as busy as bees. We had our monthly inspection to day. Sergt Jolliff came up and took charge of the Co. Corporal Alex Chisholm went home on twelve day Furlough. All quiet in front.

Wednesday, Feby 15th

Arose early this morning and found the ground covered with snow, but not very cold.

Thursday, Feby 16th

Everything very quiet to day. I have been reading the Waverly Magazine and taking things easy. I feel so relieved Joliff has charge of the Co and I have nothing much to do. Albert W. Bolen was reduced to the ranks for non attention on Dress parade.

Friday, Feby 17th

Raining this morning and rained all last night. Very muddy and disagreeable. At roll call still raining. All quiet in front.

Saturday, Feby 18th

This is a fine morning. I left camp for Picket at 9 O'Clock. I have charge of five posts. I have the boys fixing up good picket posts by digging out the posts deeper, so as to protect them in case of an attack. Things quiet in front.

Sunday, Feby 19th

Sun shining out brightly, a beautiful sabbath day and we have been lolling around in the sun all day. The Sixth Corps pickets joins us on the right. They was trying to trade papers with the Johnnies but they will not trade. I suppose they have news that they do not wish us to know. Our

Corps are not allowed to trade but the Sixth Corps boys can trade as much as they like. Was relieved and came back to camp, all quiet.

Monday, Feby 20th

Still nice weather. I went over to the depot to day. Charleston reported taken and this explains the reason why the rebels would not exchange papers yesterday. The boys are rejoicing at the good news. All quiet as usual.

Tuesday, Feby 21st

Another nice morning, I am Sergeant of the Camp Guard for the first time. The Rebs are reported massing in our front. Two nice Brass pieces are in the works loaded with grape to give them a warm reception if they should be such fools as to try that game of charging on our works. The boys are aching for them to try it, as they are spoiling for a fight they say. I think they will have plenty before long as things begin to look like there is going to be something done and that before long. There is too much riding around to mean nothing.

Wednesday, Feby 22nd

Weather good. Part of the Regiment was in the works under arms all night, for fear the Rebs might make a break. Things quiet all day. This evening we got orders and packed up, we did so and lay under arms at the works until late. A Johnnie deserter reported the rebs was going to blow up one of our forts on the right, so we turned in and slept soundly at 11 P.M.

Thursday, Feby 23rd

I left camp at 7 A.M. with a squad of twenty men and went to the picket line and slashed timber, twenty trees between the two picket lines. The rebs let us work without firing a shot. They could have killed all of us if they had wanted to. We returned to camp safely.

Friday, Feby 24th

Raining this morning and rained all night. Part of the Regiment stood at the works all night. The Regiment is divided into two reliefs and one has to be in the works at night all the time, and it is the same all along the line. I guess we will have to keep it up. It is blamed hard with no fire to stand in the cold, rain and snow all night, and a perfect nuisance as we have good abattoes and a good picket line in front and have plenty of time to get ready after the pickets give the alarm. There is no trouble about the Picket detail now. They all want to go as they can sleep there and here they cannot get the chance. They are worrying the troops to death and no good in it. Raining to night.

Saturday, Feby 25th

Still raining. I am at Brigade Head Quarters and have charge of the guard. We have nice quarters and a good fire to sit by and are taking things easy. All quiet along the line.

Sunday, Feby 26th

We was relieved at 9 A.M. Returned to camp and had Co Inspection. Nothing of importance transpiring — everything O.K.

Monday, Feby 27th

This has been a nice day. We fixed up and cleaned about our tents. The same old routine of Camp Life.

Tuesday, Feby 28th

Raining again this morning. The Camp muddy and disagreeable. We was mustered for pay. We have to stand at the works as before. I am on Camp guard.

Wednesday, March 1st

We stood at the works all night. I was relieved off guard at 9 A.M. Had Dress parade as usual. Things quiet in front.

Thursday, March 2nd

Rain again this morning. It rains as easy as rolling off of a log. Corporal Alex Chisholm returned to duty from furlough to day. No strange news from Uniontown. The same old rigmarole, stand at the works, dress parade, &c.

Friday, March 3rd

Still it rains. I went on Picket and here I am on reserve and I find it not a very nice place as the rain is falling fast. Our tents do not do us much good as we left them in Camp. The rain slacked up this evening.

Saturday, March 4th

We had a beautiful little shower this morning. We was relieved and returned to camp at 11 A.M. and found things all right but damp.

Sunday, March 5th

No rain to day. The sun is making up for lost time and is drying the mud up fast. The boys are laying around in groups enjoying the sunshine. The same old rigmarole.

Monday, March 6th

This has been a beautiful day. I took a walk around to the depot, had Brigade Dress parade this afternoon. All quiet in front.

Tuesday, March 7th

Another fine day. I am sergeant of Camp guard, had Brigade Dress parade, we stand at the works to night.

Wednesday, March 8th

It rained all night and is still raining this morning was relieved off guard, we had to stand on the works all night.

Thursday, March 9th

Our Division, the first, fixed up and moved to the rear and was reviewed by Genl Meade, Warren and Humphreys. The men looked nice. We returned to Camp at dark and at 9 O'Clock our regiment was paid off. All quiet along the line.

Friday, March 10th

Rained all last night. I came on picket at 9 A.M. and am on the reserve. Hailed and rained all forenoon, cleared up nicely this afternoon. One man of the 64th New York was shot for desertion at 12 O'Clock, rather unhealthy to desert.

Saturday, March 11th

This is a fine morning, returned to Camp at 11 O'Clock. Went over to the depot to the Photograph Gallery, sit for a negative. All quiet to night.

Sunday, March 12th

This is a beautiful sabbath afternoon, usual Sunday morning inspection. Alex Chisholm and I went to the right of the line to Fort Sampson and Gregg. They are splendid forts and well manned. Sampson has the twin sisters, Two large Black pieces and several others not so large. Gregg also has nice Artillery pieces and would give the Johnnies a warm re-

ception if they should want to pay us a visit. The Rebs are very well be-
haved lately.

Monday, March 13th

Went over to the depot and set for an ambrotype. I also got weighed
and pulled down 187½ #, 10 # more than I ever weighed before. The
weather is very nice for this month. The boys are living well now on Sutler Stuff.

Tuesday, March 14th

This is a fine morning, I am sergeant of the guard. We have to go to
the Brigade Head Quarters to mount guard, they inspect us very close.
The Sutlers are all ordered to the rear. That means the Campaign is soon
to be opened. We sit up all night at the works. There is great specula-
tion as to what we will do among the boys. Five Hundred tales afloat
and none of them from any reliable source, but we will soon know.

Wednesday, March 15th

We was relieved at 9 A.M. off guard. Have orders to send overplus
clothing to the rear. I sent one overcoat, one Dress Coat and one Blanket. The other boys the same — All this means to be ready at a moments notice to stir up the old Rebs once more and give them the finishing
touch. I hope the troops are all fat and hearty, and I think almost ready
for anything Genl Grant asks at their hands. All quiet along the line.

Thursday, March 16th

Wind and rain last night and very disagreeable this morning. In the
afternoon had skirmish Drill. The boys do pretty well for the practice
they have had. I think we will have more practices before long. By the
way things are getting very lively. Brass bands are playing, troops drilling
all the time, a continual going here and there by staff officers.

Friday, March 17th

St. Patricks Day in the morning, and it is a fine morning, weather
beautiful. This is the day of the "Irish Brigade Jubilee." Corpl Alex
Chisholm and I got leave of absence and went back to Corps Head
Quarters. We found thousands of troops there and men busy putting the
finishing touches to the race track &c &c. We found a nice track like a
Fair Ground track, but here they had four hurdles built three feet high
across the track and between these hurdles a ditch three feet deep, four

feet wide and feet long [sic]. A large platform filled with Officers and Judges and about twenty ladies. Also a good brass band. At ten O'Clock the horses and riders came in. The Col of the 7th N.Y. Dutch led the way on a large Black Stallion, Capt Brady with a fine horse and a Zouave Lieutenant came next, and then others came and arranged themselves in line, and then the word was given and away they go. Some went over the hurdles and ditches, some flew the track and ran through the crowd of soldiers. A sergeant of the 69th New York was trampled to death and half a dozen others badly wounded. The Ambulance was hauling dead and wounded away all day. The second round the Black Stallion of the Dutch Col fell over a hurdle and broke his neck and both arms of the Colonel. They sent the Colonel to the Hospital, rolled the dead horse out of the way and went ahead as if nothing had happened. Corporal Chisholm and myself sit in the Head Quarters carriage of Genl Meade on top of the hill four hundred yards away and we was hardly safe there, as one horse flew the track and nearly run through the carriage we sit in. I never seen such a time. Capt Brady beat them all, his horse carried him over nice and he kept his seat like he had grown there. On they went, horses flying the track, running over the spectators, falling over the hurdles, into the ditches, breaking arms, legs &c. We soon got tired and came back to camp. Never did I see such a crazy time. I will have to alter my mind if I ever go to see another Irish fair.

Saturday, March 18th

The weather continues good. We was on Brigade Drill to day. Genl Miles our division Genl put us through several bogus bayonet charges. In the dusk of the Evening Co "K" presented Captain Weltner with a nice new sword. We payed One Hundred and twenty Dollars for it. The Captain was taken by surprise as we had not let him know that we were contemplating anything of the kind. We sent to his quarters requesting him to come to the Company Street. Orderly Sergeant James E. Jolliff made the presentation speech. The Captain responded in a Soldier like manner. Thanking us for our gift promising us never to disgrace it or the members of the Company. He never did. He was with us until Lee Surrendered, and died very shortly after the war closed.

Sunday, March 19th

We had our usual Sunday Morning inspection. I put in the day writing letters to my friends. This has been a beautiful Sabbath day. And very quiet almost lonely.

Monday, March 20th

We were all out on Brigade Drill to day, more bogus charges. Lieutenant Brady fell in the sink, such a looking fellow after he got out I never seen. Genl Miles put us through the Drill. All quiet in front.

Tuesday, March 21st

I am Sargeant of Camp guard. The rain is falling fast. Nothing of note transpiring in Co or Regt.

Wednesday, March 22nd

We were under arms Standing in the works all night, was relieved at 9 A.M. All busy cleaning up and getting ready for Corps review which is to come off tomorrow. Things quiet in front.

Thursday, March 23rd

It is very windy and cool this morning. At 11 O'Clock A.M. we left camp for Humphreys Station a distance of four miles. When we reached the station the wind was blowing so hard we could not see one another for the dust and sand. Of all the storms I ever was in this was the worst, for one hour the sand blew in our eyes and ears until we could scarcely see. President Abraham Lincoln, a host of Ladies and children, officers of all grades were on the platform when we marched past on review. What we suffered on that stormy review no one can tell. We reached camp at 4 P.M. tired, hungry and sore eyed and our uniforms nearly spoiled. After roll call we tumbled into our bunks and slept soundly.

Friday, March 24th

We have been hard at work all day cleaning up our guns and accoutrements and getting the dust off of our uniforms. All quiet in front.

Saturday, March 25th

This morning hard fighting on the right. The rebels under Genl Gordon charged on Fort Steadman which was garrisoned by the 14th N.Y. Artillery at daylight and took them by surprise and captured the fort and turned our guns on us. We was ordered under arms at daylight. Instead of us going and reinforcing the 9th Corps the 2nd & 5th Corps advanced over the works in front of them and attacked the rebel picket line, charged and took and held it in spite of all they could do. They tried time and again to drive us out but could not do it. The 148th P.V. with seven shooters had the advance and when they started they did advance as skirmishers nicely and made the Rebs more than fall back and leave the first line. And when we came up we charged and took the main line and held it until twelve O'Clock P.M. We then fell back to the old works and stood under arms until daylight. While this was going on with us the 9th Corps charged and took back their Fort Steadman and captured all the rebs in it. Our advance was to draw the rebs away from the front of Steadman so the 9th Corps could take back the fort.

Sunday, March 26th

Everything lovely this morning. We have our fort back and took 2,000 prisoners. Very quiet in our front but heavy picket fighting on the right in front of the 6th Corps. We are under arms all the time ready for a march, but to night finds us still in the same place.

Monday, March 27th

We packed up early this morning and expected to leave for some place but stacked arms in the works. — Then took our arms and went out and had Brigade Drill and Dress parade. Still quiet in our front but the 6th Corps are pelting away all the time on the picket line.

Tuesday, March 28th

I am Sargeant of the Guard to day. Great excitement along the line, something big will happen soon sure. The sick is all ordered to the rear and all extra clothing. The Johnnies will get the devil soon or we will for the Army of the Potomac is getting in great earnest, and something will be done soon or I am no judge of faces or facts.

Wednesday, March 29th — Hatchers Run

No rest last night under arms all night. Packed up at daylight and moved to Hatchers run. The 116th skirmished all day in the rain, over runs, mudholes, brush and dead logs, first to the right then to the left, then forward and then charge. Well such a time no one ever seen, no rest at all. Rain rain and nothing but rain, if it does not stop soon we will have to build rafts to get from place to place on. At 12 O'Clock we halted and such a halt was never seen or heard of before. We found ourselves in a marshy place and not one dry inch of ground to stand on, let alone to lie down on to take sleep or rest that we so much stand in need of. We spread down our gum Blankets in the water and mud, pulled up the sides after the fashion of a dogboat and do the best you can is the word. Oh! for the morning is the wish of the troops and the rays of the shining sun to dry and warm us up.

Thursday, March 30th

Well! here we are yet, and no one lost and no old Sol to cheer us with his rays, but rain, rain. How easy rain falls in old Virginia. The ground we are on now is covered from 2 to 20 inches with mud and water, and very cold at that. We move to the right and then to the left, then forward, charge the rebel skirmish line, sometimes capture a lot of prisoners, charge up to the abettoes and have to fall back. They would not charge us, I think this is done to draw them out of their works. This is White Oak Road, and a great place for a Road it is. At noon we was relieved — yes *relieved,* and now we are behind works in the mud. But it is a great deal better than wading around knee deep in mud and water like we have been doing since yesterday morning. Only one man lost yet, John Campbell of our Co. I cannot tell about the Regiment as we are spread out so far apart. The troops work well in spurts and all think the end is nigh, and still the rain comes down steady and increasingly. While we have been busy the other troops both right and left have been doing a fair share and may be more than us. So we lay down in the mud and try to rest.

Friday, March 31st — Battle for The White Oak Road or Five Forks

We packed up and moved to the left a short distance. The sun shines out bright and warm. We are all busy cleaning up our guns and equipments. We can hear Warren with his 5th Corps picking away at the rebs trying to take the White Oak Road from them, by the roar of musketry and artillery they are having a warm time of it. We had cleaned up and got our last Co inspection when the 5th Corps 3rd Division began to fall back and here they come. I will have to quit writing as the word is Attention! At 10 A.M. our Regt fell in. Load at will was the command. The Johnnies had drove the 5th Corps back to us and behind us pell mell and all was confusion. The rebs followed to the woods and halted. We got the Command from Capt Weltner who has command of the Regiment to forward march, and the whole Division moved forward over the works down to the run which we found to be almost a river since the recent rains. Forward boys is the word and over we go but how we got over I will never tell. We moved up toward the wood where the rebels are waiting for us. As we raised the brow of the hill ("little") that hid us they poured a volley into us and kept it up so that we had to fall back across the creek again, dragging our killed and wounded. Orderly Sergeant James E. Jolliffe shot in the leg, I took his place. John H. Bagshaw wounded also Timothy McInerney wounded and Thos T. Thorndell killed. Those mentioned were of Co "K". Some of the other companies fared worse. Seven killed and Twenty three wounded in ten minutes was the list of casualties in our Regiment. We got the wounded over and back to the rear somehow safely I do not know hardly how. I have command of the Company and was busy getting them into line again. The regiment was formed again, also all the regiments of the Division, then we got the word forward Charge, double quick and over we go again. This time there is no repulse but a heavy fire is poured into us and away we go over our dead and wounded into the and over the Rebel dead and wounded. The rebs fell back slowly disputing every inch of ground, but finally we got them on the fast line and pushed them two miles as near as I could tell. All this time our boys was falling fast and so was the Johnnies. The woods was full of the ghastly Corpses of the dead, and the shrieks of the wounded and dying mingled with the crack of the musket and rumble of the artillery was calculated to impress the whole upon the mind so indelibly that it would last as long as life continued. As I was running past a wounded rebel he caught me by the Pant leg and held me so tight I had to beat his hand loose with my gun. He wanted me to help him off the field. On we went and such cheering as the Old Irish Brigade can only do. We drove them beyond the place from which they had drove the 3rd Division of the 5th Corps. So we had pitched in and finished the work they had commenced at midnight. All this time both sides was cheering as if charging one another on right, left and front. And this ended March 31st and the Battle for the White Oak Road or Five Forks. There seems to be a great determination throughout all the army to end the war as soon as possible. We have become used to roughing it and the boys does not seem to care.

Saturday, April 1st

Our Division was relieved by the 5th Corps this morning at the break of day, and we moved near where we was yesterday. We went to work and cleaned up as before and had inspection. Afternoon we moved to the front to feel for the Johnnies, but we could not find them so we moved to the left and at 2 O'Clock we charged up to the rebel works, but could not get through to the works for the abattoes. Our loss was very slight and we done them scarcely any damage. They could not get at us and we could not get at them. So we fell back behind our works. All day we have heard General Phillip Sheridan pecking away on our left. Our Division is ordered to reinforce him and away we go like mad. Closer and closer we come to the 5th Corps and Phil Sheridans Cavalry. They are having warm work. We arrive and are thrown on the left and all pitch into building breast works. Sheridan came along and pointed out the way he wanted the line to run. This is the first good look I have had of Little Phil. He is a good looking Soldier, rides well, and has a beautiful black stallion, medium size to ride on. Twelve O'Clock to night still finds us at work. The bombarding goes on lively.

Sunday, April 2nd — After Genl Lee

This morning a general advance was ordered along the whole line. We charged up and over the works after a very feeble resistance. The Johnnies fell back and in such a hurry that they left their tents standing and everything else but guns and ammunition. We followed them closely. At the South Side Rail Road they took a stand and a very firm one at that. Our 2nd Brigade had the lead and charged them and was repulsed with heavy loss. The loss of the 4th N.Y. heavy artillery was tremendous. I thought they would never get done carrying out the dead and wounded. We turned by the right flank and moved one hundred yards and then by the left flank charge was the command. It was well obeyed for at them we went like a pack of wolves just turned loose. We took the road and lots of prisoners. The sharp shooters had a red cross on their arms. Well the Johnnies fell back and we followed them closely. We captured an old black horse and we call him South Side. We carried our Blankets on him and he was a great help. We got lots of Flour, Bacon &c, but we had no time to cook for onward was the word and on we went capturing a few prisoners at intervals. They halted again at Sutherland Station and shelled defiance at us, and then we had a hot and heavy time. Our Division "General Miles" charged them, captured two guns and six hundred prisoners, and such a set of soldiers. Ignorant was no name for the poor simple devils. Talk about southern Chivalry I dont want any of it in mine if this is a speciman. I mixed among them as we trudged along. We shared our hard tack and water with them. What does you uns want to take our land and homes for was about all they knew. So on we go and at dark we halted and was so tired that I threw myself down and went to sleep for I could not cook. What I eat was in a raw state and not much of that. As I lay down I can hear the boys pecking away off to the right and left.

Monday, April 3rd

At daylight we moved briskly out onto the Lynchburgh Road and no rebels in sight at 9 A.M. but after that we took Prisoners black and white every few minutes. We kept close to the rear guard of the enemy. Sometimes when we would get to the top of a hill the enemy would be going up the next, our batteries would unlimber and shell them dreadfully. Some would stride a team and tear the wagon all to pieces, kill the mules and the wagoner, sometimes part of the mules and the wagoner would unhitch one and away he would go leaving the rest of us. We would find Bacon and provisions of all kinds but it would disappear in short metre, poor devils they find us hard provos, for we keep them on the go. We halted at 8 O'Clock laid down and slept soundly, very tired.

Tuesday, April 4th

This is a beautiful day. We started at dawn, after a very light breakfast, for our rations are short. We halted at noon and some of the boys went out on the flank to forage. Corpl Alex Chisholm and Abe Hull of Co "K" was after some very sheep, Abe chased them around so Alex could shoot them. Alex shot two of them at one shot, and out of the leaves at his feet a voice cried out, We surrender, We surrender! The boys for a moment was frightened a good deal, but soon recovered and concluded to investigate. They proceeded to tear away the leaves and came to some boards and under the boards they found a cave and in the cave they found two men. They made them come out. One of them said he was a doctor and the other said he was a school teacher. The poor fellows were almost scared to death. They concluded it was best to take them to Head Quarters — and did so — turning them over to the guard. Then they went back to get the sheep, but some one had been there before them and taken them and I am afraid there was some hard swearing done by the boys about that time, but they had captured two men and lost their mutton. We got on the go again and went along fine, halted at 8 O'Clock very hungry and tired, threw ourselves down and slept soundly.

Wednesday, April 5th

After a very light breakfast again we started on the march, the day cool and nice and the troops in the best of spirits. We halted at noon along the road, parted the column on each side of the road. Genl Grant and Meade passed with staff and bodyguard, and I thought the boys would split open they hallowed, cheered and made such a noise, threw caps at the horses &c. Poor old Johnnie Rebs I think it will soon be all up with you. We captured four or five hundred prisoners today without much effort and little or no loss. As before the boys that had anything to eat or drink gave it to them, but on we went and halted at 5 P.M. On the left the 5th Corps advanced at half past 6 P.M. and captured part of General Lees Head Quarters. Then we fell back and built works. Genl

Sheridan superintended the job. After we finished then we lay down to rest on our arms for we expected to be attacked before morning.

Thursday, April 6th

We had a small shower of rain last night, and we are very glad, we was not disturbed, we had a good rest after midnight. We started early and are pressing the Johnnies closely. We captured lots of prisoners to day, also a whole commissary train. The road was strewn all along with wrecked wagons, dismounted gun carriages left burning, caissons dumped into mud holes, guns left half burned and some spiked. The fences set on fire on both sides of the road. Every few seconds a shell would burst. In fact it was so dangerous from there that we would often have to leave the road to keep from being blown up. At one place where the road went down hill to a creek and took a sudden turn to the left two six mule teams went over and when we came along the mules and wagons was piled in a heap. Some of the mules was struggling to get up and could not make it for the dead ones that were piled on top of them. It was a bad sight to see but on we went and soon forgot it in other scenes that were rushing before us and just as bad or worse. At one place they had dismounted three guns, very large ones, and rolled them off of the road into a small run and built a dam below them so as to back the water up over them, but when we came up the dam was broke and the guns left exposed. They also burned the gun carriages. We halted at 9 P.M.

Friday, April 7th

We was up and after the Johnnies bright and early. They took a stand at high bridge on the Lynchburgh Rail Road. This bridge is three thousand feet long, has twenty two piers of brick One Hundred feet high. It is a beautiful bridge. The stream that passes under it could pass through a flour barrel — a small wooden bridge spans the water and is only thirteen feet wide. The rebels fought us for half an hour with great determination but we finally drove them across the high bridge which they set on fire at the farther end. But we were pushing them so close that our men were able to extinguish the fire after it had burned the length of two piers. They left seven pieces of artillery and forty or fifty prisoners. We crossed the little bridge and pushed on after them. Some of the pioneers cut the bridge off and let the burning part fall. I lit my pipe as we passed. This bridge is about one and a half miles from Farmville. The Rebels retreated on the Rail Road and we followed them closely for about four miles. There they about faced and gave us some shells and other small compliments which was returned with interest. While our artillery was playing on them we was busy piling up rails and old logs to stop some of their missiles. Our brigade commander and staff came up and a shell took the head off of the bugler and he stiffened and set in the saddle a few seconds, but his bugle was taken off. Another soldier got in the saddle and rode off with the dead mans brains smeared over the horse and saddle.

Our Fourth Brigade charged the Johnnies and soon had them on the go again. We supported the charging column and lost but a few men while the first lost heavily. All this time the troops on the right and left were pelting the Johnnies and the Johnnies doing the same to them and us. We halted at the position the rebels had and built works for fear the Johnnies would try to break through in the night and take us by surprise. After we finished this little job we lay down to rest. It is now midnight, tired is no name for the way we feel, but tomorrow is the last day we hear on all sides and that spurs us up and makes us bear our hardships cheerfully.

Saturday, April 8th

This morning the troops are all astir early. The Johnnies left during the night, and none to be seen this morning. We ate a hasty breakfast and was soon on their trail like blood hounds. We are and have been passing through a delightful country. We passed through Stoneville at 9 A.M. This is a small village, it has one store and one Black smith shop. Our regiment broke ranks and ransacked the place up in the store-loft, they found a large sugar hogshead full of flour. They jumped in and filled their haversacks without taking them off by scraping them full. It was a general scrabble. When they returned to the Regiment they looked like a lot of Millers for they had flour all over them. They also found several hogsheads of Tobacco and they all had a handful. This they used as whips to whip one another with.

General Humphreys and staff passed along. He said something to his aids and they all took a hearty laugh. I think it was in regard to our floury regiment. So on we go and no Johnnies in sight, but we find horses and mules given out and left by the road side, gun carriages stuck in the mud and wagons upset and broke down. All this denotes a little too much haste upon the part of our enemy and we are all in good spirits for the general belief is they are on their last legs. We halted at dark. Our Regiment went on Picket. We was posting the men when four Johnnies jumped out of the fence corner. We sent them back to Corps Head

Quarters. After we got the men posted we went to Head Quarters. We had lots of dry rails and soon you could see fires by the dozens, and the boys all busy making or getting ready to make slap jacks. And about the time the boys was ready to pan in the batter, I do not think there had been a half dozen cakes made, when fall in was the command. Well! if Regiment ever said any cuss words it was about this time for the men was tired and hungry and had their quart cups full of batter, so away we have to go. It was now 10 O'Clock and dark. After going four miles as near as I can tell we are now in the very front. We stumbled over logs, ruts and lost our slap jack batter so we have nothing to eat of any account. We laid down hungry and very tired. We can see the Johnnies Camp fire at a short distance.

Sunday, April 9th — Near Clover Hill, Lees Surrender

We had a smart shower of rain in the after part of the night. We was up early and pressing the Johnnies closely, our Division in front, and our first (1st) Brigade forms the skirmish line. At 11 O'Clock the rebels halted and formed into solid line of battle and faced about. We turned off the road by the right flank and formed in line of battle in a muddy cornfield but close to the main road and within about 200 yds of the Johnnies. There we stood the two armies facing each other, and we expected to fight the hardest battle of the Campaign. While we was waiting for orders some flags of truce came through our lines and passed to the rear. We was pretty sure now they had given up the ghost. By this time we had stacked arms on both sides. We were ready for anything and there we stood waiting, but at 3 P.M. our Division got the word attention, and an order was read to the effect that Genl Robt E. Lee had surrendered the Army of Northern Va to the Army of the Potomac commanded by Genl Ulysses S. Grant. It did not take us by surprise for we had been looking for it for some days. But when we knew it to be a sure thing what a loud, long glorious shout went up. Then the first thing I knew I was rolling in the mud and several of Co "K" boys piled on top and wallowed me in the mud and themselves too pulled one another about, tripped them up. In fact I never seen a crazier set of fellows anywhere before or since. I cannot tell what all was done but I do know that I had to work for two good hours getting the mud off of me. All was busy doing something and such confusion and carrying on was never seen in so short a time. Then the artillery opened. I think there was not one piece but what belched forth the glad tidings, those that were captured and all. It was one continual roar for miles and miles.

Monday, April 10th

We had rain last night. This morning both armies busy cooking and eating what little grub we have. We have stacked arms a few yards apart. The boys in the Blue and in the grey are trading everything that is tradeable. Hats, Caps, Penknives, Coffee, Sugar, Tobacco, Hardtack is scarce. It looks like a fair or big muster in old Fayette Co. I gave Jacob Allamon five hard tack and told him to give them to the first Rebel Orderly Sergeant he seen. He did so, and brought me a five Dollar Confederate States Note for a keep sake. They meet at the Provo line and do their trading. I am busy making report of casualties in Co "K" since March 31st. Since orderly Sergt Jolliffe was wounded I have had charge of the Co as Capt Weltner was in command of the Regiment. 1st Lt Cope and 2nd Lt Springer are still in prison. The late hostile armies seem to have forgotten they were enemies yesterday morning, and are mixing and chatting the hours away in a very friendly manner. So the time flies. I feel to day that it is good to be here, when I look over our thinned ranks and miss the boys that stood side by side with us let it be rough or smooth. If we could only have them here to day to see what they helped to make possible; but alas! they are sleeping that long last sleep that knows no waking, scattered in unknown graves among the battlefields of Virginia or absent in the Hospital with shattered Health, wounds or amputated limbs.

Our rations that were due us to day came up and were given to the Johnnies and we wait another day without murmuring, for we were very short ourselves, and that makes me think that we are all Americans of the Old School of our Fathers. Oh! shaw, let things go. The Fair is still going on. The Blue and the Grey are all glad it seems to me that the cruel war is over — what a change a few short hours has made. The Shades of night comes on, all is quiet, all quiet on the lines, all quiet, and we try to sleep but cannot for the war is over and we feel so glad, so proud of ourselves, and so sorry for our comrades that have fallen by the wayside, that sleep is almost impossible.

Tuesday, April 11th

This morning it is cool and cloudy, and we are up early and busy as bees getting ready for to take the back track. So we fall in, fall in, start back, that sounds nice — and on we go through a nice country, pass nice farms at long distances apart. Ladies give us water as we pass, and they are glad also. Seen one young lady with an infant whose arms are just long enough to push her curly hair back, as the ringlets fall over her face.

Her sister carried the water, she was very beautiful indeed. But on we go chattering in fours. We marched along fast and encamped near the place we camped April 8th. Tired and hungry we threw ourselves down and slept soundly.

Wednesday, April 12th

This is a beautiful morning and we got on the march early, and reached a point where we could see Farmville at 4 P.M. We halted and unfurled the old Tattered and torn but much loved Flags. At 5 P.M. we marched through with drums beating, Brass Bands playing, and our old Colors flying. The place was full of all kinds of people, citizens, soldiers and negroes, male and female, old and young. Our Division the first has the lead, we passed through and massed Divisions, stacked arms. I looked back and seen the veterans coming. All had the step and that sideways dodge that only drilled troops have. It was a grand sight to see. You could see them for a mile or so as they come, their guns bayonets and equipments shining in the sun. We fell in at 6 P.M. and moved near High Bridge that the rebels had set on fire on the 7th and our pioneers had cut off and saved all but two spans. We went into camp and threw ourselves down and slept the sleep of satisfied conquerors.

Thursday, April 13th — on the March to Berksville Station

All up early and on the move. Our Division the 1st raced with the 2nd Division for Berksville Station. The officers had a bet which would reach it first, so on we went like race horses. We struck the Rail Road and thought we was lucky, but before we went two miles we would have been glad to get off and take the mud again as it almost broke our backs, one short step and then a long one. One of the worst places we ever marched was through an up and down grade cut. Nice clear water was running down by the side of the ties, we took our cups and dipped up and drank it and thought it was pure and nice, and when we reached the middle we found that we had drank the essence of two dead horses. The Cavalry had a fight here and threw them into the cut and they was rotten. I tried to belch it up, but it was there to stay, gag, gag was all we could do. Col St Clair A. Mulholland was at the head of the Brigade and our regiment had the lead. Some 6th Corps wagons was crossing the tracks and had one wagon standing on the Rail Road and another driving on above it, which blocked our way and stopped us. Our Col (of the 116th P.V. St Clair A. Mulholland) ordered them taken away but the train master said he wouldn't move them as he had orders to cross. The Colonel drew his revolver and told him if he did not move them he would kill all the mules and him too, he shot the leader and was aiming on the next but the teamster drove them off and we passed through. The Colonel would have surely done what he said. We were thus delayed a few minutes, but on we go, and beat the 2nd Division one hour. I was so stove up and tired I threw myself down without stopping to cook any supper. During the march we passed many Rebs plodding along looking crestfallen and sad. Poor Devils I pitied them. Lt Zadoc B. Springer came to the Co to day. He was captured at Reams Station or Weldon R.R. Aug 25th, 1864.

Friday, April 14th — Berksville Station

This is a beautiful day. We stopped right in the underbrush, but went to work and soon had it cleared away, and this evening after a hard days work the place looks like a little city. The country is very nice, everything is pure and clean. We lay close to the Rail road. The boys are healthy and cheerful, and are busy beautifying our Camp. We are tired tonight and seek our old friend wool Blanket with many thanks. So lights out.

Saturday, April 15th

We are still at the same place. The trains are busy coming and going, taking away the Johnnies as we have no use for them now as paroled prisoners. Hundreds of them are Lying around loose waiting their turns to take the trains. Some rain fell last night and it is not quite so pleasant in camp to day. We are getting rested up and feel much better as the soreness is about gone.

Sunday, April 16th

This is a beautiful Sabbath day and finds us at the old stand. We cleaned up and had Sunday Inspection, the first we have had time to have since March 31st. I received a letter from Sergt James E. Jolliffe, he is well but his leg is stiff at the knee and he thinks it always will be. I am still acting orderly of our Co ("K") I am tired of it and wish Jolliffe was here.

Monday, April 17th — Assassination of President Abraham Lincoln

Another beautiful day. We had monthly inspection. The boys are all happy, cheerful, and noisy. Jumping contrabands in blankets, playing Banjos, Violins and old Broken note accordeons.

At dress parade this evening "The Assassination of President Abraham Lincoln" was read to us. A silent gloom fell upon us like a pall. No one spoke or moved, our sorrow was so great that we could scarcely realize what had happened. I always thought that he was most loved by all the Army and people of America, but I am now sure of that. The "Stars and Stripes" was quietly lowered, and old torn shreds of Flags almost slipped out of the hands of the Color Sargeants. The Regiments was quietly dismissed and we moved away slowly to our quarters, as if we each had lost a near and dear friend at home. Quietly, quietly we went to our rest. Was anybody glad, if he was he made no sign, and well for them they did not, for they never would have reached home alive. No drill, No Dress Parade. No Nothing, all quiet, Flags at half mast, lonesome was no word for us. It was like going from a busy City to a fastness in the mountains, what a hold Old Honest Abe Lincoln had on the hearts of the soldiers of the army could only be told by the way they showed their mourning for him.

Tuesday, April 18th — Berskville Station

The weather is still beautiful. We packed up this morning and moved across the Rail Road, about the same distance from it as we was before, onto a beautiful farm high and dry, and are all busy beautifying our new Camp, after which we lay around mostly in our tents all quiet and lonesome. That Silent Gloom still pervades and hovers around our Camp. No Drill, No Dress parade. We are now fixed up in pretty good shape again, the Johnny Rebs laying around the Station in hundreds waiting transportation south.

Wednesday, April 19th

The weather still continues to be fine. The Flags are still at half mast. Twenty-one Minute Guns were fired to day in honor of the burial of President Abraham Lincoln at 12 O'Clock noon. There has been no Drilling or duties performed except those that were strictly necessary since we heard of his death. The effect of the news seems to hang over the army yet, but all do their duty quietly and without confusion.

Thursday, April 20th

We had a sprinkle of rain last night but it soon dried off. We have commenced to drill from 9 to 11 O'Clock A.M. and from 2 to 4 P.M. Sergents drill together, and Corporals together. Co "K" has 14 Enlisted Men, Commissioned Off. 2, aggregate 16 Men. So the rigmarole goes on. Drill. Eat. Sleep. Clean up Camp. Camp Guard &c.

Friday, April 21st

To day Cloudy but no rain. Our Colonel St Clair A. Mulholland Drills the Commissioned Officers, and it does us good to see him make them toe the mark, like they make us do it. *We do enjoy that officers drill.*

We had our first dress parade this evening since the news came of the assassination of the President. Our Regt the 116th P.V., the 183rd P.V. and 66th N.Y. had Dress parade together, and all three did not make a full regiment. The 66th N.Y. would make one good Co. Drill, Inspection and Dress parade fills up the time and keeps us busy.

Saturday, April 22nd

A beautiful day again. We are drawing clothing to day which takes time and patience. Things go on much the same, Drill four hours each day. Fixing Camp and Dress Parade, Colonel Mulholland presented us to day with a new flag, and gave us a good long address. Our old Flag has nothing left of it but the fringe and stuff, and it looks like rats had gnawed it. The old Flag was sent to Philadelphia for safe keeping, the boys hated to see it go. The Colonel did not forget to refresh our memories as to where and when the Old Flag had waved.

Sunday, April 23rd — Berksville Station

This is a beautiful sabbath day. We had our usual Sunday inspection, after which I took a tour through the camps to see the troops and seen many old friends and comrades. I spent the evening writing letters to relatives and friends.

Monday, April 24th

Still beautiful weather, we had our usual 4 hour drill, also Brigade Drill, nothing new, regular old song.

Tuesday, April 25th

To day 16 guns fired at intervals of thirty minutes from sun up to sundown, and had parade of the whole army at 10 O'Clock A.M. So on we go closer to home as every day goes by.

Wednesday, April 26th

Weather still nice and pleasant for April. Drill, Drill, Dress Parade. Commenced Pay rolls, job that takes time and patience, also Monthly Reports, and Evening Reports.

Thursday, April 27th

The weather beautiful, same old routine of Camp Life. Our Capt Jno R. Weltner went home to day on a furlough.

Friday, April 28th

The Usual Drills, Dress Parade &c. Still making out Pay Rolls. Great rejoicing this evening, news is that the Rebel Genl Johnson has surrendered on same terms as Genl Lee did, and the troops are in great glee to night. Well! I cannot tell all they are up to to make things lively so I stop.

Saturday, April 29th

Weather still fine. Boys all busy washing and cleaning their Clothes for the sabbath day. Finished the rolls this evening. I wrote to Orderly Sergeant Jolliffe to day. Abe Hull came up to day, had been absent wounded and sick.

Sunday, April 30th

We had our usual inspection and mustered for March and April pay. James Collins went home on a 20 day furlough, Albert W. Bolen and Thomas B. Williams came to the Regiment to day.

We had a good noisy time. The 66th N.Y. discharged and went home on the 5 O'Clock train, and we went down to bid them good bye, and a happy lot of boys they were.

Monday, May 1st

We had a hard rain last night, but has cleared up and is a fine day. We had Drill, Dress Parade, and Marching orders to Manchester, which is opposite to Richmond the rebel Capitol, and the boys received the order with great shouts of Joy. So we are all busy to night getting ready for the move on to Richmond.

Tuesday, May 2nd — Berksville Station and Jettersville

We have been busy all day getting ready for the move. We packed already but did not get on the move until 3 P.M. The 116th our Regt and the 183rd P.V. guard the wagon train. Most of the troops moved this morning. To night finds us near Jettersville. Wagons are all parked, Guards posted, and we are speculating around the Camp fires as to what comes next.

Wednesday, May 3rd — on the March to Richmond, Va.

We were up early and started on the march. The nights are cool and days pretty warm. We moved by the side of the Rail Road. We passed a little Saw Mill. Some of the boys let the water on the wheel and she was going up and down and no log on. It put me in mind of old Dave Browns Mill near New Salem. We passed the Appomattox Court House. This is a beautiful country we are passing through to day. We camped on the banks of the Appomattox River, and we are all tired to night.

Thursday, May 4th

Packed up early, crossed the river at 7 A.M. and had a nice march through a delightful country. By the roadside was gathered all kinds of people, all colors and sizes gazing at us as we pass. While we halted for dinner I laid down by a tree and fell asleep, I had a bad headache and could not eat my dinner.

I was wakened by the chatter of a lot of young ladies. They were very nice looking and could ask about as many questions to the minute as any I had come across in my travels. Why does you uns all go 4 here and 4 here all along the road. The Rebs goes here and there, over the fences and every where. Whats that on your cap that horn and letters, they look so nice. The rebs has old Hats, Caps and no marks on them. And a host of other questions all of which I answered the best I could. They talked the Negro Brogue. On we go, we halted at 6 P.M. and rested until eleven P.M. Then away we went again and are still going at 12 O'Clock.

Friday, March 5th — Manchester

We traveled all night, and this morning finds us at Manchester. It is a very nice little town. The James river runs between it and Richmond which we can see over on the hillside. It looks like quite a large City.

It is just one year to day since we struck the first lick of the campaign to capture Richmond at the wilderness ("Evening of May 5th, 1864"). Was she worth the powder, and the lives lost, was it for the best, who can tell, not me I declare. I feel so good now, I think I would do it over again. But how many brave boys are laying by the wayside. Echo answers how many. 76 men that does not answer at Roll call, 14 Enlisted Men and 2 Co officers respond and answer to Their names, as we drop off to sleep I feel very sad.

Saturday, May 6th — from Manchester through Richmond

This is a beautiful day and all the boys are up early and fussing around as we cross over to the late rebel Capitol on our Pontoon Bridges as the Rebs had burned their Bridge.

This day one year ago we was pelting away at the Johnnies in the battle of the wilderness. There we go, we pass over the Pontoons, the taut stretched lines that hold them give back and fourth. As the current strikes the boats the men all stagger like as if we were intoxicated. We finally strike the graded stretch, pass the burned district and find that few streets look like streets now. We pass Old Libby Prison and Castle Thunder, now the windows are filled with miserable looking faces. Roughs of all nations I think. The Prisons are gloomy looking and if I had my will they would be laid low before another night passes.

But our friends [are] the Colored People, the poor darkies carrying water and give us to drink. All ages, sex and sizes all busy as nailers. The day is warm and we drink much and they bring more and more. How pleased they look, how happy they seem to be. We's glad you's cum! We's glad you's cum is their shout all along our line of march. It seems to me I could pick the Union people from rebels by the look on their faces, but on we go, the side walks and hills crowded all along the line with a motley crew. We could not see far back for the crowd was jammed up close and we merely had room to pass. We marched to the outskirts of the city, halted, stacked arms and rested for three hours. I went to the 85th P.V. which was doing Provost duty. We had a grand old shake all around, Ed Chick gave me grub and filled me up full and gave me two loaves of bread to take along. Bradley gave me a Silver Dollar.

The time is up, Fall in! Fall in! and we take our places and move off. We have passed through Richmond and as we stood and gazed at the many forts and works so solid and so strong and firm, and so well manned and mounted with huge guns, one Fort had four 100# guns, it would have been hard to storm. They was fixed in good shape and no mistake about that, but we passed through with the Stars and Stripes floating well out, Brass Bands and Drum Corps almost countless. So on we go and marched three or four miles and turned off the nice level road into a beautiful clover field and camped for the night, and tired is no name for us. But every day brings us nearer home, and we bear it with cheerfulness, and we drop off to sleep with thoughts of Home, Sweet Home.

Sunday, May 7th — near Richmond

This beautiful sabbath finds us trudging along on our way. The country is beautiful, nice Farms, Scenery &c. Charley Yauger has a dog he brot from Richmond, tied with a rope, and we call him Nick Whiffles and his dog Calamity.

Near Hanover Court

We pass Hanover Court House, crossed the Chickahoming River and camped on her banks for the night. The boys are having a glorious time bathing and enjoying themselves in the river and in various ways, and as usual we lay down tired and sleepy as we have nearly as hard marches as we had before the surrender of Lee.

Monday, May 8th

We was on the go bright and early, and one hour was all the rest we got to day. As usual we are passing through a beautiful country and we camp on the banks of the river Po after crossing over. The Second Division came up later but did not cross over but camped on the other side.

Tuesday, May 9th

Up early and started out again at a good 28 inches [sic], and passed through a nice level country. We passed an old Grist Mill. The Miller came out and gazed at us. He put me in mind of Father as he was a miller for 40 years. We crossed the river again and halted for the night near Old Spottsylvania. Threw ourselves down and slept soundly.

Wednesday, May 10th

Up early and on we go, passed Massapoak Church and reached Fredericksburgh at 12 O'Clock noon. We found it a terrible tumble down place, scarcely one house but looked damaged in some part. One small Frame was perforated on all sides with bullet holes, looked like two Bushel Balls had passed through it. One large brick a cannon ball had pierced through both gables, and the holes there yet big enough to throw a dog through. The stone wall where the old Irish Brigade was hurled against with such fearful loss, crossed where Joe Hooker had his Pontoon Bridge laid over. We passed through and the usual throngs was look[ing] on. Up the grade on the other side we passed through Falmouth at 1:30 O'Clock P.M. and went four or five miles and halted for the night in a nice woods, and all tired as usual but feel pretty well generally.

Thursday, May 11th — on the go.

Up and at it again, we cannot see much of the country as the roadside is woods, underbrush &c. We had a nice days *rainy* march and at

5 P.M. we camped for the night, all wet through and through and a cold rain at that, everything so wet we could not build fires. Night cool, and we are very much demoralized, tired and hungry, and I have a bad headache.

Friday, May 12th

This is a nice morning. One year ago to day we charged at Daylight at Spottsylvania and captured Genls Steward and Johnson and a host of Prisoners, and nearly cut the rebel army in two, helped to shoot off the Eighteen (18) inch tree with Bullets.

Hip, Hip Hoorah for the Second Corps,
With Hancock in the saddle,
They are the boys to make the noise,
And make the Rebs Skedaddle.

That twelvth of May in Sixty four,
Quite early in the morning,
The gallant boys of the Corps,
Gave Early a little warning.
 Hip, Hip, Hoorah &c &c.

Genl Barlow led the Club,
That marked the first Division,
And Genl Miles the first Brigade,
That made the first incision.
 Hip, Hip, Hoorah &c &c.

The Irish Brigade was always there,
And charged square through the line.
And made the rebel prisoners shout,
Clubs are trump this time.
 Hip, Hip, Hoorah &c &c.

The Jersey Blues where were they,
Fighting on the right,
And punching the Johnnies through the pine,
With all main and might.
 Hip, Hip, Hoorah &c &c.

("So I give the old song as I transferred it to my Diary.")
We captured 30 guns and 3,000 prisoners and fought from early morn

until late at night. On we go passing through a very poor country, looks like part of the mountain in Fayette County about Fall City or Ohio Pyle but not so hilly. My head is better as I get warmed up. We halted and Bivouacked in a nice field, and I feel pretty good, but all are tired and go to rest quietly.

Saturday, May 13th

Got on the march bright and early. Halted two hours to let a wagon train pass, then on we go, country still barren looking. We crossed Acquia Creek, then we commenced to ascend the hights, very steep and at the Top or nearly so there are two Forts and very strong works built in 1862. It is a very strong position and one when properly garrisoned could not be taken without great loss. We stacked arms and rested awhile, got on the go again, and at Sundown we halted for the night. We could see the Dome of the Capital at Washington City. Such chattering and congratulations to each other went on, and how good we feel to night, for we are in hopes our hard marching is over and that we will soon be speeding home on a fast train for we have done much trudging along.

Home, Home, sweet Home, there is no place like Home. But we are all well and as far as I can say in excellent spirits. So mout it be.

We have lots of visitors this evening and lights are not out at Nine O'Clock sharp, but finally at a late hour we go to tents and sleep.

Sunday, May 14th

This beautiful Sabbath finds us in the same place, on the hights near Alexandria Va. but not regularly encamped. And the Citizens I might say from every place are here, hundreds of them, and the questions are countless. They ask about friends, relatives and where such and such troops are. You can see Soldiers Surrounded by Citizens listening to the marvelous tales of this that and other fights, skirmishes, and charges with bayonets, clubbed muskets, Hair breath escapes &c &c.

Monday, May 15th — Camp Distribution

Near Alexandria and in sight of Washington D.C. we struck tents, packed up and moved to Fort Bernard this morning early. The timber was slashed and burned in 1862. The Underbrush has grown up thick and makes a one horse wilderness. We can hardly find room or space large enough for our tents, but we all went to work with a will and soon cut off the sprouts, and upheaved stumps, stones & logs, and this evening we have quite a nice Camp. We are high and dry. Nice clear water gushes out in various places through the white pebbles, it is pure, sweet and good. The view from this point puts me in mind of Kreepps Knob at West Brownsville, Washington Co Pa. We can see for miles.

We have been so busy all day we have not had time to attend to the Citizen Folks from Washington, that looked while we worked, sweat and tore up and rooted the scrubby under growth out. They have grub of all kinds to sell to the poor soldiers and at Fabulous prices. Pies 50 cents apiece, Bread 35 cents pr loaf and everything else in proportion.

Tuesday, May 16th — near Alexandria

All up early and busy as bees, Grubbing and Cleaning, getting Camp in shape, washing Clothes &c &c. Major William A. West of Uniontown to see us to day. 1st Lieutenant James D. Cope came to us to day, he was captured on June 22nd near Petersburgh Va. He took command of Co "K." I have been Corpl 1st, 2nd and Orderly Sergeant since March 31st 1864. Things are very lively here, almost like a big city, Thousands and Thousands of troops scattered over miles, Horses and Mules by the hundred acres, Hundreds of Colored Contrabands that followed the army. Paying and receiving visits makes things lively, so time goes on.

Wednesday, May 17th

Up early, no drill, nothing but Camp guard and fix up camp. The underbrush, stumps and sprouts have all disappeared and soon our camp will be in the best kind of shape. It looks now quite different from what it did three days ago. The weather has been dry and nice, so here we are.

Thursday, May 18th

One year ago to day in the charge on the rebel works near Spottsylvania I was struck with a Minie Ball a few yards from the works. The ball went through my blouse pocket, hit a Knife, Spoon and Fork in one handle and ten rounds of cartridges. I was knocked senseless for sometime, when I came to my Regiment had gone on over the works, late in the evening got back to our support. Battery K of heavy Artillery was part of it, Jim Black, Cooney, George Claybaugh, Bony Mitchell, Ganny Chew, and lots of others I knew was there, I was awful glad to see them as I was hurt pretty bad. The Ball stopped on my belt plate. I had to turn my gun in and got a carbine and carried ammunition in my pocket. I had to pass to the Hospital but never used it but stayed with the Regiment, could not wear a tight belt until June 2nd. Had a steady rain all day, no visitors and stayed in our tents all day.

Friday, May 19th

The weather still cloudy but no rain. We had Co Inspection to day. My Overcoat, Dress Coat and Blanket came, also all the rest of them. Things dull, the rain and wet keep the visitors away, and it is rather lonesome.

Saturday, May 20th

This is a beautiful morning. Had Company inspection at 9 A.M. and Brigade at 2 P.M. Commenced to rain soon afterwards, and I made out my monthly report of Co "K."

Sunday, May 21st

Rain, Rain and we are all in our tents, writing letters, playing cards and sleeping the time away.

Monday, May 22nd

Get ready for the grand review at Washington. We drew new clothing, and are busy as nailers getting ready, and it takes no little work to get ourselves in shape. We look around every way we can see Thousands upon Thousands pegging away, cleaning guns, equipments, washing clothes, awful busy indeed.

The Army of the Potomac, Shermans Boys and Phil Sheridans Troopers all bent on the same point. So we work away and try to make ourselves look the best we can. So we lay down and sleep out as usual. I have been looking at the troops passing and repassing for days and our turn comes tomorrow.

Tuesday, May 23rd — on review

We packed up early and marched to the long Bridge, and it is well named for it is a long 1¼ mile. Rested. At 10 A.M. passed over and up Thirteenth Street near Pennsylvania Avenue. Rested half an hour. Such a din of people, packed every place, except in the middle of the street. So we fall in, and on we go.

Talk about big Things, this takes The Cap sheaf off of all big times. The White House and Public Buildings was covered with Bunting and Flags, Distinguished Men, Women, and Officers, both Military and Civic. When the Old 116th passed by with her thin ranks and old torn Flag, nothing but Staff and Fringe, all had been shot away, and the Staff looked like rats had gnawed it, we got a good old send off. Them boys have seen hard service, we could hear on the sidewalk as we passed. The shouting was loud and long. We seen Orderly James E. Jolliffe on his crutches and his right leg stiff at the knee. And others, many others that had been cut down with shot and shells from the ranks from the Wilderness to Lees Surrender. We got through at 5 P.M. We returned to Camp, tired was no name for us. Everything was so vastly Big that I cannot tell what a day this was.

So we reach Camp and go to rest and are thankful that our day is over. And for three days and a half this has been going on, Shermans Vets, Sheridans Cavalry, and the Army of the Potomac. They pore through the City as if there was no end to it.

Wednesday, May 24th

The day after our review. This is a beautiful day and we are lounging around and not over yesterdays big tramp. This is Shermans day and from daylight the troops are going to show off in grand array. It has been a continual come and go all day until dark, it was a mighty host. The day was hot, and I know how they feel I have been there. I would have liked to see them but I was too near played out. Nothing of importance to day as we have a day of rest which we need.

Thursday, May 25th

Still the weather is fine but warm and dry. The Boys (Co A) that was on provo duty at Division Head Quarters reported to the regiment to day, and I think we will be discharged soon.

The First Brigade of our Division had a Grand Dress parade to night, each gun had a candle in the muzzle, I tell you it was a grand sight. The evening still and they was just far enough off to look nice, they had rows of candles on the ridge of the tents all lit up and them going through dress parade moving through the other made it a grand sight. At twelve O'Clock the show was still going on as if they knew no such thing as Rest or Sleep. I for one have to turn in and get some rest as I am not over the 23rd yet, so I lay me down and sleep.

Friday, May 26th

This is a very dull day in camp as the rain is pouring down the near way. It always seemed to me the rain could come with the least preparation in this part of the Country of any place in the world. Lt James D. Cope came to day and received a warm greeting for we had not seen him since the 22nd Day of June 1864 when he was taken prisoner.

Saturday, May 27th

This is another day of rain. Rain and still it rains. Will Ramsey and

Alex Woods called on us to day. We just lay in our tents, talk, write letters, make out reports and let the rain fall.

Sunday, May 28th

This is a beautiful sabbath day except a little mud. We had our usual Co inspection by Lt Jas D. Cope, the first time since he was captured, after which we all run around here, there and everywhere, general visiting day.

Monday, May 29th

All busy as nailers to day cleaning up for the review tomorrow. Everything quiet and nothing worthy of note.

Tuesday, May 30th

This is a beautiful day, and at 12 O'Clock we moved out in grand style to Bailys X Roads. It was a grand sight, the old 2nd Corps never looked better (even on the 23rd of May). Genl Hancock is to review us to day. We was all marshalled to our places, Parade Rest was given, and we stood at ease, and while we waited and was looking for Hancock, his old Darky rode up the line leading the old gay Dapple Brown. (Hancock came out in a closed carriage.)

And we give three times three for the old charger and the old horse seemed to understand for he reared, walked on his hind feet, went side ways and cut all the monkey shines imaginable. I think the old Darkey thought we was cheering him, we could have thrown a loaf of bread down his throat without taking off the crust. — Attention and we all get to our places. Genl Hancock, Genl Meade, Genl Humphreys, Gov Curtin of Penna and a host of Generals and civilians came down the line, and we give them a good old fashioned send off. It was a grand review and went off in good style, and the last for the old Iron 2nd Corps. We returned to camp at 5 P.M. all well pleased with our days work.

Wednesday, May 31st

I have been busy all day taking Invoice of ordinance and Camp equipage, so busy that I hardly know what has been going on.

Thursday, June 1st

Still beautiful weather and the regular old routine of Camp life, Drill, Dress Parade &c &c. Finished ordinance reports.

Friday, June 2nd

I got a pass to day and went over to the 14th Pa Cavalry, seen George Tuit of New Salem and Jabe McCloy and others of my old acquaintances. Got a horse and we went to Alexandria, seen the afternoon show and stayed for the Theatre at night and had a grand good time, all round, and got back to camp at midnight tired and sore.

Saturday, June 3rd

Still nice weather but very hot. McCafferty (our Sutler) treated the Regt to Ale &c &c. I did not indulge, the *boys very noisy* to night.

Sunday, June 4th

Still very warm. Part of our Regiment whose time is out went home to day. Capt Weltner under arrest for being absent with out leave. We had our usual Dress parade to night. *Very warm.*

Monday, June 5th

Troops leaving for home from all parts of the army. I am not very well to day.

Tuesday, June 6th, to Monday, June 12th

The same old rigmarole of Camp life, with no change to the 12th.

Tuesday, June 13th

Weather still warm and fine. Tom Williams and Dick McClean got discharged to day, Tom wounded in the foot, Dick on the 18th of May 1865 in the arm. His arm had to be amputated near the shoulder. Capt Weltner still under arrest and papers not come yet.

Wednesday, June 14th

We are all getting ready for a rigid inspection to day that is coming off tomorrow. Dick & Tom went home to day.

Thursday, June 15th

We had a hard rain last night. We had our monthly inspection to day, and our usual Dress parade this evening.

Friday, June 16th

This is a beautiful day, same old Rigmarole.

Saturday, June 17th

Weather is good, had orders to move, but was countermanded and here we are.

Sunday, June 18th

This is another beautiful day, have our usual Sunday Inspection, Company and Regiment small. After inspection we all took a swim. The boys built a dam and domed up the run and made a pretty good swimming hole. I think one or two thousand were in and soon the water was like very thin mortar. I felt like I had been sand papered. We looked the color of half blood indians.

Monday, June 19th

We struck tents this morning and packed up and all are ready to move, when the order was countermanded and the boys tried which could get off the most cuss words to the square inch.

Tuesday, June 20th

We had a nice little shower of rain last night but pleasant to day and we lay around loose, very dull.

Wednesday, June 21st

Weather nice and warm, had drill. The 53rd has marching orders and are fixing up the rolls. Bolen and Yauger came back, been to the city on a (Bolen pass) *knapsack drill.*

Thursday, June 22nd

Weather still beautiful but rather warm. We had our usual drill, go over the hill in the hollow and lay in the shade and call it drill.

Friday, June 23rd

We had our usual drill to day. Abe Hull died at Hospital with Diarrhoea. Col Mulholland and Capt Weltner had quite a quarrel to day. Chews of Tobacco passed, but no one wounded.

Saturday, June 24th

All quiet on the line, the same old rigmarole, Drill, Dress Parade.

Sunday, June 25th

Another beautiful day, we had our usual inspection and Dress parade.

Monday, June 26th

Commenced to rain this morning and has kept it up all day. We lay in our tents, read, write and cat nap, and speculate about when we will leave this beautiful hilly country. We are tired of gazing at the Dome of the Capitol eight miles away.

Tuesday, June 27th

A beautiful day, and are all busy making out pay rolls. Sergt Sembower and Henry Hull are detailed at Provo Head Quarters from Co "K."

Wednesday, June 28th

I am detailed to take charge of Brigade Pioneers, so I left Co "K" this morning and here I am at Genl Pierces Head Quarters in charge of 20 men from different companies and Regts. I relieved Lieut Taggart to be captain of Co I. I like the place very much, no drill, Dress parade or nothing. We are close to the Baily Residence, under a row of very large spreading oaks, and get water from the Baily well, ("which is very deep and cool") and I like the change very much. Nothing to do but eat, sleep & Read and write, have a good cook.

Thursday, June 29th

I have the Pioneers busy all day beautifying our camp, and a splendid one it is. Alexander Berwick and I tent together, I am very well contented.

Friday, June 30th — near Alexandria, Baileys X Roads

I went over to the Regiment (116th P.V.) a short distance and was mustered for May and June pay. I found the boys all O.K. I returned to pioneers camp.

Saturday, July 1st

A nice shower of rain this morning, makes this a nice day. One of the brigade staff told me to day that 2nd, 5th and 6th Corps was consolidated into one Corps, the 6th 1st Division, 2nd Corps 2nd Division, and 5th Corps 3rd Division, making the Provisional Corps. What a corps that will make, they are all of the genuine American Stuff.

Sunday, July 2nd

The weather very warm, we lay around in the shade and watch the troops, some drilling, others being mustered out and going home, some changing camp &c &c. I am so well contented I do not care if I stay until late in the fall.

Monday, July 3rd

Troops all striking Tents to day and moving out to form the Provisional Corps. We (the Pioneers) struck tents with the rest and went to the Regt — General Pierce said he wanted me at his Head Quarters and would have me detailed. So I lay me down with Co "K" boys once more.

Tuesday, July 4th

This is a most beautiful day. I run around, laid by and wrote letters, and read Isabel Vincent that Capt Alton loaned me. The boys all over the hills are having Homemade fire works and enjoying themselves as best they can on the grand old fourth. We still have many visitors coming and going.

Wednesday, July 5th

Good! I get my detail to take charge of 2nd Brigade 2nd Division of Provisional Corps. We are back under the same old oaks, our tents pitched and feeling very good, nothing to do and plenty of time to do it in. We get drinking water from the Baily well, and a nice little stream of water passes close in front. In fact we never were so well fixed since I donned the U.S. Blue.

Thursday, July 6th

This is a beautiful day but warm. I have a horse to ride if I want to when I please. One man cooks for the whole thing and he knows his business. Any amount of troops leaving for home every day. (I am in no particular hurry now.)

Friday, July 7th

Still fine weather. I went down to the Regiment (116th P.V.) to day (horse back) and set on a stump and looked at the boys drilling in the hot sun. Came back and the chin is that we are to be disbanded again and be sent home.

Saturday, July 8th

This is a beautiful day. I went over to and had a long talk with Mrs. Baily. They own 600 acres of land, but the soldiers has made the fences scarce. She is the mother of seven sons.

Sunday, July 9th

I went down to The Regt. The boys are very anxious to go home. For my part I am in no particular hurry (I am fixed) and would just as leave stay until fall.

Monday, July 10th

This is a nice day, had a slight rain, rather a dull day and we lay back under the Oaks, read, sleep, eat and write. We are eating our white bread for the first time since Feby 29th 1864.

Tuesday, July 11th

Nice day. Officers and Clerks all busy making out discharge papers. I passed the day reading and laying around.

Wednesday, July 12th

Weather still keeps nice. I go over and have a talk with Father Baily and his wife. They have the colored Brogue and I pass the time away nicely.

Thursday, July 13th

Weather cooler and very nice. I went to the Regiment to day. They have the reports and rolls all ready. I came back and disbanded my Pioneers but I liked the old boys too well to not do all I could for them. I sent them to their Companies and Regiments. In the evening I went to the 116th Regiment Co "K." Lt Cope ordered me to take charge of Co "K" as orderly Sergeant. I told him I was a disbanded Pioneer. I always tried to do my duty.

Friday, July 14th

We are busy getting ready for home, *for home*. That sounds well and a happy set we are, and at 12 O'Clock M. we was mustered out and have to leave in the morning for Washington City. It is now 12 O'Clock Midnight and while I write the boys everywhere almost are tearing up and burning everything that will burn and a great big bonfire is blazing making an illumination that lights the old Hills around Alexandria for miles and miles.

Saturday, July 15th

I could not sleep last night or rather this morning. So Hezekiah Dean and I start for Washington City as I promised to call and see Uncle Thomas Clear who lives on 13th St. He has been clerking in the Treasury Department for years. So Ky and I light out and we come to the Long Bridge a Sentinel says halt and show your pass. I have no pass but I tell him a straight tale and he knows Uncle Thomas and where he lives and lets us pass over. And not far we come to the brown front and we lay our accoutrements on the portico. I knock and Uncle comes to the door, reaches out his hand and pulls us in and the catechism commences. Aunt Sarah and Seven or Eight cousins greets and wants us to stay a few weeks. I promise to come back from Harrisburgh and we hear the boys coming, we rush out and on we go. We get on the cars at 9 A.M. and on we [go] cheering and getting cheered at every house, village and hamlet by the way. What a time had we all the way on our glorious return. My thoughts often goes to the poor boys that lay by the wayside from the wilderness to the surrender of Lee April 9th. If we only had them along then our cup of Joy would be full.

Sunday, July 16th

We reached Harrisburgh at 5 A.M., got off the cars and marched through the City quietly to Camp Curtin, pitched our tents — all in good shape. Went back to the city, ran around and visited the different places of interest. Lots of Pa Regts here in Camp waiting for their eagles.

July 17th — Harrisburgh

We got up early and got on the go. We took a turn around the city and found many things to interest us. Some would get their pockets picked, the city is full of pick pockets, fine ladies of the loose persuasion, Theatres and Playhouses all in blast. This is a very gay place to sow wild oats and lose stamps and health. We got to camp at midnight, tired.

July 18th

Wes signed the pay rolls to day after which we put in the day going from place to place seeing the sights, so at midnight I turn again, tired is no name for me.

Many of the boys are picking out suits of clothes and have the Jews to lay them back until we get our pay.

July 19th

This is a nice morning. I think the boys have two or Three Thousand dollars worth of clothes laid up on few shelves. At twelve to day, we got our pay and discharge, got our dinners, got on the One O'Clock train, and away we go leaving the Jews saying cuss words. We nod and cat nap on the train.

July 20th — Pittsburgh

We arrived at Pittsburgh at 2 O'Clock A.M. Went to Hare Hotel, threw ourselves down on sitting room carpet and slept sound. Got up at 7 A.M., got breakfast, went out and bought what we needed, and seen the sights, and at one or two O'Clock got on the Uniontown train and we reach Uniontown at 7 P.M. The Platform was jammed with people, friends to greet us and their friends. I seen many that would never greet them now as we had left them by the wayside. I got my supper and at 8 P.M. I got on the Mountain Hall City or Boss Rushs so on I go through Monroe up the long tedious mountain Pike. I lay over on the seat and snooze and at twelve we are still snailing up the hill.

July 21st

I arrive at Boss Rushs at 2 A.M. this morning. I threw myself down on the floor and at daylight our old friend Boss woke me up. I could smell the ham cooking in the kitchen and the coffee, it made me hungry clean down to my toes. I got fixed up with a good wash of the pure Mountain water, and then such a breakfast as I put my self outside of only Boss and his folks can get up. After doing full justice to the breakfast I start for the Ohio Pyle Falls, nearly all down hill. I arrive between 8 and 9 A.M. I find them all in good shape, and I get a warm reception. I take off the old Army Blue and put on the Citizen Clothes and feel well satisfied with myself, and feel that I would do it again if they should want three hundred thousand more. After dinner I go down to the saw mill, I file the saw and start the old saw mill and make the saw dust fly. Buckwheat Cakes and honey (wild) has to suffer and all else that is eatable, that appetite of mine still continues. Grey Squirrel and Red Squirrel Pot Pie &c &c — Hardtack a thing of the past.

Letters

March 2nd, 1864 — Camp Copeland

Dear Mother,

Alex and I are well, only I have a bad cold. We sent Two Hundred Dollars apiece home by William Hunn to give to Father, but he has left home since. You will have to get Uncle Isaac to go and draw the money and deposit it in the Fayette County Bank, in Fathers name. We have 75 or 80 Dollars to send home yet which was our Government bounty, but we will not send it now until we get a furlough. I think we will get a furlough the last of this week. We are in Camp Copeland now, we come out last night, it is 10 miles from Pittsburgh on the Pittsburgh & Connellville Railroad. We got out and marched up to Camp and stood in line for about an hour and a half, and it was pretty cool for the snow was about 4 inches deep and we had nothing to eat since noon, and then only a piece of bread and fat meat with a little coffee. You can give this little order to Uncle Isaac and he can get the money from Mr. Hunt. I would have wrote sooner only I had no chance, my money was all greenbacks and Alex's is Greenbacks and Pittsburgh.

(*Notes in Margin:* Was Sworn into U.S. Service Feb'y 29th 1864. Left home for Pittsburgh Feb'y 26th.)

March 4th — Camp Copeland

Dear Mother,

Alex and I are as well as usual, excepting slight colds. Uncle Isaac come down last night, Tom was not here and Uncle went down to the city this morning. Tom had gone to Pittsburgh yesterday afternoon. We have five in our mess, all acquaintances and first rate boys, Dick Mc-Clean, James Collins, Cousin Tom, Alex and myself. I don't know whether we will get a furlough or not, but I think that we may get one next week. I send 80 dollars and Alex 70 making $150.00, which can be put in the Fayette Co. Bank in Father's name. I will write as often as possible. It is not a very handy place to write, as you have to set down and put the paper on your knee instead of a desk. I want you to save all our letters. When you write direct your letter to Braddocksfield P.O. Camp Copeland, 116 Regt Inf'y P.V. We are not organized as a company yet.

Write soon. Your Son Daniel Chisholm. I send this letter by Uncle Isaac.

March 4th, 1864
Brother Alex's Letter

Dear Mother,

I take this opportunity to write you a few lines and hoping they may find you well. I have spent 3 dollars of my government money, I send you $70 in this letter, a $50 and a $20 Greenbacks, by Uncle Isaac. We have comfortable quarters now. Capt Conner said that he thought we would get a furlough this week or next. I do not know whether we will or not. We belong to the 116th Regt P.V. The regiment is near Washington I heard, I do not know that it is so. I bought a pair of boots, paid Nine Dollars for them. There is about 5 or 6 Thousand soldiers in this camp. It is the muddiest place you ever saw. The soldiers are coming in by squads and Companies, and some going away. They have the greatest way of punishing the soldiers here I ever seen, they tie them up by the thumbs just so they can touch the ground, they killed one man this way the other day. We have the best set of fellows in Camp in our mess, 5 of us, James Collins, Richard A. McClean, Tom Williams, Dan Chisholm and myself, Alex Chisholm.

Write soon. Alexander Chisholm — your Son.

March 10th, 1864 — Alexandria Va.

Dear Father,

We are as well as could be expected excepting colds. I suppose it will surprise you, when I tell you that we are in Alexandria Va waiting to be sent down front to our regiment. At noon at Camp Copeland on Tuesday the sergeant came around to our barracks and told us that we had to leave at four O'Clock that afternoon. We started at four and reached Harrisburgh at 3 O'Clock next morning and went to the Soldiers home and got a good breakfast of hot coffee and light bread with a piece of beef. We started early in the morning again and arrived at Baltimore at 11 O'Clock and got our dinners at the Soldiers Rest. We started again for Washington at Eight O'Clock at night and arrived there at a quarter of twelve O'Clock, and unslung our knapsacks at the soldiers rest and spread our blankets on the floor and went to sleep and had a first rate sleep for I had not slept much since we started. We got our breakfasts and started for Alexandria, we came here on a Steamer. It was quite a change for we had been on the cars since we started from Camp Copeland. It was only Seven miles. I got a glimpse of Capitol as we marched out towards the Potomac river. We seen some very nice residences through Maryland as we came along. There is a great many Pine trees scattered through the fields. We did not get to see much through the cities, for as soon as we got inside the building that we were to stay in there was a guard placed at each door. We was very glad when we heard that we had to leave Camp Copeland. It was the muddiest place I ever seen. We do not know exactly yet when we are to go, but they say we will go to Brandy Station, were the regiment is stationed. It is sixty five miles from here and only about One Hundred from Richmond, so we will be apt to see the elephant before long. I will not tell you to write, because it would be uncertain whether we would ever get it or not. Alex is getting along first rate. Some of the boys begin to feel a little blue. I want you to get me twc flannel shirts, you had better get the goods and have them made. I want them to come up high in the neck, for I don't expect to wear a collar much. I have a government shirt on now. When I looked in the looking glass I hardly knew myself, for the Collar was the largest part about it. I want a silk Handkerchief and a pair of Boots. I want them made at Paines for he has my measure. I want them made middling broad, so that they will be easy on my feet, and would also like to have some Paper Collars, size 13½. I want the Boots made of heavy calf skin. Alex got a pair at the Sutlers and paid Nine Dollars for them, and they are beginning to run down. When I write again I will tell you where to send them and how.

March 13th, 1864 — Alexandria
Dear Father,

We are getting along first rate, we are still quartered at The Soldiers Rest in Alexandria. We get plenty to eat. The guard wakens us up at Five O'Clock in the morning, and we get ready for our breakfasts and eat before daylight. We have Bread, Pork and Coffee for Breakfast & Supper, and for Dinner we have Bread and Soup. I expect that tomorrow we will be moved to our Regiment. We have been here since last Thursday. There are a great many troops going through here to their Regiments. We are in a building with guards around us, and we can not get out unless a guard goes with us. It is the best place I have been since I left home. We have excellent water and a good chance to keep ourselves clean, Towels and Soap found us. The Dining room will accommodate one thousand men at a time. We haven't an officer with us yet. The Company elected John Weltner Captain. A part of Genl Kilpatricks men are in the same building with us, and the balance of them are camped on a hill about a half a mile out of town. They have been on a raid and they say they were within a mile and a quarter of Richmond, and destroyed a great many Depots and Rail Roads. There is a great deal of stealing going on here, last night one man had 42 Dollars taken and another 59 and a few nights before one had 400 Dollars stole from him, and every night some one loses a cap, overcoat or knapsack. I think Pittsburgh is about as mean a place as could be called a city, Harrisburgh is a nice place and Baltimore is the nicest City I have seen yet, I want them boots made wide at the top so that I can wear my pants on the inside of them, and the shirts without collars, so that I can wear paper ones, and a good Silk Handkerchief. You will have to get them on my good Credit or on Fathers and I will pay him when my two months pay is due. I cannot tell you where to send them to yet, nor I cannot tell you where to write to yet. It isn't very good writing for I have to use Alex back for a writing desk, and of course he doesn't sit very still.

March 16th, 1864 — Alexandria
Dear Father,

We are still at Alexandria and getting along first rate. There hasn't been any of our Company in the Hospital yet. We are still at the Soldiers Rest, and I think it is a Soldiers Rest for we cannot get out for to get tired. I seen two Indians yesterday. They were the first I had ever seen. They were sharp looking fellows. They came from Lower Canada and talked French. I seen the Hotel where Ellsworth was killed for taking the rebel Flag down. I seen the residence of the Rebel General Lee as we came down the Potomac to Alexandria. When you write I want you to give me Uncle Joseph's address, and let me know when you heard from Uncle Tom, also from Grandmother, how she liked the pictures and what she said about them. I seen George Darby the other day, he was sorry we had not enlisted for the 8th Reserves. When you write let me know whether Weltner is in town, and if he is what he is doing. We heard through some of the boys that left Camp Copeland since we did that Capt Conner had gave his commission as first Lieutenant over to James Cope, and that he had a part of a Company recruited and intended to join it with ours and make a full company. I wish they would so that we could have our officers here.

The Susquehanna river at Harrisburgh is a very wide river but the Potomac beats anything I have seen yet in the way of rivers. I want you when you send that box to send another towel and 1 pr Woolen Socks, for the government socks are so large that they wrinkle and hurt my feet, and all the Cotton ones I have. I don't know how much more I will think of before I can tell you where to direct it to. I want you to write and tell me how you all are, and if you got my money all right. Alex says to tell you we are gay and happy still. You will have to write very soon for I do not know how long we will be here.

Your Son, Daniel Chisholm. Co "K" 116th Regt Pa Vol's — Alexandria Va.

March 20th, 1864 — Camp Briggs
Brother Alex's Letter
Dear Father,

I take this opportunity of writing to let you know I am well, and hoping you are the same. We are ½ mile from Alexandria, we have encamped on the banks of the Potomac, just our Company. It is a beautiful place. The boys have all caught bad colds laying on the ground but are getting better. I want you to send me a Ten Dollar Greenback for they wont take any other kind here, I must have it, address Camp Briggs Care of Capt McGraw.

March 24, 1864 — Camp Briggs
Dear Father,

I received your letter dated March 18th last evening, and was glad to hear from you for more than a week. I wrote on the 13th so that it takes about 10 days to write and receive an answer. I haven't been well for about a week, I am getting better now. It was coming out to camp and laying on the damp ground. It gave me a very bad cold, and I was very sore all over. I think I may get along well enough after this. We are camped on the bank of the Potomac, about half a mile from Alexandria. It is a very nice place. But the wind blows most all day. 20 of the boys was sent to Brandy Station to guard a lot of recruits down front to their regiments. Alex and Tom was with them. I expect we will stay here until after the draft is over. We can see the Capitol very plain from where we lay. The Potomac is about a mile and a qr wide here.

You will have to send us that box as quick as you can for I expect I will be nearly barefooted before we get it. Send me 1 or 2 Bob Sellers Cough Syrup, for I cannot get it here, send me my best black necktie and razor. We have plenty of Paper, Envelopes and Stamps for the present. Tom dont need a pair of Boots, he got a pair in Pittsburgh before he left. Let me know whether our clothes ever got home yet or not. I bought a little looking glass and left it in my coat when I boxed it up. If you have got them yet, I wish you would send the glass in the box. It is lonesome in the Camp without the boys. As for keeping John Weltner's Books it is not so. He hasn't any to keep yet. He promised me I should be Company Clerk. But I think it is a little doubtful. If I was you I would not say anything about it to him. You will have to send the box by Express To — in Care of Capt Mcgraw, Alexandria, Va. You will have to send us five Dollars for neither one of us has a cent to pay the Expressing. You must write immediately. You can send it in the letter and let us know a little of everything that happens and how you all are. I think I will stand it better after this. Write as soon as you get this and tell me how soon you can send the box for we need it. Alex ought to have a silk Hdchf.

April 4th, 1864 — Brandy Station Va.
Camp near Stevensburgh about 4 Miles from Brandy Station

Dear Father,

I received two letters from you five or six days ago, the next day after we arrived here and was very glad to get them. They were addressed to the Soldiers Rest and had been forwarded. We are both well and getting along first rate. The day we came here it was raining and the ground was very wet and muddy, and as soon as we got into Camp The Capt said that we might get as good a spot as we could and pitch our tents which of course was very poor. However Alex, Tom and I put our three little shelter tents together and tried to keep dry in them, but it was an impossibility, and went around to some of the old soldiers tents and asked them to take us in, and all succeeded in getting places. But the soldiers in the tent Alex was in got contrary and told him to march out, and he went to the Meeting House where he got to stay in the dry until next morning. The boys I got in with were splendid fellows, and made a rousing fire for me to dry by for I was wet to the hide, and made me a cup of warm coffee to drink. The reason that I did not write sooner was that the first day we had to try and fix our quarters as comfortable as we could, and that evening at roll call Alex and I was called on to go out the next day at eight O'Clock as pickets, and that was the roughest duty I have been called on to do. My Boots has gone entirely up the spoon. My feet was wet up to my ankles for four days. Alex and I was on the same post the first two nights. I had the pleasure of seeing one reb across the river on an entrenchment. The third day it snowed and was very disagreeable, especially to my feet. As soon as I got to Camp again which if it had been another mile farther I could not of made it for my feet was awful tender from the mud and water, I got a pair of Boots of one of the boys by paying six Dollars, worth about three but they will last me until I can get them from you. We have moved since I told you to direct the box to Alexandria and it is a little doubtful about us getting it if you have started it. If not send all you can by Springer & Jolliffe that you can and address the box to Co "K" 116th Regt Inf P.V.

Washington D.C. I will try to write once a week after this. You will have to send me ten dollars, for I had to borrow the six to pay for my boots. Write as soon as you can and let me know about the box and Weltner and whether you got a letter from me while I was in the rest, with a picture on the envelope of our troops shelling the Guerrillas out of the woods along the banks of the Mississippi.

(In a letter dated April 5th, 1864 from Bro Alex it stated we arrived at Camp near Stevensburgh on March 29th, spoke of there being much rain, Mud and Slush and that Abraham Hull was laying in a tent ¼ mile from Camp with the Smallpox.)

April 8th, 1864 — Camp near Brandy Station, Va.
About 4 or 5 Miles from Brandy Station, near Stevensburgh.
Dear Father,

I received your letter dated March 28th and was glad to hear from you, and that you were all well as usual. Alex and Tom are hearty as bucks excepting Tom has a sore throat. For my part I never felt better in my life than I do at present. I think the sick spell I had at Camp Briggs was from lying on the ground and not being used to it. It gave me a most powerful cold and upset me pretty generally. But I have been hearty ever since, and have been on duty nearly every day since we arrived here. I kept my fine shirt, I forgot to put it in the box. We received the box to day and was very glad of it. I had no sooner opened it than I off with my Government Shirt & *Collar*, the largest portion of it and on with my new Flannel one, and it fit up to nature. The Boots were a fit also, but they are too light for the service they have to do. I think they were cheap, perhaps the cause of that is that I haven't seen any thing since I left Baltimore but what they asked their prices for. The sutlers here sell butter at 50 cents, Eggs 60 cents pr doz, Cheese 40 cents per tb[?]. We have splendid quarters here, we just finished building our log hut to day and after this we will be in the dry. There is five of us in together. If your lungs are sore you had better go to the doctor and get something for them before it runs too long. I think the move from the old shop to the stable was a very good one as it will be handier to the house. As for the sugar Benjamin sent us it was very good and I will write him a letter. As for the $5.00 you sent in the letter to care of Capt. Mcgraw it came all right. We sent no shirts home with our clothes. I tell you it is a nice thing to receive a box here, it puts one in mind of home. I shall wear my other boots as long as I can. Alex will need his against he gets them [sic]. The ones he bought in Camp Copeland has not worn well, although he has worn them twice as long as the other boys that got theirs at the same time. I heard that there was 8 or 9 of our boys taken prisoners that belonged to an old Uniontown Company. I do not know what Company it could be. We received the other $5.00 in the box, making the $10.00. I sent for $10.00. If you have not started it yet you need only send $5.00. I will have to have it so I can pay the money I borrowed for the boots. I think I have written about 12 Letters home, I dont know whether you got them all or not. I wrote one home and gave it to the guard at the rest to take to the office.

Your Son, Daniel Chisholm.

April 18, 1864 — Camp near Stevensburgh, VA
Brother Alex's letter, Extract from.

We are in regimental Camp. The first night had no quarters. There was a cold rain turning to snow in the night about 10 O'Clock. The next day or two we put up quarters, then done Picket duty, going to Kellys ford, a distance of about 7 or 8 miles from Camp. The weather was very cold and raw and they would not allow us to have any Picket Fires.

April 27th, 1864 — Camp near Brandy Station
Dear Father,

I received your letter dated April 20th and one the day before from yourself and Jennie, and was glad to hear from home. The letter that Jennie wrote was nine days coming. I had not received any since we got the box. I am sorry that you sent anything in the box that Uncle is sending to Thomas, for it has not come to hand yet, and very likely never will. Alexs boots has not come. I wrote to the Ex Agt at Alexandria but did not receive any answer. Tom, Alex, Dick McClean and most all the boys are well. I was sorry to hear of mother having the headache, but hope she is as well as ever before now. It would do me a heap of good to get that box, it makes my mouth water to read about it. I have the office of 4th Corporal. I had the chance of being hospital Steward but refused it. James E. Jolliffe is our Orderly Sergt, Warren S. Kilgore 2nd, Edward Pence 3rd, Wm Sembower 4th, Hezekiah Deane 5th, James Collins 1st Corpl, Steven Beckett 2nd, Daniel Crawford 3rd, myself 4th, Robt Brownfield 5th, Saml A. Clear 6th, George I. Cruse 7th, Dick McClean 8th, T. B. Williams, Co Clerk. We had Division Drill yesterday, we come up in line of battle and charged bayonets on double quick for about half a mile. It made some of the boys puff and blow. But I think if the enemy had been in front of us they would have had to skedaddled. We went through the full motions of a battle and retreat. Genls Owens and Barlow was present. We have very nice weather here now.

I was at preaching Sunday. I could not say church for it was out in the open air, beneath the broad Canopy of heaven. I wrote a letter to Sarah A. Williams a few days ago, I addressed it to Harrisville, Harrison Co. Ohio. I suppose they will get it if they have not moved. We will move before long from here, we do not know what hour, so we keep ourselves in readiness for the march. I am going to keep as light a knapsack as possible. You said something about buying the house you live in. It has been some time ago and I forgot whether I wrote to you about it or neglected it. You do just as you see fit with the money. I think it is the best thing you could do with it, to put it into property. If you do buy, buy a good house, Morgantown St is the nicest Street in town, and the house you live in is well situated. You could have the stable for a shop and you would always be handy to home. I want you to keep an account of the money each one of us draws and what the boxes costs us, and keep all the letters we write home. There has been three of our Company died since we left town. They have been talking something about stopping the soldiers from writing home. If they do, write on for we will want to hear from home.

Your son Daniel Chisholm.

May 1st, 1864 — Camp near Brandy Station
Dear Father,

Alex, Thomas & I are as well as usual. Also all the other boys of the Company. We got the box in due time and had a feast of course. The cheese and Rusk were excellent. It made us almost forget that we were soldiering. Dick McClean divided his molasses with us and we our honey with him. I received a letter from Cousin Sallie A. Williams, they were all well, and Uncle Tom is going to write me a letter before long. I have not wrote to Uncle Joseph yet, as I am afraid he has moved before now. Burnside has come up to Brandy Station with Forty thousand men, we will be very apt to move before long and when we do we will be apt to see the Elephant. We were mustered yesterday for our pay, we will be apt to get it in a month or two. We have had Division Drill nearly every day for a week. There is five Regiments in our Brigade, the 63rd, 69th and 88th New York, 28th Massachusetts and ours the 116th Pennsylvania. It is called the Irish Brigade. Alex's Boots has not come yet, and I am afraid never will. I sold my hat to one of the boys for two Dollars and a half. I would not of sold it, only I had no good way of carrying it, and I got as much for it as I paid a year ago. I suppose things begin to look like Spring about town once more, and that the people are beginning to purchase their Summer goods. But here there is no change, you see nothing but government Blues. I heard it said that the Army of the Potomac drawed a hundred and Eighty Thousand rations making for about 125,000 abled bodied men for service. I guess I will bring my letter to a close. It is a very pretty day here.

Write soon — your Son, Daniel Chisholm.

May 13, 1864 — Spottsylvania
Dear Father,

I and Alex are still in the land of the living. Thomas Williams was wounded in the foot. I suppose you will think it a long time since we wrote. It has been nine days since we started from camp, and seven days we have been fighting. At roll call this morning there was but twenty of our Company left, Dick McClean, Alf Bailes, Ed Pence are here, Sembower is missing, Daniel Crawford wished me to tell you to tell Wilhelms that he has got through so far without being hurt. Our Col was wounded and Lt Col Dale was killed yesterday. There has been a great many of our men killed. We charged over the rebel breastworks yesterday morning and took a great many prisoners, twelve cannons and Maj Gen'l Johnston and Gen'l Stewart besides several Brigadier Genls. This morning the report is that the rebels have fell back and that Burnside has taken forty pieces of Cannon. I and Alex have escaped so far better than I expected to, for they have fell thick and fast on each side of us. I got a letter from home the other day and was glad to hear from you. I wish you would write as often as possible for I like to hear from home if I cannot write. Since I commenced writing Simbower has come in. I guess this is about all I can write at present. I do not know how the fight may terminate yet. I would like to see a late paper. Our Corps charged en Mass yesterday morning and we become very much mixed up, a few of our regiment got to the left and was mixed up with The Diamond Division (3) of our Corps. Alfred Bailes and myself were The only ones of our Company that were near Lt Col Dale when he got over the second line of Rebel Breastworks. It was near some Oak trees. He was about twenty feet from the works, had his sword raised and was commanding forward boys, forward boys. At that moment the enemy commenced to enfilade or shoot down the line along the breastworks we had charged up to. I told Alfred Bailes we could not stay where we were without being killed, and the troops had begun to fall back to the first line of works. There was a great many men killed as we got back. We did not see our brave Lt Col afterwards, he was a good man. Of course he was killed or captured, as no one could live when the leaden hail was hissing like the continued buzz of a swarm of bees. I am anxious to see the illustrated papers. I wish you would send me several with accounts of the battles in. I will write every chance I have. Write soon. So good bye to you all — maybe for the last, [*sic*]

Alex says to tell you that he is well, for the present it is all he can say. The most of this letter was wrote by putting the paper up against his back. It has been raining and is very wet and damp. The Capt says for you to tell Charles Seaton that he is well yet. Lts Cope & Springer and Orderly Sergt James E. Jolliffe are still with us.

May 19th, 1864, Thursday
Parks A. Boyd. The first man killed in Co K May 5th. Cap shot off of my head May 5th

Dear Father,

We received your letter dated May 7th, and was most thankful to hear that you were all well as usual, We have been having a hard time of it since we left Camp. We started on the night of the 3rd of May about Eleven O'Clock. Marched that night, the next day and the evening of the fifth we engaged the enemy at Black Oak Swamp or the Wilderness. Our Company in this their first engagement stood up and done their duty. We had one man killed, Parks A. Boyd, and 2 or 3 Wounded. I had the front part of my Cap shot off by a Minie Ball, It knocked it off of my head and made me feel a little strange about the top knot. I would like to send my Cap home if I could get the chance. The next day we marched forward in the fore part of the day and built breastworks. The enemy attacked us about Four O'Clock in the afternoon. They intended to charge on us but they met with too warm a reception. We had another man killed in our Co, George W. Hanan, and several wounded and missing. The breastworks were not sufficiently covered with earth, we had not the time to do it before they attacked us and they caught fire in front of our regiment and we had to fall back a piece but the enemy was retreating and we soon rallied. That night I and five others were detailed as Pickets and stationed in the woods. Afterwards there was a stronger force stationed behind us and we were ordered up to their line. I marched up safely but the man next to me got behind and when he come up he was fired on and wounded in the arm near the shoulder. It was Jacob Allamon from New Salem. I suppose you have heard of the grand charge we made on the morning of the 12th. I was in it. Alex was not. He had been out on Picket and had not got up in time. We took it was said Eight Thousand prisoners and drove them out of their breastworks. We took two Generals and Twenty one Cannon. Our Company lost two more men killed, Milton Rathburn and Joseph Smith. Smith had Captured a rebel Flag and was jumping on and tearing it from its staff when I persuaded him to quit and take care of it and told him he would get to carry it to Washington City. He was killed shortly afterwards. We had four wounded and several Missing. Our Lt Col, Dale, has been Missing since. I and Alfred Bailes seen him when he got over the second line of works. He was trying to get us to charge farther but we had went as far as it was possible for us to go and I am almost positive that he was killed right there. Our Colonel was wounded on the Picket line and carried to the rear on a stretcher. Capt Mcgraw is acting as Col. Weltner was sent to the rear on account of his health. We had a big fight yesterday, May 18th, Spottsylvania, charged on the enemy and drove them from their works. Two more of us was shot dead, Poor Dan Crawford and William Conn, both shot through the head, Dick McClean, Robt Brownfield and two others wounded. Dick was wounded in the arm, Thomas Williams was shot through the foot and they say it was a very ugly wound. There is much more I would like to say but I have not room. I think you had better buy the house if you can get it at anything like a reasonable price.

Your Son Daniel Chisholm.

May 19, 1864
Brother Alex's Letter

Dear Father,

We received your letter dated May 7th, and was glad to hear from home and that you were all well. We have had a pretty rough time of it since we crossed the Rapidan river. We had a fight the next day, I believe it was at what they call black oak swamp or the Wilderness. The fight commenced in the evening, it was pretty sharp until dark, then again the next day. One of our men was killed in the first fight. He was from the mountains, he was a very civil man. Dans Cap front was shot across, it was a close shave indeed. The rebs made a charge on our breastworks, but I think it must of been a sorrowful charge for them, as I think we must of killed a great many. They fell back in a hurry, more of a hurry than they came up. We have been fighting we may say all the time. Yesterday we made a charge. I suppose you heard about the great charge when we captured so many prisoners. That was Seven days ago. The charge we made yesterday we drove the rebs back from their entrenchments. They killed a good many of our men and wounded a good many. Daniel Crawford was killed and a boy by the name of Conn. Dan Crawford fell right the side of me, shot through the head. He never spoke or even moved, a slight groan and that was the last of poor Dan Crawford. Dick McClean was wounded in the arm so they say. I did not see him after the fight. Robert Brownfield, Sheriffs Son, was wounded 4 or 5 days ago in the foot by a grape shot I guess, making an ugly wound. I did not see him. He was sent to Fredericksburgh, then to Washington I suppose. We have a hard time of it. We have done more fighting than a good many troops that have been in for three years service. Our Company numbered 70 men when we left Camp, now it numbers about 30, several missing and the rest killed and wounded. We was relieved by General Berneys troops last and sent back here to the rear to rest. We had the largest Corps in the army of the Potomac but now I guess it is the smallest. It has made two charges on the enemies works, beside the regular fights. Dan was not in the charge yesterday; he is clerking for the adjutant, now he can stay in the rear. It is easier than carrying the musket. I was glad he was not in the last charge. They say the Rebs shot rail road iron at us. I did not see any. I am well as usual, Dan is well too. we are resting near to Spottsylvania Court House. You can see on the map where it is. I must now stop as I am getting tired.

Your Son — Alex Chisholm.

May 20th, 1864 — Camp near Spottsylvania Courthouse
Dear Father,

We are still laying here. That is in the same place that we were yesterday. I wrote you a letter yesterday but it may have not been mailed yet. Last night we were ordered to pack up and fall in and started off at a double quick for about a mile when we about faced and marched leisurely back to camp. I afterwards learned that the rebs guerillas had captured our wagon train and that our boys had recaptured it. After we got back to camp Alex spread his gum blanket and we laid down with two shelter tents for our cover. I had my gum Blanket stolen from me after we left camp, and neither one of us has anything but what we have on. Alex got his knapsack burnt the time the breastworks caught fire, and I had to throw mine away in a retreat. I was on picket about a mile from Camp and the enemy commenced cross firing on us with their Artillery. It was the same time our Colonel was wounded and Thomas Williams shot in the foot. We had a large field to cross and the shell, grape and canister was flying thick. I was tempted to throw it away before I did, but I thought of the shirt that came from home and carried it until I could run no longer, and it had to go. There was a man shot in our division this morning for throwing down his colors on a charge the other day. He was a Sergeant. It was a hard looking sight. But it dont do to show the white feather here, and there must be some examples made. I did not get to see Thomas after he was wounded, but understood from some of the boys that did, that he had a very ugly wound. Dick McClean had to have his arm taken off above the elbow and the doctor says Robt Brownfield will have to have his taken off. We crossed the Rapidan on the fourth of May. It received its name from a woman that lived on its banks by the name of Ann and she was a very rapid Ann. I don't think it is worth while to bother about Alex's boots now, I think we can get them after awhile. You need not send that money now for it would be uncertain about me getting it. I wrote you a letter about a week ago just after we got out of the big charge. I did not write much for it was raining and I didn't feel much like writing. I hope we will get to lay here for a day or two that we may have a little rest. It has been 17 days since we started from Camp, and mighty little we have had in that time. Alfred Bailes, Wm Nycum, Wm Sembower and Edward Pence are all right yet. There has been a great many killed and wounded in the late battles. Six Killed and Fourteen Wounded in Our Company and Missing. A great many has returned that was slightly wounded. Our Brigade lies in a cornfield, and the corn is up very nice, but I dont think it will do much good after we get out of it. There is a splendid looking dwelling mansion to the right of us with everything nice about it. It puts a fellow in mind of civilization after getting out of the wilderness. I want you to write as often as you can and send me as many late papers as possible. I will write every chance I get —

Your Son Daniel Chisholm, Co "K" 116th Regt P.V.

May 31st, 1864 — Camp 10½ Miles from Richmond
Dear Father,

I received Your letter dated May 17th and was glad to hear from home. Alex and I are enjoying good health with plenty of appetite to destroy our rations. We are laying behind breastworks this morning. Yesterday morning our Brigade went out to support the skirmish line and came in last night. We can hear the locomotives whistling on the Richmond Railroad. It is thought they are running up reinforcements. Tell mother not to fret about us boys, that we will take as good care of ourselves as we can. We all have our chance to run. I think there will be a great deal of hard fighting between here and Richmond, as it is getting near the Capital. The 16th Penna Cavalry was within 4 or 5 miles of the city, they could hear their Bells ringing. I understood that Butler was up within 5 miles and fell back of his own accord. As for Thos being with us, he was sent to the rear as soon as he was wounded, and I understood since that he had to have his foot taken off. I expect that he is either in a Washington City or Philadelphia Hospital, I have not had any letter from him. If they have at home I wish when they write to him they would tell him to write to me, that I have several letters for him. I am sorry to hear that Jenny has not been well. But hope she is well before now. Tell her to write to us. The fruit will be plenty here, especially peaches, cherries and all kinds of berries. The Rebs have any amount of corn planted and it looks well. It makes some of them look mighty black at us to march through their corn, wheat and orchards. It has been a good while since I last wrote to you. It is hard to get paper and I haven't any way of carrying any. I wish you would send me a paper once a week at least. I wish if one of the town papers had a list of the killed, wounded and missing of our company that you would send it to me. I would like to see The Standard. Write soon and often as you can.

Your Son, Daniel Chisholm.

May 31st, 1864 — Camp 10½ Miles from Richmond
Brother Alex's Letter

Dear Father,

I thought I would write you a few lines while I have the chance. We have been short of rations for the last 2 or 3 days, but we drew last night, and I made a strong cup of coffee, fixed a piece of meat and 2 or 3 hardtack which strengthened me very much. We lay about 10½ miles from Richmond, the rebs Harbor. If we can get 3 or 4 miles further Richmond is gone up. I think when we get those siege guns at work it will make them think the world is coming to an end. Our artillery is playing on them every few minutes but they seldom answer. I seen William Knight the other day, he said they was within 5 miles of Richmond. I heard Tom Williams had to have his foot taken off. I expect it is true for they say it was a bad wound. I was out on the same line but I did not see Tom. The balls flew thick and fast around me but did not hit me that time, but I cannot tell how soon they may for a fellows chance is slim sometimes when the grape and canister fly as thick as hail. Tell Hanson Rutter to write me, and all my little pardners, tell everybody to write. Tell Mother not to be uneasy about us boys, we will do the best we can. We have now two months wages coming to us. That will be 82 Dollars. They have raised privates pay from $13 to $16 per month, so much the better.

Your Son Alexander Chisholm.

June 8th, 1864 — Camp Near Gaines Mill
Brother Alex's Letter

Dear Father,

I take this opportunity of writing you a few lines to let you know that we are well at present. We received your letter May 30th and was glad to hear from home. We are at what is called Cold Harbor, 11 Miles from Richmond. The rebs are very strongly fortified here. There was a flag of truce sent out last night to bury the dead, it went out at 6 O'Clock and stayed out until 8 O'Clock. The Pickets dare not fire at each other now, the order was issued last night. I believe it is a good thing. I was out to the outer works this morning. The Johnnies are stepping around as thick as bees. The distance between the lines of works at the nearest is about from 50 to 75 yds, you can see Their batteries plainly. We have our batteries massed in front of us. The rebs have tried to charge our works for 3 nights now before last night, but did not come any speed. Our works in front is about 10 feet thick with a strong line behind it, but I suppose they have just as strong as we have. We made a charge on the enemy works on the third of this month, and our movement was not commanded right and we gained nothing but lost severely. This is The 2nd brigade I am speaking of. The first brigade took the enemies works and battery. I guess we should of acted as a support for them, but some mistake was made through some of the officers. In our Company we list 1 killed, and 4 wounded. Lt Zadoc B. Springer got a slight wound across the bowels which makes him unfit for duty for a few days. I never had balls to whistle so thick apast me no[r] never want them to whistle half so thick again. Dan was in the charge, he helped a wounded man off, so he had not quite so hot a time. We charged down into a ravine under the bank like and the rebs batteries opened and we could not go any farther without being all killed or wounded, as they had a cross fire on us. We laid under this bank about 1½ hours when we was ordered to fall back. We done so under a shower of bullets. I think charging is played out now after this, it will have to be done by undermining their works and seiging. Our men have dug under their works now some place along here so they say. Mother says she would like to have us some shirts. Those shirts are good yet but not very clean You may depend. Alfred Bailes is well and hearty, he has a bad boil on his neck. Cannot Uncle Isaac tell Thomas where we are or whether he hears from us or not, I should think he could as we have been writing often. About the money — if you see a good chance to use the money Dan and I both think you had better do so, as it would save you of paying rent. Where we live is a beautiful place, and I like the place better than any place I know of but you cannot give too big a price. Do you think the property is worth any where near $600.00 Dollars, and how much do you think it would take to make it a nice place, that is to repair the house and yard in order. You know there is good water handy and an alley back which is not at all places. I dont think it would take much to make it a comfortable home. You can study and talk it over between yourselves, you and mother and tell us in your next letter if we are spared to receive it. No more at present. Write soon.

from Your Son Alex Chisholm.

June 8th, 1864 — Camp near Cold Harbor or Gaines Mill
Dear Father,

Alex and I are well as could be expected and getting along first rate. We received your letter dated May 30th, also the Papers you sent us before I neglected saying so in the other letter. We had an Armistice yesterday to bury the dead, it commenced at 6 and ended at 8 O'Clock P.M. which has been the only time for 5 days that we hardly dare to stick our heads out from behind the breastworks for the shells, solid shot and Balls. I am sorry to hear of mother straining her foot or ankle. I think she ought to have a girl help clean house and do the heaviest of the work. Tell Jenny to take good care of herself until she gets entirely well again, and to learn as fast at school as she can, also to write to us and tell us a little about everything and what she is studying at school. Tell mother not to be uneasy about us after battles for if not killed or wounded we will always write as soon as possible. I was clerking a while for the adjutant while his clerk was in the hospital but he has returned and I am at the same old business. I am glad to hear you have a good garden. There is a garden or what was one in the rear of our breastworks but it dont look much like one now. I am glad to hear that carpenters have plenty of work. When you write tell me the price of best Muslin & Calico. Also Sugar and Coffee. I do not know who it could have been that knew about me being shot through the Cap. I wish you would say which one of Baily's girls it is that is dead, I think it must be Jennies teacher as I forget their names. I think Mother must be becoming quite spright in her old days that she can take an extra turn at the hoe. I am sorry that you do not get any word from Uncle Joe. If you do and write to him, I wish you would ask him what Corps, Division & Brigade he belongs to. Our boys was in another charge on the third. But it didn't amount to anything, only getting hundreds of men killed and wounded. We had two killed and four wounded in our Company. I was only in the beginning of it, Charles Yauger was wounded next to me and it fell to my lot to take him off of the field. Lt Springer was wounded across the bowels by a Minie Ball. Our Colonel was wounded again while on the Picket line. Our Adjutant was wounded and Capt of Co G in the Charge. We haven't heard of Lt Col Dale since the Charge of the 12th inst (May). Our Regiment has lost a great many men. The fight of the 3rd was on the same ground that the Penna Reserves fought on the same day of the month two years ago. There has been an order issued that there should be no more firing on the Picket line after this and everything is quiet except of the boom of Cannon on our right. Colonel Burns that commanded our Brigade in the Charge was killed, Col Kelly commands it now. It is a very pleasant part of the country through here, very warm in the daytime and cool at nights. Genl Barlow that commanded our Division is now Maj General, he commands the Ninth Corps. He is the second General that got his third Star by the fighting and bravery of our Division. Alex and I think you had better have the boots sent back as it will be a long time before we could get them. I think $600.00 is too big a price for the house. If you see a chance to use the money to a good advantage use it. Write & Soon and often.

My love to all — Your Son, Daniel Chisholm.

June 21st, 1864 — Hospital, City Point
Dear Father,
I am in the hospital at City Point with a slight wound received on the Evening of the 16th in a charge on the rebs breastworks. It is about half way between the knee and ankle. The wound was so slight that I did not go to the rear until the 19th and would not of went then if it had not been for Alex and the other boys. I went back to the rear and the doctor dressed my wound and had me to get in a wagon and sent me to City Point. Alex was well when I left but I can't tell how it is now as there has been heavy fighting since, and they were in the front. Edward Pence was wounded through the thigh and across the hand, Alfred Bailes in the mouth, it knocked two or three of his teeth out and came out below his jaw injuring the bone. It is a very ugly wound. Stephen Beckett, in the foot. Pence's wound is very severe. The three men mentioned were all wounded the same day I was. There is an awful lot of wounded here and they are still coming in. There was 80 wagons loaded with wounded came in to day. They are sending them to Washington City as fast as they can. I have not heard what they have been doing at Petersburgh for two or 3 days. They had taken The N.C. Rail Road and was tearing it

up before I left. I wrote a letter to Jenny on the 12th. We started for Petersburgh that evening, we marched that night, the next day and the next night until about 1 O'Clock without stopping long enough to cook our Coffee. It was very disagreeable marching. The dust was so thick it almost suffocated us. I have not received a letter from you since May 30th. I have heard some talk of Army Correspondence being stopped for sixty days. The other boys receive letters most every mail. I would like to have one too, though there may be one on the road. Alex may have received one before now at the Regiment. I could not of wrote this letter if it had not been for the U.S. Sanitary Commission. They gave me the paper and Envelope and said they would pay the postage. I would like to know where Thomas Williams is that he doesn't write to us. I suppose Dick McClean is at home. I think I will be able to go back to the Regiment in 3 or 4 days. Write as soon as you get this and as often as you can for we are always anxious to hear from home, enough so to drop everything and run to see if there is a letter for us when the mail comes. The wounded soldiers are well cared for. We get Coffee and a piece of meat and some farina, Soft Crackers and Lemonade through the day to eat & drink. I believe that this is all at present.

Your Affct Son — Daniel Chisholm

June 28, 1864 — Hospital, City Point Landing, Va
Dear Father,

I am still in the hospital. When I wrote to you last I did not think that I would be here more than a week at the farthest. But I have been here nine days and the slight wound don't look any better than when I came. It has been exceedingly warm for the last two weeks. We had a small shower of rain last night which makes it some cooler to day. I have not heard much from our Corps since I have been here. I did hear that they were going into summer quarters for twenty days to have some rest which they very much need, but I do not know how true it is, as I think they are too close to Petersburgh for much rest. There has been a great many of the wounded sent off to the cities. But there is a great many here yet, there is a good many sick coming in. I guess the principle matter is they are worn out. I begin to think I look a heap better than when I came here. I have had the Diarrhea for three or four weeks but the doctor has been giving me pills and I think I will get it stopt before I go back to the Regiment. I do not know what they are doing out front. There was some heavy firing last night. I heard it said that Grant has got his six sisters in position to shell Petersburgh. They are large Guns that he used at Vicksburgh. I spent the last money I had the other day, I gave a quarter for a pie, and a half a dollar for a can of currant jelly. If I had three or four dollars I would have some delicacies, as I do not relish Hard tack and Coffee of my own make when I can get something better. But since I have been in the hospital I have had plenty of soft bread, Tea and Coffee, Farina once in a while, some jelly or canned Peaches and a drink of Blackberry Wine, Milk Punch or Lemonade. I guess there is no chance of getting any money here, if I find there is I will write for some. Sutlers sell awful high, $1.25 for a can of Peaches, 50 and 75 cents for a very small can of jelly, so the less money a fellow has the better it is for him for he is mighty apt to be tempted. I have seen some of the boys pay a Dollar for a six cent loaf of bread and a quarter for a hardtack. But I don't love them that well, although I have been hungry enough. There has been a great many of the hundred day men come out front, I guess they will get to see the elephant to their satisfaction. I would like to hear from home very much but dont know that I will be here long enough to get an answer, so I cannot say for you to write to me. But write to Alex for he would be glad to hear from you and tell him where I am —

from your Affct son, Daniel Chisholm.

"For right is right since God is God,

And right the day must win.

For to doubt would be disloyalty.

For to falter would be sin."

July 1st, 1864 — Hospital, City Point Landing
Dear Father,
    I am as well as usual, my wound appears to be a long time about healing as it is more sore than it was for the first week or so. I could have been sent to Washington City if I had wished to go. But I told them that I would as lief stay here until my wound got well. There was a continual roar of Artillery last night. It sounded as if they were large guns. I heard some of the nurses say that it was our men shelling the rebs to keep them from laying their pontoon bridge across the river. I suppose you will have a happy fourth of July at least I hope so. I don't know what kind of a one I will have or Alex. I would like to hear from him very much. It is thought we will have some hard fighting about the fourth. I believe that this is all at present. It was hardly worth while to begin

writing for all I had to write, as it was of very little importance. But I have nothing else to do —

Your Affct Son — *Daniel Chisholm.*

July 4, 1864 — *Hospital, City Point Landing, Va*
Dear Father,

I was quite sick last night and this morning. My Stomach has been out of order for a week or so. I vomited up what I eat for my supper about 3 O'Clock this morning, and continued vomiting until about 10 O'Clock. I could not eat any breakfast but eat a tolerably hearty dinner. I think I will be all right in a day or two. Everything is apparently quiet out front but we do not know what they may be doing before night. Genl Grant rode along below our tent yesterday. I did not get to see him. He says he could take Petersburgh and Richmond at anytime but he would have to lose a great many men, and that he can take it a great deal easier by laying still and watching them. He has two of the Rail Roads that Lee got his supplies on, and we have cannon so placed that he cannot get supplies up on the other only at night, and he is going to take it some of these days. Then Lee will have one of these three things to do, Retreat, Surrender or Fight, and he cant fight very long without something to eat. I am getting awful tired of the hospital and hope that I will soon get out of it. All the worst cases have been sent away to the cities, and what is left will be ready for duty in a short time. Mother I suppose I eat a heartier dinner than I would of on account that it was a lady that prepared it for me. She was so kind it made me almost feel that I was at home. It consisted of a half slice of bread toasted and well buttered with a cup of good warm tea and one soft cracker. I have concluded to have you write me a letter whether I get it or not. But I doubt not but what I will get it. Let me know about Alex whether you have had a letter from him and how he is getting along. Hezekiah Dean started for Washington City yesterday, he is sick. The Stars and Stripes float gaily from all the ships and boats to day. There was one Hundred Guns fired down at the Point. The Cars make numerous trips out front every day. The Engine is named Genl Grant. You will have to write immediately or I will not get it.

Your Affct Son — *Daniel Chisholm.*

(Extract from letter of Brother Alex Same date. Spoke of being down the line to see some of the boys, Joseph Sturgis, John Stevens, Henry Benton, and took dinner with them in Fort Steadman.)

July 7th, 1864 — Hospital, City Point, Va
Dear Mother,

I have taken up my sheet of paper and pencil for the first time to write you a letter. And I almost feel ashamed to own it, but better late than never. It is a very pleasant morning, rather warm but there is a very refreshing breeze from the river. And my bed is at the end of the tent next to the river so I get my share of it. I have got over my little spell of sickness, and feel as well as common. My wound is a long time about healing up, it is just three weeks to day since it was done. I guess the doctor thinks it fractured the bone, I mean the Ball did, slightly, although he did not say so. The nurse said it had the first time he dressed it. If it did that may be the cause of it not healing sooner. Mother your boys have seen some pretty hard times since they left home in the last of February. Indeed if I had of known the privations, suffering and hardships which a soldier had to undergo, I would have gave up in despair and said I could not stand it. But there is nothing like trying. When we were on Division Drill near Stevensburgh and had to double quick for about a hundred yards, I had to fall out on account of my hip and wait for the ambulance but I did not get into it, I took my time and walked to camp. But I was not fit for duty until we started on the march. I expected to have to fall out before we went a mile. But my spunk kept me in my place in ranks, as it has done many a time since when I was scarcely able to drag one foot after another. Many a time I have thought of the good meal of victuals I could have at home prepared by your hands, after marching a day and night with only a dry hardtack to eat without time to cook a cup of coffee or even rest.

I have become so used to laying on the ground without anything under or over me that it does not effect me in the least. I think if you were to see what was the little fancy clerk at Cheap Corner No 1 about five months ago you would hardly recognize him. I think he is a little taller but not much heavier, and is sunburnt and tanned until you might think he had seen a little of Africa. Had a good color for all that and looks as if he enjoyed the blessing of good health. And Alex has been extremely handy. Nothing that he eats no difference what it is, a dozen green apples or a piece of raw fresh beef, it has never hurt him yet. I have been all day writing this so I will stop now and finish tomorrow.

July 8th. It is another very pleasant morning. I would like to hear from Alex very much. Mother I want you to write me a good long letter. And if Tomatoes, Blackberries, Raspberries, Whortleberries and every other good kind of thing is plenty, I want you to have a good many of them put up in cans. For I feel as though I could eat enough next winter if I live to make up for what I didn't get this summer. So I have to bring my letter to a close with the wish that it may find you all in good health and that I was with you for breakfast.

Your Affct Son, Daniel Chisholm.

(July 8th. Extract from Brother Alex's letter. In Camp near Petersburgh. Spoke of their being only 9 men left in the Company for duty.)

July 10th, 1864 — City Point Hospital, Va.
Friend Joseph M. Hadden,

Having more time to write letters now than since I left home, I have come to the conclusion to give you a short letter. It will be the first one I have written to any one excepting home and to a cousin since I left town so you can judge that I haven't been carrying on a very heavy correspondence, and If I wasn't in the Hospital it would be very doubtful about you getting this one. I suppose you are having a good time this summer teasing Dry Goods, as it has been a fine time for wearing them. Well Joseph I have seen some pretty rough times this summer, and had several narrow escapes. At the battle of the Wilderness I had the front part of my cap shot away by a minie ball. On the sixteenth of June I was wounded about half way between the knee and ankle, on the shinbone slightly. At first I did not think it would be necessary for me to go back to the hospital, and ran around on it through the bushes and brush getting it hurt several times until the nineteenth when I went back to the Division Hospital to have it dressed. They dressed it and started me to City Point where I have been since. The wound has been very slow about healing but I think it will not be long getting well now. Edward Pence, Stephen Beckett and Alfred Bailes were wounded at the same time. Our company is a very small company to what it was when we left town. Marching went pretty hard with me at first especially with that lame hip. But I became hardened to it. Like a green soldier does always, I started with a heavy knapsack, but it didn't bother me long for I throwed it with all I had except what was on my back, and that wasn't very much. The least a soldier carries the better it is for him. We can hear the cannons very plain from Petersburgh and heavy musketry. It was very noisy up that way last night. I think the days of Petersburgh are numbered and that she will fall with a mighty crash.

Well I believe I will stop writing as I have nothing of any importance to write. Give my best respects to Mr. and Mrs. Hadden and all the boys and tell them to write to me.

From Your Friend, Daniel Chisholm.

July 11th, 1864 — City Point Hospital, Va.
Dear Father,

Seeing that it is another very pleasant morning, and I have nothing else to do but to write, I will try to give you a few lines. There is one of the Sanitary Committee that takes particular delight in furnishing me with paper and Envelopes, so I have no want for them. I wrote a letter yesterday to Joseph Hadden which is the first one I have written to any one excepting home and to cousin Sallie A. Williams. There is some very heavy cannonading out front this morning, and there was a good deal of musketry last night. My leg is getting along first rate. It will not be long until I will have been here a month. I will go over to Dr. Burmasters if I live about tomorrow to see about that letter. I caught cold in the snags of teeth in the front part of my mouth. My upper lip swelled considerably, so much so that it made me think of Joe Wares when I looked in my glass. I wrote Mother a letter on the 7th and 8th and I want you to get her to answer it. The provision wagon brought a Bbl of Cabbage, Potatoes & Beans to the Cookhouse opposite our tent yesterday evening and I seen one of the Ladies with a fat piece of pork so I suppose we are going to have Potatoes & Beans cooked with fat Pork which will be a real treat. You have no idea the hankering a soldier has after such things after being fed on hardtack, Coffee & Fresh Beef. It will be apt to go a little hard with me at first again when I return to my regiment, after laying on a bed and getting little delicacies. I believe I have written all I have to write at present. It dónt amount to much, but it is all I have to do to pass the time away.

From your affct Son, Daniel Chisholm.

July 16th, 1864 — City Point Hospital, Va.
Dear Father,

I am getting along first rate. My leg is getting well fast. I would like to hear from Tom Williams very much and from Alex too. I have not had a letter since I have been here. We have very pleasant weather here now. It is a great deal cooler than it was a week or so back. Genl U.S. Grant rode around through the hospital streets yesterday. He recognized a private soldier and stopped to shake hands with him. A crowd began to gather around him and he had to move on or he would have been surrounded. I have been amusing myself by looking at the picture and reading about Mrs Caroline Chisholm. I will tear the leaf out and send it to you the one that has the picture on.

I gave my Cap to one of the Sanitary Gentlemen to Express home to you. It is a hard looking Cap. It has seen about as many hardships as any other cap in this summer campaign. When you get it have it dusted off and put in a hat box. If you place the brim toward the west you will have the position it was in when the ball passed through it, as I had just shot the load out of my gun and turned to reload. The ball carried away the P.V. and the 6 leaving the two ones. The boys used to ask me if I belonged to the 11th, and to what state. The letter K and the Club our Corps mark are still on it. I asked him how much it would cost me to send it home. He said nothing as the Sanitary always sent such relics free. It was a very airy Cap. When I used to have to double quick it would flop up and down like a bellows. He said it might have to lay in Washington City awhile.

It is just a month to day since I was wounded. There was cannonading over towards Bermuda Hundred this morning for about fifteen minutes. It is time for me to bring my letter to a close.

My love to you all from your Affct son, Daniel Chisholm.
N.B. Let me know in your letter whether you got my cap.

July 18th, 1864 — Camp near Petersburgh
Brother Alex's Letter

Dear Father,

I now sit down to write you a few lines, to let you know that I am as well as common. I hope that times may find you the same. There is still some fighting going on out front, mostly cannonading. James Collins and myself are trying to be transferred. James wrote to his father to attend to it. That is Col Collins I mean. We want to go to the 14th Penna Cavalry. There is a good many boys I know in that Regiment. I would like it better than the marching. The Company has 20 men in it so James says. The Cavalry men looks as fat as you please. Pat little [sic] boy on a raid got 7 watches; his box he carries his curry comb in, he got it full of gold and silver. They have plenty to eat always. I got a letter from Dan the other day, his wound was pretty well healed up, he was still at City Point. At that rate he will soon be up with us. Write soon. Tell me all the news. This is not a long letter, as it is all of my Ink.

Your Son — Alex Chisholm.

July 23rd, 1864 — City Point Hospital, Va.
Dear Father,

I received your letter of the 17th to day, and was glad to hear from you. My wound is getting along very nicely. If I had of known it would have been so long healing, I would have went to Washington, and very likely I could have got a furlough for thirty days, and had it extended.

The reason I suppose that Alex did not send my letters to me was that I wrote to him to take good care of them until I got up to the Regiment. I was glad to get the $5.00, it came unexpectedly. I wanted to get my shirt and Pants washed. I wore the shirt from the time I put it on in Camp until I came to the Hospital without having it washed, which is the longest time I ever wore a short without washing. It surprised me to hear that flour was $11.00 pr Bbl and that other necessaries were in proportion, $2.12½ is too small wages for a Carpenter when everything is so high. The Carpenters out to make a strike.

Keep an account of the money drawn by each one of us separately. I sent Home $280.00 and Alex $270.00. You can say to Mother that I release her from the task as I acknowledge it would be rather a hard job for her to write. Glad to know that your job at Dr Fullers has lasted so well. Have they got into their house yet. I was sorry to hear of the death of John Haddens wife. I am sorry that I was not with the Regiment when the Dr wanted me for steward, as I would have layed a hold of it. $30.00 is respectable wages. I hope that mother will have a pleasant visit to the Renshaws. The old man must be very frail. I am sorry to hear that Thomas Williams wound was not doing so well. I wrote a letter to him the same day that I answered yours. I believe there is nothing that I want that you could send me. If there was it would be rather risky about me getting it. I suppose Jenny has grown to be a slapping big girl. I hope she is learning fast at school. I believe I have nothing more to communicate at present.

From Your Affct Son, Daniel Chisholm

July 29th, 1864 — City Point Hospital, Va.
Dear Father,

I am well and getting along first rate. The Second Corps has been on the battlefield again and a lot of them came in wounded last night. After marching twenty four hours to Turkeys Bend near Malvern Hill they made a charge on the rebels works, and carried them with a small force, capturing fifteen pieces of Artillery — and some prisoners. There is said to be from twenty to thirty thousand Cavalry with them. I suppose they have gone to do something big — For if there is any dirty work to be done in the Army of the Potomac she has it to do. There are a great many sick here at present, there is a boat load being sent away this morning. Enclosed you will find a ten dollar Confederate Note, it is the genuine. Take care of it as it one day will be a curiosity, when it will be of no more account than so much brown paper to the Confederate States of America. My wound is doing well.

from Your Affct Son, Daniel Chisholm.

August 12th, 1864 — Camp near Petersburgh, Va.
Bro Alex's Letter
Dear Father,

I received your letter several days ago, and have not had time to write until now. I received a letter from Dan last night, he said his wound was still healing, also that there was 2 Boats laying waiting to take loads of wounded that evening or next morning. He says his name was taken down to go. It is best for him to go as I think he can get a furlough perhaps if he tries for one. It is a great pity about T. B. Williams foot being so bad. Tell Thomas that I have had a good many bullets to sing a-past me, but none but one to touch me. One day I was on picket and was shot through the Coat sleeve, down next to the wrist taking the skin off a little, it stung a good deal. Poor Edward Pence is no more, his loss in our Company is great. He was beloved by every one that knew him as a good soldier and clever man. Capt. Weltner is with us now in command of the company. He says we will go to Washington inside of 10 days and that is the report now. They are giving us all figures for our Caps and Corps Badges and rigging us up with everything we need. I never hear from Bailes or any of the wounded boys. They tell me that the Johnnies is paying you another visit or trying to get down into our part of the country. I hear that they are fortifying about town and that they are running soldiers all the time up to town. They ought to get the old 2nd Corps up there, better known by the rebs as the butterflycorps. The first sight of the red club they would skedaddle. I hope the people will not be so easy scared this time. I would feel very safe if the rebs was 20 miles off. All do for the best.

Your Son Alex Chisholm.

August 13th, 1864 — Sickles Barracks Hospital, Ward P, Alexandria, Va.
Dear Father,

I am now in the Hospital at Alexandria. I have been here for about three days. My leg looks tolerably well, I think it will do better here. But I don't like the place as well as I did City Point. I received your letter of July 30th. I am glad that you have come to the conclusion to buy the house as the money is as good in property as anything else and fifty five dollars is a big rent.

I suppose young Brown hadn't the dimes, and so he couldn't get to California, he should have counted the cost before he started. I am glad to hear that Thomas Williams has got home. I am sorry to hear that it will take so long for his foot to get well. I wish that I could be with the Company. I am very tired of the hospital, it is anything but a pleasant place. If Thomas Williams is at home on furlough and has to go back to the hospital he had better try and be transferred to a Philadelphia Hospital, as he would fare much better and be in his own state. The Chestnut Hill is said to be the best Hospital.

I think the stable might be fixed to answer for a shop first rate, and it would be handy to the house. The job of Dr Fullers has been a good long one.

I like the figure of Mothers dress very well. But it is rather coarse for forty cents pr yd. Goods is very high now I suppose and it must be very hard on the people that are very poor.

I believe you had better send me ten dollars, as I want to buy a shirt, two pairs of socks, and get some Photographs taken. And a knife for myself and one for Alex with a spoon and fork attached to it, he has wanted one ever since he has been out, and a few other little notions. I received a letter from Alex the same day that I received yours. He was well.

from your Affct son. Daniel Chisholm.

August 20th, 1864 — Sickles Barracks Hospital, Ward P, Alexandria, Va.
Dear Father,

I just received your letter dated Aug 16th and was glad to hear from you. Times must be very hard as goods are so very high. I think you need not pay Col Brownfield or Haddens either just now, nor until we get our pay on the last of this month. I will have 5 months pay coming to me at Eighteen Dollars per month, a Corporals pay, and the bounty install-ment which is fifty Dollars making One Hundred and Forty Dollars. And Alex's will amt to One Hundred and Thirty Dollars, making in all $270.00. And as far as mine is concerned you can take it and use it whenever you need it. I think you had better see about the house as soon as you can, and if you can get it for Six Hundred (of course try them at Five fifty at first) buy it, and the other Hundred can be paid when we get our money.

I would like to have a furlough very much but think it useless to try to get one, as I have seen others worse cases than mine try to get them but failed. Since I have been here the Gangrene has been in my wound but I believe they have got it out now, it eat right smart of a hole in my leg — but it looks a great deal better now. It was a very slight wound in the first place but the proper care was not taken of it, and it has been running off and on ever since. I am glad to hear Thomas Williams is getting along very well. Tell him to write to me.

I am glad you got my Cap all right.

Old Mr. Wests death must have been quite sudden.

The $10.00 came to hand all right. Tell Jennie to write to me. The second Corps has been fighting again and I feel anxious to hear from Alex. I wrote him two letters since I have been here, and sent him a paper this morning. But haven't had time to have an answer from him yet.

Your Affct son, Daniel Chisholm.

August 28th, 1864, Sunday — Ward P, Sickles Barracks Hospital, Alexandria, Va.

Dear Father,

I received your letter dated Aug 23rd yesterday, and was glad to hear from you. It will be very lonesome for Mother and Jennie if you have to go to Pittsburgh for work. You did not quite understand it about the five months pay. The way of it is this, that when we received our first installment of the bounty we were paid one months pay in advance, the bounty being sixty and one months pay thirteen, making Seventy Three Dollars. And since the first of May I have been getting Eighteen Dollars making Seventy two and Thirteen for April makes Eighty five and the second installment of the bounty forty Dollars makes a hundred and twenty five and in another month I would have the third installment coming to me — I do not know how it is about the State pay that belonged to other states. I do not think I will stand much of a chance for a furlough and another thing it would cost me a good deal. But if I and Alex should be alive next winter we will try and get each one of us a furlough at the same time so that we can both be at home together, but that is looking too far ahead. The Morning Chronical has just come around, and I see that the second corps has been engaged again. And from what the paper says I judge that we have lost heavily, and I shall be very anxious until I hear from Alex. From what Jennie says he came very near getting a ball on the picket line. There was a boat load of wounded came here last night. There is about twenty wounded rebels in this ward and they say that they are getting tired of fighting. If Jenny has had her Photograph taken send me one. If you should go to Pittsburgh to work write and give me your address. Jenny and I will have to keep up some correspondence. I received a letter from Tom W. the other day.

Your Affct Son, Daniel Chisholm.

N.B. Always let me know when you heard from Alex.

September 12th, 1864, Monday Morning — Sickles Barracks Hospital, War P, Alexandria, Va.

Dear Father,

I received your letter dated Sept 4th several days ago. I had just written one to Jenny or I should have answered yours immediately. My leg is still about the same old thing. I was glad to hear from Alex they were in a very hot place on the Weldon R. R. Sherman done a big thing in taking Atlanta. It will be Grants turn next. If he succeeds in taking Petersburgh and Richmond this campaign, next spring will be the last of the Southern Confederacy. Apples are certainly very plenty, Butter is worth from 70 to 80 cts here, Carpenters get 3 Dollars per day. I think it is pretty near time some of my old chums was beginning to write to me. Father I will have to call on you for one more dollar. I expect you begin to think that I am death on spending money, but send one Dollar and I wont bother you for any more soon. I expect to get two months pay soon. And then I will send you the money to pay Brownfield & Haddens. The paper boy has just been making the rounds, and has been singing out that the Army of the Potomac has advanced, Captured a large lot of prisoners, and that there is a battle going on now. I hope that they will be successful, and that this fall may witness the downfall of the rebellion. I have nothing more to write of at present. It is rather cool this morning. We have had a good deal of rain lately. You need not send me more than One Dollar.

Write Soon — Your Affct Son, Daniel Chisholm.

Aug 30th, 1864
Extract of Bro Alex's Letter

This letter was written just after the fight at Ream Station, on the Weldon Rail Road. Lieut Zadoc B. Springer was captured along with many others of the Regiment, Newton Umble was among them. In this fight we were outnumbered 3 to 1. At that time we were tearing up the Rail Road, burning the ties &c and were surprised. We had burned about 6 miles. The enemy suffered awful, being literally mowed down, only for great numbers they would not of drove us. I seen Steward Stearns of the 16th [*sic*] Pa. Cavalry, to day or rather the day of the fight. He was pulling Peaches off a tree filling his pouches. We was flanking the right side of the road at this time. Huckleberries were ripe and plenty, I ate my fill as we passed through the woods. Our Butchers had several Beeves killed and Dressed ready to supply us, when attacked they fell into the Rebs hands. Captain Crawford and Capt Taggart were both killed here. They commanded the Regiment at the time. Taggart was a local Preacher and a very good brave man, also Crawford was a good man.

Sept. 21st
Extract of Bro Alex's Letter

Spoke of a salute fired this morning in honor of Sheridans Victory in the Shenandoah Valley. I think Abraham Lincoln will be the choice for President in place of Genl McClelland.

Nov 11th
Ext from Bro Alex's Letter

In this letter I have heard that Dan is at home from Hospital on furlough. While writing hear Old Genl Butlers guns a booming away down at Dutch Gap Canal, being dug through a neck of land at a bend in the James river. It was a failure as no boats ever run through it.

Oct 19th
Ex from Bro Alex's Letter

Left of Petersburgh, spoke of not getting my box yet, also of going on fatigue duty. Also spoke of buying a watch. I also got a pair of boots from home.

Nov. 20th
Ex from Brother Alex's Letter

At this time we are laying on reserve back of main line, what is left of us. All is quiet except strong Picket firing all the time, It is ugly getting around on account of so much rain.

Sept. 16th, 1864 — Sickles Barracks Hospital, Ward P, Alexandria, Va.
Dear Father,

I received your letter dated Sept 11th yesterday morning, also one from Alex dated Sept 12th. He was well excepting a bad cold. Sorry to hear that mother is bothered with Neuralgia, but hope she is better before now. I received a letter from Thomas and another from Alex dated Sept 10th this morning. He had no postage stamps and it laid in the Alexandria P.O. a day or two and so got behind hand. He says they have a great deal of hard duty to do. They are still in Camp, and are detailed most every day to work on forts. He says that Col Mulholland has got the papers signed for taking the regiment back to Philad'a to recruit up again. But I suppose it is only a Camp rumor as such things generally are. Capt Weltner is on the sick list again, and "K" is left without one of her Commissioned officers, without even an Orderly Sergeant. I was sorry to hear of Capt Taggarts death, as he was one of the nicest and bravest Capts in the Regiment. We have had considerable rain here and it is beginning to be right cool of nights. Alex seems to have been coming the sharp on us, for he wrote to both of us for money at the same time, and I sent him all I had and half of my Postage Stamps, and now I am out of money, Postage Stamps and have very few friends. But if I get that dollar I wrote for I will be an independent boy once more. A soldier hasn't any business with but a very small amount of money, because if he is where he can he will spend it as long as he has a cent. There is boys here that has spent in the last two months as high as 50 and 60 dollars, or a dollar and more a day. There is going to be some hard fighting, down with Grant some of these days. They are not holding off so long for nothing. Next Monday the 19th will be the draft, and when it is over and you know who is drafted in the borough I wish you would give me a list of the names, that is if she hasn't filled her quota. Co K is a very small Co now. I hope there is something in it that Col Mulholland is trying to get them to Philad'a to recruit. There was a man shot here to day. He was a bounty jumper and helped several men to desert. He said he had made about Twenty Thousand dollars by his bounty jumping, but he paid for it dearly in the end.

Saturday Morning Sept 17th. It is a beautiful morning and very pleasant. The Doctor passed through examining us to see who was able to go front. He looked at my leg and said that it was no go.

Your Affct Son, Daniel Chisholm.

Monday, Sept. 19th, 1864 — Ward P, Sickles Barracks Hospital, Alexandria, Va.

Dear Father,

I received your letter of Sept 15th this morning and was glad to hear from you. My leg is about the same. I am hearty able to eat my rations and feel first rate. I am sorry to hear that the Dr in Washington had not received Dr Robinsons Certificate but hope it will be all right yet, and that Thomas will get into the Pittsburgh Hospital for it is so much more pleasant to be in ones own state and so near home. Butter is from 70 to 80 cents pr # here. I have not received either of Thomas Haddens Letters, but the one he addressed here may come to hand yet. Grant has not taken Petersburgh yet and I suppose will not try to for some time to come because every day he delays it Lee's army becomes weaker by desertions, while ours is growing stronger by recruits as well as by convalescents returning to their regiments. And every once in a while he has the impudence to attack our works with his forlorn hope only to return to his own frightfully mutilated, and his men discouraged at their useless work. I hope Grant wont attack them yet awhile because I think they are working their own destruction. To day is the day of the draft, and any a poor Copperhead will have a sore head when he hears that he is one of the doomed, and has to fight for his country so much against his will. When you write let me know who was drafted. I have not received any letter from Alex since I last wrote you. And I cannot answer Tom's letter until I know where he stops. I received the One Dollar Bill all right and set down immediately to answer your letter. I don't think that the Second Corps has been engaged lately except on the skirmish line. The Rebs made quite a raid near City Point, and captured a drove of cattle and took some prisoners. It is reported our men recaptured them. I believe that I have nothing more to write of at present.

Your Affct Son —Daniel Chisholm.

Sept 24th
Extract from Brother Alex's Letter

Orderly Sergeant James E. Joliffe had gone to Division Head Quarters to clerk for the Quarter Master.

Sept 30th, 1864 — Camp Near Petersburgh Va
Brother Alex's Letter

Dear Father,

I received a letter from you yesterday, you said you had sent my Boots by J. West. I am glad to hear that, for it would be uncertain about getting them as we shift about so much. I will see Johnny soon and get them. I got the suspenders this morning safe in the little box. I am well and hearty. We are doing Picket duty. Our Regt had drawn New Rifles, they are very good ones. The Picket lines is pretty hot all the time. You ought of seen me knock 2 Sand bags off the Rebel Works. I can knock a Johnny every clip at 4 or 5 Hundred yards with my rifle. They are Springfield's. I got payed for 6 mons 89 Dollars. I did not get any bounty this pay day, me nor Corpl Patterson. We will get ours next pay day. Some of the boys got their bounty 2 installments 80 Dollars. The next pay day I will get 3 installments, and my monthly pay which will be a good pile. I put in fifty Dollars in this letter. I cannot send any more as I owe the sutler pretty smart. I would as leave the government would have my money as any one else, it is safe. I have hardly time to write at all. Write Soon.

Your Son — Alex Chisholm.

Octr. 16th, 1864 — Ward P, Sickles Barracks, Alexandria, Va.

Dear Father,

I am enjoying good health at the present time. My leg is nearly healed up, and I reported myself for duty to the doctor this morning, and expect to leave this afternoon or tomorrow. So you need not write to me until you hear from me again. I expect it will go very hard with me laying on the ground, until I get used to it, as it is considerably cooler than when I left my Reg't. I cannot send you that other Five dollars now, so you can use the 10 as you are a mind to. I bought a pair of Boots, Shirt, Cap and two pair of socks and had to pay Seventeen Dollars for them. I bot of a Jew and he asked me twenty one dollars for the lot. I think I got them as cheap as they could be had. But Goods of every description are very high. I had a half dozen Photographs taken and Paid Two and $^{50}/100$ Dollars for them. They are not finished yet, and if I do not get them before I leave, they will be sent to me and I will send you one in my next letter. And if you have written to me before you get this, I have a friend here that will get the letter and send it to me. I sent a Newspaper to you a few days ago, and wrote on a little slip of paper for you to send me one, and let me know how you all was. And on last Thursday I sent Four Pictures. When you write let me know whether you got the Ten dollars, Pictures &c all right. It is with my own free will and accord that I am going to my Reg't. In fact I could stay here as long as I want to. For my name has been taken down and sent into Hd Qrs as a clerk, and the young mans place that I was to fill is going to leave this week, on account of his time being out. I have been writing for one of the Drs a good deal, and was one of the asst clerks of the Election held here for Pennsylvania boys to vote. And I have got so that I can write a pretty fair hand when I take a little pains. And while I am at it I will tell you how the Election went, out of Sixty Six votes polled, there was Ten of them Democratic. So no more at present.

from Your Affct Son — Daniel Chisholm.

Octr 21st, 1864 — Augur Gen'l Hospital, Near Washington City. D.C.
Ward 2.

Dear Father,

I am well and getting along first rate. But only got myself out of the Hospital to get into it again. I was sent to Camp Distribution on last

Monday, and was to leave for the front on Tuesday morning. But all that come there have to go through an examination, and the surgeon pronounced me unfit for duty, and I had to go to the hospital again. I was examined yesterday for the Invalid Corps and don't know what conclusion the surgeon came to. But I don't think that he put me into the Invalids for I put as good a face on matters as possible. My leg has been sore for so long that it has turned to something like an Ulcer, and all it wants is healing up. And I will be as sound and fit for duty as ever I was. If I had some of Mother's home made salve I think I could cure it myself quicker than any of the Doctors, and if I get any place where I am likely to stay for some time I will send for some of it. But I don't think that they will keep me here long. It is only a temporary Hospital, where them that are disabled for life and cannot do duty in the Invalid Corps get their discharges, and those that can are put into it, and those that are sick and have wounds not healed up yet are transferred to the hospitals, and I hope that the last will be my fate, for I don't like the place at all. If I had of known what I was doing, I guess I would have been satisfied where I was. We have good news from Sheridan again this morning. I had my Photographs taken before I left Sickles Barracks, but could not get a pass to go down town to get them. But one of the Clerks promised to get them and send them to you. I had them taken just as I was, without even putting a collar on. Not being used to have one on I forgot it. If you get them I want you to send one to Alex. I dont know what kind of looking things they will be, and if they are not good ones you need not let any one see them. I will want about Three of them myself. I never would have had to be in the Hospital, if I had of went to the Hospital as soon as I was wounded instead of marching and doing duty on it three days afterwards. It has learned me a lesson, a wound is not to be trifled with, no difference how slight it is. We have a very good Doctor here. He is a Frenchmen and of course is very polite in his manners. I may be kept here until my leg gets well, and as soon as you get this I want you to write to me, for I have not heard from you or Alex for over a month. I will write to Alex tomorrow morning. I expect he begins to look for me pretty strongly, for I wrote to him that I expected to be there before now. We have been separated for a long time. But not as long I hope as some. It has been a rare chance when there has been two brothers in the same Co that they both escaped, without one of them being killed, or maybe both of them. And when you write tell me when you heard from him and how he was. Marking Co and Regt across the Envelope, so if I am not here it will be forwarded to the Regt.

Your Affct Son, Daniel Chisholm.

Novr 3rd, 1864 — Camp near the flank Breastowrks, near Petersburgh Va.
Brother Alex's Letter

Dear Father,

I seat myself to write you a few lines to let you know that my health
is good and that I got my money and box safe. The box had been wet
and the Cakes were molded so they were unfit for use, it was a spite.
The other things were all right. The weather set in bad yesterday with a
kind of sleet and rain, which makes it very disagreeable. The Third Division relieved us 3 days ago, and we moved up about 2½ miles to the
left on the inside flank Breastworks. We put up our tents as good as we
could without logs. We expect to put up good quarters as soon as the
weather will permit. It is coming time now we may expect bad weather.
There may be some fighting yet but I dont think there will be much. Well
election time is drawing nigh at hand and I think old Abraham will be
elected without any doubt. The Democracy keeps a good deal of crow-
ing as if that would elect Little Mack as they call him. But let the wild
World wag as it will, vote for old Abe still. Old Abe is the man that fears
no noise so far away from home, his head is level and his clothes fit him.
How is Jennie getting along. We was mustered for 2 Months pay the last
of last month, and expect to be paid soon. Two months at $18.00 pr
Month $36.00 The two installments of bounty $80 Dollars which makes
$116.00 due me. It seems as though I am a good deal of expense to you,
but it seems as though I cant help it. If you need any of my money I
want you to use it, as much of it as you want, it is for you. Have you
seen anything about the House lately. I will try to get a furlough this
winter to come home. This is a pretty big undertaking, but if I can get
some one to lag for me a little perhaps I can get one. How is mother's
health now and how is your own. I have not heard from Dan for some
time — but expect a letter soon. I hear Mr. Biddle is married, is it so.
Also that Mr. Wyatt is dead and Mr. Uriah Hook, people is dying fast
about town somehow lately. Well write soon.

Your Son Alex Chisholm.

On the day I left my company the 19th day of June 1864 on account
of my wound becoming so much inflamed and painful (I having received
it on the evening of the 16th Thursday) that I could not stand it any
longer, our Second Lieutenant Zadoc B. Springer handed me a pocket
book that my Brother had taken from the pocket of Daniel Crawford
after he was killed on the 18th day of May 1864, at Spottsylvania, my
brother having given it to the Lt to send to Crawfords wife the first opportunity, and as I was going to the hospital the Lt thought I would likely

be able to get it home. My Brother was next man to Crawford when he was killed. He never spoke after he was shot. The Minie Ball passed through his head. I was very sorry to leave my Company and did not do so until my wound compelled me to. It was done on the evening of the 16th day of June 1864, about 5 O'Clock or between 5 and 6 O'Clock, and I was in a fight on the 17th, 18th and 19th. In all that time I did not have a chance to give my wound any attention whatever. The weather being very warm, and being on it most of the time running through underbrush, building breastworks and doing whatsoever I was called on to perform it put it in bad shape. When I started to the field Hospital it was with the intention of having my leg dressed and then going back to my Company. The first thing the Doctor done after looking at it was to ask me when it was done. When I told him, he said that I should have attended to having it dressed and taken care of by coming to the hospital at once, and that now I might lose my leg as it was in a very serious condition. He ordered the nurse or one of the attendants to take my gun and accoutrements and the Dr spent a couple of hours trying to get my wound cleaned out, the Blue goods in my pants had been shot into it. After he was done one of the nurses picked me up and put me into an army wagon and I with others was taken to City Point, 12 miles away.

This is a copy of receipt taken from Mrs. Crawford when I handed her the Pocket book when I had arrived at home from the hospital on Furlough.

Received Uniontown Novr 10th 1864 of Daniel Chisholm, The Pocket Book of my husband Daniel Crawford, containing Nine Dollars intrusted to his care by Lt Z. B. Springer.

Signed Margaret A. Crawford.

Novr 17th, 1864 — Ward F, U.S.A. Genl Hospital, Pittsburgh Pa.
Dear Father,

I would have written to you yesterday, but I had the Headache all day, caused I suppose by getting up so early. I was admitted into the Pittsburgh Hospital without much trouble, also Alfred Bailes. I will have to cut my letter off pretty short, for I neglected writing until it is almost time for the mail to start out, and I dont know whether it will go to day or not,

from your Affct Son, Daniel Chisholm

N.B. Thomas Williams and Dick McClean are getting along first rate.

Dec. 1st, 1864 — Pittsburgh Hospital

Dear Father,

I received your letter dated Nov 23rd one week ago to day and should have answered it sooner, only I thought I would wait until I received one from Alex. I received one yesterday, and he was well as usual, and appears to be in good spirits. He says they are in Winter Quarters, about two hundred yards from where I was wounded, and all they have to do is to drill four hours a day, and they get plenty to eat. He says that he would like to have a fifteen day furlough very much But thinks that he cannot get it now, on the account of there being so many married men, that are trying very hard for furloughs. He says that he will not try very hard or bother very much about it now, for long as he has good health he dont miss it much. He says that the company numbers fourteen men. He says he wants me to go down town and buy him a fiddle worth about 7 or 8 dollars, a good pair of warm gloves. Also some chestnuts and other nick nacks. But [I] think that I shall respectfully decline so far as the fiddle is concerned. But the next box you send him it would be well enough I think to send him the Gloves and Chestnuts. But the fiddle would be a dead loss, and I think I can make him think so too. I was sorry to hear that you had hurt your back but hope that it is better before now. The doctor thinks that my leg is healing up, but I don't see much heal about it. I dress it now with Brown sugar with a damp Cloth over it. I heard that Cope had been wounded in two places, when you write let me know the particulars. Tom Williams, Dick McClean and Alf Bailes are all well as usual. Tom has got so he can walk quite well with a cane. I believe I have nothing more to say at present,

your Affct Son, Daniel Chisholm.

Decr 5th, 1864 — Pittsburgh Penna "Hospital."

Dear Father,

I received your welcomed letter of Decr 1st, and was glad to hear from you and that you were all well. My leg is not much better than it was when I was up home. Sometimes it looks a little better, but it soon breaks out again. I like this hospital very well, it is rather a dirty place though to what I have been used to. We get a plenty to eat, and when I get that I can get along.

There is a young man in the same tent with me from the mountains that knows Uncle James and appears to be pretty well acquainted over that way. I didn't question him very much about it for fear he might come out on me for having relations in the rebel army. I am glad that they have got one of the boys tight anyhow.

I have written three letters to Alex since I have been here, one of them ready to mail this morning. I have received one from him and expect another soon. If I stay here I will try and get a pass about New Years if I can.

There is nothing I need at present that I know of, unless it would be some butter or something of that kind, and I can get along very well without, for it wouldn't last long, I have too many friends here. I guess I have nothing more to write of at present. Write soon and let me know what the news is in town.

Your Affct son Danl Chisholm

Decr 13th, 1864 — Camp near Petersburgh Va
Brother Alex's Letter

Dear Father,

I now seat myself to answer your last letter received Decr 12th, dated 5th Decr. It found me enjoying good health considering the weather. We have had some cold rainy weather lately and a small skift of snow. We left our quarters on the 9th and went up to the left, that is our division the 1st. It was to attract the Rebs attention so as to draw the force from Genl Warrens front down about Stony Creek, he had his Corps there, and sure enough we did draw their attention. Genl Warren advanced some 20 miles and tore up some 20 miles of the South Side Rail Road and done some other damages. He has returned to camp.

Yesterday evening I got my Gloves, safe. I think $2.80 was a big price for such Gloves as those. They fit pretty well. You done better than I expected by Mr. Clawson. I suppose he hadn't done yet had he. I would like to have got a crack at that cousin of mine Peter as you call him, I would have put one Johnny out of the road.

I think we will be paid some time in next month. I have $150 coming next pay day. Good for that.

I just came in off of Picket this morning. I went on yesterday morning. We have good times on Picket now to what we had before Petersburgh. We now and then see a Johnny at a distance lurking around like a wild beast in the forest. I can hardly hold my old rifle from bearing on them. Tell all my friends to write soon. This is all this time.

From Your Son — Alex Chisholm.

Decr 30th, 1864 — Pittsburgh, Penna
Dear Father,

I received your letter of the 27th yesterday morning, and was glad to hear from you so soon, and from Alex too, and that he was well. I do not know why he does not write to me. There was no letter here for me from him when I came down. I received one from Cousin S. A. Williams. They were all as well as usual.

I am glad Capt. Weltner has got back to the Company again, and that they are in their winter quarters for it has been very cold yesterday and to day.

I got along first rate coming down. The engine run against a stone laying on the track, and bent the cowcatcher up considerably which detained us some.

Tom and Dick are here yet. Tom has gone up home on a pass and I suppose that you will see him.

I had no trouble in getting from the depot to the hospital aside from getting into the mud something less than a foot.

I am sorry Alex has got into the habit of smoking, for it is a very bad habit, worse in the army than any other place, for a soldier soon learns to never be satisfied without he has a cigar or pipe in his mouth smoking to pass the time away.

The news are very cheering for the soldiers out front now. I heard some of the boys saying that we had taken Wilmington, that it said so on the bulletin Board. We will see about it when I get a paper. I think Alex ought to write to me for I have written five letters to his one since I came here. I wish that you would mention it in your next letter if I do not get one before you write.

The paper does not say as reported that we had Wilmington and I believe they will have to abandon the taking of it for the present, it appears to be too strongly fortified. I will bring my letter to a close for the present.

Your Affct Son, Daniel Chisholm.

Jany 10th, 1865 — Pittsburgh Pa.
Dear Father,

I wrote a letter yesterday to Jennie, and seat myself this morning for the purpose of letting you know we had an examination yesterday and that I was marked to go away, I suppose to the hospital that I came from. We may go away to day, and maybe not for two or three days. You needn't send anything to me by Tommy as it is very likely I will not be here when he comes back. You can tell Tom to get my letters when he comes back, and keep them for me until I write to him for them. If anything should happen that we don't get away as soon as I expect I will write again as soon as I arrive at whereever I have to go to.

From Your Affct Son. Daniel Chisholm.

(I was expecting to leave hospital at Pittsburgh in a day or two from above date, see letter from Pittsburgh date on back July [sic — apparently meant January?] 12th, 1865.)

Jany 12th, 1865 — Pittsburgh Pa
Dear Father,

I received your welcomed letter this morning dated Jany 10th and was glad to hear that you all were enjoying good health. I mailed you a letter on the same day I believe that yours was written. I was not sent away as soon as I expected but may go yet this afternoon. They took my bedcard this morning. So I suppose it will not be long until they will be starting me.

I received a letter from Alex dated Jany 6th. I forgot whether I had recd it before I wrote to you last or not. However it will not do any harm to say that he was well and getting along first rate. He told me all about his corporalship, he is sixth corporal. Lt. Z. B. Springer promoted him to 1st and Capt Nolan then commanding the Reg't, afterwards killed, reduced James Collins then 1st corporal to the ranks and Alex took his place. Weltner was not with the company then, but as soon as he came up he reinstated Collins and Alex had to fall back to the rear and take the Sixth Corporal, after marching and fighting at the head of the Co all summer. Collins has since been promoted to 5th Sergt, a position which Alex deserved and would have had if either Cope or Springer had of been with the Company.

Cousin Tom is married and Aunt and mother has kicked up a row about it. I knew that he was going to be married some time ago. I think if Uncle and Aunt can be satisfied, that the balance of us ought. I think they had better come to a treaty of peace. I am glad to hear you are going to have a turkey and would like to help eat it very much. I expect that I could get a pass if I would try but dont think it worth while as it is such a short time since I was at home, and it wont do to be running home too often or I might get something pinned to my wings like Tom. It will not be worth while to start anything to me while I am here for I don't know how soon I may be sent away. If I get some place where eatables are not very plenty then I will call on you. I have nothing more to write of at present and will bring my letter to a close.

From Your Affct Son — Daniel Chisholm.

(Last Letter wrote from Pittsburgh before going to the front.)

Dec. 20th, 1864
Extract from Alex's Letter. My bro.

Camp on the extreme left of Petersburgh, in Winter Quarters. The boys are in good humor. The news from Sherman is very encouraging to us as he is victorious and considered a good General. Steven Beckett came up last night, we have now 20 men for duty, 1 Commissioned officer, Capt Jno R. Weltner, 4 Sergeants, 4 Corporals. The Capt came to us from the Hospital to day and looks well now. I have a cold at this time, caught it while up at Hatchers run. It was very cold and we had no tents with us. A good many of us got our hands and feet and ears frozen. William Sembower has the chronic Diarrhoea, suffers much with it. George Ganoe is going home on a furlough his father being very sick. He complains of his relatives not writing to him.

Jany 14th, 1865
Extract from Bro Alex's Letter. Camp on Left of Petersburgh.

Orderly Jolliffe has gone to the Hospital sick with some kind of fever. Sergeant Clear is acting orderly in his place. Capt. Weltner has promoted James Collins to 5th Sergeant. There is a good many Reb deserters coming over now. Our lines are about one mile apart on our front with a large wood of Pines and ravines between making it a good place for deserters to come over under cover, and of still nights we can always hear them. We all think the backbone of the rebellion is broken, and the end near. The sooner the better, I am glad Old Abe is elected President. Our Regiment gave 4 Majority for Genl McClellan.

Jany 30th, 1865
Extract from Letter of Bro Alex

Brother Daniel came up to the Company from the Hospital. His wound is not healed yet. He is doing light fatigue duty now. Orderly James Jolliffe also came up from the Hospital. He is not stout by any means. I am hauling logs to build a shanty for the three of us. Dan, Joliff, and myself. Size about 9 ft square. I received the box of cigars and had many friends while they lasted.

Feby 2nd, 1865
Extract from Letter of Bro Alex

In your letter you wished to know how many men was in the Company. There is Jolliffe. Clear. Dean. Sembower. Collins. Beckett. Paterson. Bolen. McInnerny. Bro Daniel. Myself. Seese. Campbell. Hager. Ganoe. Bagshaw. Hayden Hall. Hull. Moore. Allamon. Frazier. Thorndell. 22 men at this time, but few of us left to stand another Summers Campaign.

Jany 20th, 1865 — Camp. Army of the Potomac.
Dear Father,

I suppose it will kind of surprise you when you find that I am with the Regiment again. I got here yesterday. I left Pittsburgh on the 13th. Left the Hospital on the 12th just after I mailed my last letter to you. And put up in the Girard House for that night and the next day until the next morning. I didn't expect to be front so soon but the Doctors marked me for that and I thought I would come out and see how the boys were getting along. I had to go to the Dr this morning. He excused me from pickets so I will have nothing but Camp duty to do, and that will not be very hard. The boys are all getting along first rate. Alex has got to be a very large boy, and has excellent health. We are in camp (Winter Quarters) along the breastworks, and the Pickets are out about ¾ of a mile.

The rebs are deserting every night in squads. They are a miserable looking set, with scarcely enough clothes to cover their nakedness. I don't think they will hold out much longer. I would like to have a couple of Dollars if you can send it to me. I have nothing much to write of at present and I don't expect you can read what I have scribbled.

Your Affct son, Daniel Chisholm.

(Arrived at the front on Jany 19th, 1865, from Hospital at Pittsburgh.)

Feb'y 12th, 1865 — Camp. Army of the Potomac
Dear Father,

I suppose you are beginning to look for a letter from me, but I have been so busy for the last week that I have not had time to write. My health has been good since I have been here and my wound appears to be about the same old thing, though I believe that if I had to have stayed up on the left two or three days longer that I would have had to left the regiment again. But we are back now in our winter quarters, the same ones that we left. James Joliffe, Alex and myself bunk together in a new hut that we just got finished yesterday. It is very comfortable, only it smokes us out now and then. We had it pretty hard for the two or three days that we were up on the left. Although we were not engaged. It came so near though that part of the Regt on our left was engaged. The enemy charged three times on the 2nd and 3rd Divisions of our Corps but were successfully repulsed each time. It rained one day and night besides sleet and some snow which made it very disagreeable being without shelter.

The Adjutants Clerk having gone home on furlough I have his position until he comes back. And I hope it wont be long for it keeps me too busy.

I left Pittsburgh on the 13th of last month and got to the Regiment on the 19th. It wasn't a very pleasant trip I assure you. It was cold and I was with a very hard lot of men from the time I started until I got to City Point, the most of them being Deserters and Bounty Jumpers, and it isn't very pleasant for a wounded soldier to go marching through the streets under guard with a lot of shirkers hand cuffed. I stayed all night in the soldiers Rest at Washington. There was about one hundred Rebel deserters there, and I talked with several of them that had been in the army since the war first broke out. They all appear to agree pretty well that the South is about to play out.

Our line of works is very strong with a great many forts all along every three or four hundred yards apart. They are building a very high lookout about a quarter of a mile from where we lay. I have come to the conclusion that I would like to have a small piece of cheese, a roll of butter and a small sack of Buck wheat flour, and some of that sorghum molasses, a few rusk and about 2 pies and some small sheets of letter paper and envelopes. If there is any other little thing that wont take up much room and is good to eat that you think of you might slip it in. I concluded to send for it now on the account that I might not have another chance of getting it while we were in comfortable quarters. I don't want a box, But a little one with a good deal in it, For Alex has an appetite that is hard to beat.

When I got to the Regt he was in his bunk asleep, and it surprised him a good deal when I wakened him up and he seen it was me. He has got to be very tall and is pretty straight. The boys were all glad to see me. James Jolliffe was at the field Hospital sick, but he is with the Company now although not able to do duty yet. I must bring my letter to a close as I have scribbled about enough. It is very windy to day. Give my best respects to all friends and write soon.

Your Affct Son, Daniel Chisholm.

Feb'y 13th, 1865 — Near Hatchers Run, Va — Army of the Potomac
Dear Father,

I suppose you will get over your surprise somewhat before you read this, as well as mother. I suppose it will surprise you both more than when I came home. As I discover it is a very hard thing to get a furlough from the front, I did not expect Alex to get a Furlough so soon as what he did when he first made application. I hope that he may get home all right, and that he will have a good time of it.

I want you to write to me as soon as you read this, and let me know if he got home all right, and how you all are. Regimental Clerk keeps me very busy, and if I dont answer your letters right away you will have to excuse me. The boys are all well and getting along first rate. Everything appears to be quiet since our move on the left. Alex can tell you all about that and a great deal more.

My health is all O.K. and I am beginning to get fat. My wound is the same old thing as Alex can tell you. I am writing on a half sheet of paper, I dont want you to take it as an insult as I would do if any one should send me one. Soldiers are excusable in time of war and scarcity of paper. Alex can bring some with him.

I just happened to stop to study or rather concentrate my ideas, when I made the discovery that I had a whole sheet. This paper is very thin. Send good paper. I have not much to write of as there is not much news here now. I wrote day before yesterday but I suppose you will get this about The same time.

Your Son. Daniel Chisholm.
Co "K" 116th Regt Penna Vol's, 4th Brigade, 1st Divsion, 2nd Army Corp,
Army of the Potomac.

1865 — Camp 116 Regt P.V.
Dear Father,

Being at leisure this evening I have concluded to drop you a few lines. My health is good, able for the full allowance of hardtack and Salt Horse. I suppose Alex is at home all right before this time and in his full hight of enjoyment. I would say to him that we had Regimental inspection to day, again by the Brigade Inspector and the boys all come out with their white gloves on, muttering and growling as they always do on inspection day. There was a good deal of picket firing night before last, occasioned it is said by six Hundred Rebs coming into our lines in front of the Sixth Corp.

Wm H. Sembower received his furlough and starts for home tomorrow. Those boots I sent home I intend for you to have repaired and keep them for a Sunday go to meeting pair, and there was a pair of suspenders in my overcoat pocket for you. I wrote to Thomas Hadden for a Vest and Suspenders and a pair of Gloves. If he lets me have them on my terms Alex can bring them with him.

I want you to send me in the box or by Alex about fifteen or Twenty cents worth of Glycerin. I got the little bottle I had broke after carrying it about a year. Would like to have some postage stamps and I am completely out. It is about Nine O'Clock and I am scribbling away like a fine fellow. James and I are keeping Bachelors Hall. We have a New and Good Hat. We have added two barrels to the top of the chimney and the cat [?] disappeared several days ago.

This is full of nothing. You must excuse it for this was wash day the first one I have seen since I left home. Capt and all the boys are as well as usual. I see by the late paper that Sherman is going to rock at the cradle of the Rebellion ("Charleston").

I will bring this to a close —

Your Son, Daniel Chisholm.

Feby 24th, 1865 — Camp 116th Regt P.V.
Dear Father,

I received your welcomed letter of Feby 17th day before yesterday, and was glad to hear you were all enjoying good health and that Alex arrived at home all right. I suppose he is enjoying himself now, but will be on his way back before you receive this. There is some talk of our paymaster being here but I dont care if we dont get paid for a couple of weeks yet, then we can get two months more pay beside another installment of the bounty. I will then have three hundred and thirteen dollars coming to me and Alex will have enough to make it something over five hundred. We settle up our Clothing Accounts this year. I will come out in debt about fifty one cents.

There has been very heavy cannonading going on to our right for the last half hour. There is something wrong over in rebeldom and it wouldn't surprise me if we would have to move before long. There was several Rebs came in last night, one first Lieutenant. He said that they were on a move.

The news just came a few minutes ago of the fall of Wilmington and Charleston has gone too. We received the news of Charleston being evacuated day before yesterday. The Major had the Regt to fall out and give three cheers, and they did give three hearty, rousing cheers with a good will.

I think you have made a good thing as regards the house, hold them to their bargain, don't let them slip.

I would like to have a Waverly Magazine occasionally with the American Standard.

General Lee I understand says that our high Lookout a little to our right shall not stand very long. So I suppose he will commence shelling it some of these days. We can see their cars on the South Side Rail Road on a clear day, and they have lately placed some large guns to shell them. There is a considerable Camp of them opposite our front.

They say Lt Springer has been exchanged. If there is anything of it let me know it in your next letter. Also whether mother and Aunt Martha has come to a treaty of peace yet, and when Thomas was at home. I must bring my letter to a close as it is nearly time for the mail to leave. Excuse bad writing as I have been putting it down double quick. If you see Dick McClean tell him to write to me.

Your Affct Son, Daniel Chisholm.

March 7th, 1865 — Camp of the 116th Pa Vols, Army of the Potomac Brother Alex's Letter

Dear Sister,

I am seated in my lodge this pleasant afternoon and not having anything to do particularly, I thought it proper to write you a few lines to let you know that I am well, also Dan is very hearty. Dans wound is sore yet. If we should have to go on a move which I think will not be unlikely, he will have to go to the rear. The weather here for 4 or 5 days past has been very fine and if it holds out we will have a move soon undoubtedly. The boys are in good spirits. Uncle Sam is feeding us well now and the boys are getting fat the most of them. I was out on a scout three nights ago. The object was to find out whether the Rebs put sharp shooters outside of their videttes to watch the videttes so as to keep them from deserting. We got up to their videttes as close as possible. It was a moonlight night and we could of seen their sharpshooters if they had of had any out. Deserters says that they put out sharpshooters. There was a sharpshooter out of the 148th Penna with me, he had a Seven Shooter, he was a Sergt. The Capt of the line picked on him and me and of course we could not refuse. They have been signalling all day from a station close to our camp. Well I must now close as I have to go on Dress parade.

Write Soon — Your Bro — Alex Chisholm.

March 9th, 1865 — Camp 116th Regt Pa Vols. Army of the Potomac.
Brother Alex's Letter.

Dear Mother,

I am seated in my ranch this morning and have not got anything to do at the present times so I have come to the conclusion to write to you to let you know that I am well. Also that Dan is well. His wound is about the same. It does not seem to heal much. The adjutants Clerk has returned from his furlough and has taken his old position and Dan is helping him. It keeps them both pretty busy. We expect our pay this week at the farthest. We had a nice rain here last night, it makes it pretty muddy.

You ought to of heard us cheering here last night. It was about Eight O'Clock when they called us out and read us the news that 13 hundred of Earlys troops were captured and 40 officers with Early himself. If this be true it was worth cheering for. We still lay in our old position, all goes on same as ever. Stillness reigns over Rebel and Yankeedom, but how long it will be so I cannot say. Perhaps Genl Grant knows.

I am going to get a memorandum of all the boys that were killed in the Company and missing, stating the place & battle that they were killed in. Has George West finished my photographs yet. If he has not tell him he need not. Well I have not much to write about this time, so I will now bring my letter to a close.

From your Son, Alex Chisholm.

March 12th, 1865 — Camp 116th Regt P.V. Army of the Potomac

Dear Father,

I received your welcomed letter of the sixth inst this morning, and was happy to hear that you were all well as usual. Alex is well, in good spirits, and getting along first rate. He arrived here the evening of the second, the day that his leave of absence was up. He has written home twice since he returned. I believe he had a good time and enjoyed himself splendidly while he was at home. We have had beautiful weather for the last three or four days. And everything begins to look as if spring was approaching with her mantle of green.

I seen a man shot yesterday for desertion, belonging to the sixth Corps, and there were two hung the day before.

I have not received my box yet, but expect that it will be here in a day or two.

Lt Z. B. Springer has been exchanged, and I suppose that he is at home on leave of absence against this time. Capt Jms R. Weltner received a letter from him a short time ago, and he expected to be at home soon then. Hezekiah Dean received a furlough and started home two or three days ago. Wm Sembower has had his extended. The boys have all been very lucky so far in getting furloughs. The adjutants Clerk has returned but I still write some for him. I have good times and get along first rate. It is very little I do. I am beginning to think that I am rather a dear boarder to Uncle Samuel, and if he was to look into matters a little I think he would be of the same opinion, but if he is satisfied I am for they say soldiers wages are going to raise from sixteen to twenty Dollars per month. We were paid on last Thursday and Alex mailed One Hundred Dollars in his letter to you yesterday. He had due him One Hundred and fifty two dollars. His transportation from Washington home and back amounted to seventeen dollars and thirty two cents, and he owed the Sutler Ten dollars which left him one and twenty four. I received seven months pay and two installments of the bounty, amounting to Two Hundred and One dollars. If I send it by mail I will wait until I hear from you so that I will know whether you received Alex's all right or not. James Jolliffe is in for a pass to visit City Point, and if he gets it I will have him to Express it for me to you. If you get it all right you will not have to borrow to pay for the house. You had better have it attended to as soon as possible, if Searight has had the Act passed so as to enable Wilkinson to make the Deed. My leg is still about the same thing, otherwise I have good health — never felt better in my life.

I would not be surprised if we were to receive marching orders now at any time for I think the spring or Summer Campaign will open early. Genl Sheridan has had another victory in the Valley. We will be apt to hear from Genl Sherman again soon.

I cannot get my commutation money unless I was at Pittsburgh to get my furlough myself. It is not worth while to try by sending an order for it for there would be no account taken of it.

I must bring my letter to a close. I wrote on the large sheet of paper because I had no small. Alex has wrote up all the paper he brought with him. I guess he wrote a letter to nearly everybody he seen.

Your Affct Son, Daniel Chisholm.

March 3rd, 1865
Extract from Bro Alex's Letter

I have been home on a short furlough and got back to the Regiment. Met Thos Williams and Dick McClean in Pittsburgh and was with them a day. Then took the train for Baltimore and Washington City & Fortress Monroe. Arrived in Camp on Thursday, found the boys in good spirits. Sembower came home on furlough while I was at home. I had a Photo taken at Lingos while I was home.

Arrived in Camp on Thursday.

March 11th, 1865
Extract from Bro Alex's Letter.

We have got our Pay. Dan Received $201.00, I received $152.00. I owed $17.00 Transportation, $11.00 Sutler Bill, $25.00 to Saml Clear. So I will send you two $50.00 of the Amt. Dan will send his by Ex.

March 26th, 1865 — Camp 116th Regt Pa Vols. Army of the Potomac.
Dear Father,

I received your welcomed letter of March 19th after looking for one anxiously for sometime, was glad to hear that you all were tolerably well, and hope ere you receive this that mothers boil and sty may have disappeared, and left her in her usual good health. I am sitting comfortably in my tent writing by candle light. You will see by the papers that the Army of the Potomac done something yesterday. I hardly know what yet, but it was a noisy day all along the lines. I know nothing but reports and can say nothing as to the correctness of them. You can judge how near they are by the papers. It is first reported that the Rebs charged on the Ninth Corps. Our men fell back, and let them follow them on, let them take all the prisoners they wanted until they got up as far as Meade Station. There they turned around and was going to take their prisoners back, but the Yanks were too sharp for them, and had marched a line of battle in the works behind them and in turn took them prisoners. The Sixth Corps charged but did not succeed in taking the works, although they took some prisoners. It is reported that Genl said that we had taken four thousand prisoners, and seventeen stand of colors. Our Corps was pretty hotly engaged. The second Brigade suffered considerably, the one we used to be in. There was no one hurt in our Company or regiment. I started to go out with them, but couldn't go it far, and had to turn around and come back to camp again. The boys returned about One O'Clock at night and fixed their tents up to day. I dont think we will stay here long. I was glad to hear you had heard from Uncle Joseph. I suppose Lewis Reahard is quite a business man. Is he the youngest of oldest of the two boys. If I were you if I could hold Wilkinson to the bargain I would do so, for you will not get another such a bargain in Uniontown, or a house as pleasantly situated in good society.

I received a letter from Thomas Williams to day from Pittsburgh. He was well and said nothing about being sent away. Sembower returned to the Company all right and Deanes time is up to night. I expressed to you One Hundred and Fifty Dollars on the 18th of this month, and send you the receipt of this letter. I would have sent it sooner only I was waiting to get a letter from you. I also mailed five to Jenny, and intend to send some to mother as soon as I hear from what I have sent. I want you to write as soon as you get this and let me know how you all are and about the money. I wrote to you and Jenny both since I received a letter from home. I must bring my letter to a close as it is taps and lights have to go out.

Your son, Daniel Chisholm.

NB, My leg is about the same old thing.

March 31st, 1865 — City Point Hospital, Va.
Dear Father,

I embrace the present opportunity of writing you a letter. I am again in the Hospital at this place. I was examined by the Brigade Surgeon, and pronounced unfit for duty, so I had to leave again although I was sorry to have to do so. Alex, The Capt and all the boys was well when I left the Regiment. I do not intend to go farther than here if I can help it. There is a great many sick and wounded here at present. There was very heavy cannonading night before last, some yesterday, and pretty heavy to day at times. The rumor here is that the rebels charged our works and were repulsed three different times.

We have had a good deal of rain in the last two days. There was a good many wounded of the fifth corps came down yesterday. They were engaged it is said eight miles beyond Hatchers Run and that the second corps was engaged yesterday.

There has been a great many improvements made here since last time and the place begins to almost look like a small city. There is trains running from here day and night to the front.

I want you to write as soon as you get this, and let me know if you got the one hundred and fifty dollars that I expressed to you, I sent you the receipt for it in my last letter, and whether Jennie got the five I sent her. I would send mother fifteen dollars now only I do not take my letters to the office myself, and do not know what kind of hands they have to go through.

I wrote to Alex day before yesterday, and am going to write again this afternoon. No more at present —

Your Affct son, Daniel Chisholm. Ward 8, Section C, 2nd Division, 2nd Army
Corps Hospital, City Point, Va.

April 1st, 1865 — City Point Va.

Dear Father,

I seat myself to drop you another few lines. I am enjoying reasonably good health, but have a very sore ankle. I suppose it came from a sprain. It is swelled considerably, but begins to feel some better than what it did. It is my left ankle and between it and my sore leg it makes quite a cripple of me. My leg is about the same.

There was a great many wounded came down from the front this Evening, and I am sorry to say that the old One Hundred and Sixteenth was in the engagement and suffered considerably. There was four wounded out of Co "K" from town. There was James E. Jolliffe 1st Sergeant, Corporal Timothy McInnerny in the arm and Thomas Thorndell wounded in the bowels. Joliffe has a pretty bad wound in the leg. He thinks Thorndell was fatal. Brother Alex was all right when Joliffe last seen him. They were fighting about two miles from the South Side Rail Road.

> *from your Affct Son, Daniel Chisholm. Ward 8, Section C.*
> *2nd Div 2nd A.C. Hosptl.*

(Tells about James E. Jolliffe being wounded.)

April 4th, 1865 — City Point Va.

Dear Mother,

I seat myself this pleasant afternoon to write you a short letter. I have just been out looking at a squad of Johnny prisoners passing by, about two thousand in number. They were taken in and about Petersburgh. I suppose the news of the capture of Petersburgh will be stale before you get this. There was seven thousand three hundred prisoners brought down yesterday. They were said to have been taken on the South Side R Road, and the report now is that we occupied Richmond yesterday morning at a quarter of Eight O'Clock. I do not know how true it is, but it is pretty generally credited here, and I would not at all be surprised if it was the case.

Sergt James E. Jolliffe was sent away this morning up north to a Genl Hospital. I have not heard from Alex since I have been down here. I have wrote to him three times.

We have fine weather here. I suppose you have commenced making garden before now. Have a good garden, plenty of tomatoes, peas and Lima Beans, for I wouldn't be surprised that we would be home to help you eat some of them.

Mother that twenty dollars that I was going to send you has dwindled down to ten, but father can draw you ten out of the bank, and that will make it all right. I was paid Two Hundred and One Dollars, sent home $150.00, loaned Alex $15.00, sent Jennie $5.00 and now send you $10.00, paid $5.00 towards getting the Capt a sword, and $2.00 for a Co memorial, paid $6.00 of an old debt, and spent $3.00 and have $5.00 left, and intend to send it to father for him to pay Haddens what I owe them.

Well we have glorious News, too good I am afraid to be true, so I wont mention it until I hear more of it, and it has been made official. And I hope it wont be long for then the war will be over.

Your affct son, Daniel Chisholm. Ward 8, Section C.
2nd div, 2nd A.C. Hospital.

(Sergt James E. Jolliffe was sent north from Hospital here this morning.)

April 7th, 1865
Extract from Brother Alex's Letter

I wrote sitting behind the works at Gravelly Run, after a hard fight of a few hours duration. We lost Lt. Brady killed, also our Priest was killed. We made a charge on the Rebs and was repulsed the first charge, then reformed and charged again and drove them back quite a distance, about one mile capturing a good many prisoners. Brady, myself and two others were in a Rebel Rifle Pit and Brady was standing up when he was shot dead. I went on the skirmish line and got seven articles which I sent home. We lost 28 men wounded, in our Regiment, Thos Thorndell wounded, Timothy McInnerny shot in the Arm. Major McGraw was wounded, also myself slight in shoulder.

April 11th, 1865 — Ward 7 McClellan U.S.A. Genl Hosptl, Philad'a Pa.
Dear Father,

You will see by this that I have been transferred to a Genl Hospital again. I arrived here day before yesterday, "April 9th," but we were not landed until yesterday at noon. It was the first boat load of sick and wounded that has arrived here this spring, and there was a large crowd of citizens, ladies with refreshments, and little boys eager to carry your knapsack while they asked you a host of questions. Everybody seemed to be in a good humor, and rejoicing over the good news from Grant (The surrender of Genl Lee and his army), who has knocked the main prop from under the rebellion. One more such a push and our ship of State will be calmly sailing on the still waters of Peace.

My leg looks a great deal better than when I left the regiment. I dont know whether the good news is having any effect on it or not, but it looks a great deal better and I am in hopes that I will get back to the Regiment in a couple of weeks.

This is a splendid Hospital, ahead of Pittsburgh for accommodations.

I got to see the City of Wilmington, Delaware, and Fort Delaware where there are so many rebel prisoners.

I have not heard from you nor Alex by letter since I left the Regiment. I am going to write to Alex this afternoon, and I wish you would write to me as soon as you receive this and let me know when you heard from Alex, how he was getting along, &c.

What is the news about town, and how are you and Wilkinson making it about the house. I am a little anxious to hear whether you received the money that I expressed to you or not, and I mailed $10.00 to mother from City Point.

How does the news seem to operate on the minds of the Copperhead community of Uniontown.

Well I must bring my letter to a close.

Your affct Son, Daniel Chisholm.

(Arrived at Philada from City Point on April 9th, 1865.)

April 20th, 1865 — Ward 7 McClellan U.S.A. Genl Hospital, Philada Pa.
Dear Father,

Having not received any word from home for so long I have seated myself again to write you a short letter this evening.

It has been nine days since I came to this Hospital, having arrived at the City on the 9th of April. I last wrote you on the 11th of April. If you received the letter and answered it, I suppose I will not get it for it only takes the mail two days at the farthest to go and two to come. I wrote to Jennie on last sabbath and will look for an answer tomorrow. I have also written twice since I came here to Alex, and have not received any answer yet. I am very anxious to hear from Alex and how you are getting along at home, and would like to hear whether you received my money all right. If I receive a letter I will answer it immediately, and I would like to have you answer this one right away for it is about a month since I heard from you.

It is quite cool this evening and has been raining most of the afternoon.

I made a short visit to the City yesterday for the first, and took a walk up Chestnut Street. Philadelphia is a nice City, everything looks nice and clean, a great many of the buildings have the woodwork on the outside painted white, that do in Pittsburgh. [sic] There dont appear to be much news this evening, excepting that it is reported that the guerrilla Mosby has surrendered with his band of robbers and murderers. It is said that the Second Corps is guarding the Rail Road from City Point to Richmond. If they are they are having pretty good times.

How is the Oil business getting along in old Fayette, have they struck oil any ways near town. Well I must bring my letter to a close. It is longer than what I supposed it would be when I commenced writing. I hope to receive a letter from you soon.

Your affct Son, Daniel Chisholm.

April 20th, 1865
Extract from Letter of Brother Alex

We are in camp three miles above Burkesville Junction. The weather is fine and we are getting rations now regular. I have not got any letters from you since we started on this Campaign. We have had it pretty rough, so much rain. One day we marched 21 miles through the mud. Poor old Abe is dead. If it could be left to us to end the assassins life it would be rough on him, I got a letter from Dan day before yesterday. He was in McClelland Hospital, Philada. His leg was getting well fast. William Sembower and I are bunking together. The Country up here is fine. The Apple Trees are about to bloom. There is a good deal of Oak timber in this part. We are 53 miles from Petersburgh, and about 50 from Richmond. Genl Lee could not hold out any longer as he was well hemmed in.

April 23rd, 1865 — Ward 7 McClellan U.S.A. General Hospital, Philada Pa.
Dear Father,

I received your long looked for letter yesterday morning, and was glad to hear that you were all well, and that you had received Greenbacks all right,

I was sorry to hear of Grandmother Chisholm's death.

I am afraid that in the end you will come out minus a house, but there is nothing like holding on, and if talking will do any good go in strong, and scare them into it if possible. It is the only way. It is no use to try law for it, it would only be a waste of money, for you have no written agreement to show, and I dont think that the letters would amount to much. But if I was you I would do all in my power to hold the property without going to law. Six hundred dollars is enough for the property, for it needs a great deal of repairing. It will not be long until property and everything else will begin to come down.

I am glad to hear that Lt James D. Cope is at home. Do you know whether Lt. Zadoc B. Springer has returned to the Company or not.

I was in the City yesterday at the time of the arrival of the President Abraham Lincoln's remains, and seen more people together at one time than I ever expect to see again. The streets and side walks were crowded so that it was scarcely possible to move, and every door, window and house top was crowded with spectators. The car or hearse that drew the Presidents remains was a magnificent affair. I cannot describe it, but it was very large, and was arranged very tastefully and appeared to be covered with black silk Velvet, it must have cost a great deal. The Coffin was a very nice one, it cost one thousand dollars. His remains lay to day in state at Independence Hall. The building is shrouded in mourning.

I am very anxious to hear from Alex, I expect a letter from him every day. I sent him a Harpers Weekly containing a picture of the Assassination of the President. It rained some yesterday but the sun is out to day and everything looks bright and green. I would like to have about ten dollars, and I want to buy a pair of shoes, Cap &c. I would not have needed it if I could have stayed with the Regt. I dont always write a full letter but I think I can make up for that by writing a few extra ones now and then. You appear to be getting pretty good wages now. I must bring my letter to a close as I have nothing more to write of at present,

Your affct Son, Daniel Chisholm.

April 29th, 1865 — Ward 7. McClellan U.S.A. Genl Hospital, Philada Pa
Dear Father,

I received your welcomed letter this morning, and was glad to hear that you were all well. So far I have received two letters from you including the one received this morning, and one from Jennie with a few lines in it from you. I answered all, and sent in Jennie's a letter from Brother Alex. I suppose you have received a letter from him before this.

I am glad to hear that Wilkinson has come to the just conclusion to let you have the property. I think you are very lucky in getting it for six hundred dollars. I don't think I shall try for a furlough at all for it is not so very long since I was at home, and transportation would cost something from here home. Booth has been shot, better taken that way than not at all, but it is a great pity they could not have taken him alive. I have not been to the City for several days. The next time I go I intend to visit the water works. I will expect another letter from you in a day or two. How much money is there in the bank now. We will be mustered here on Sunday for two months pay, but it is very doubtful whether

I get any or not without my descriptive list. I will bring my scribbled letter to a close, as it is getting late.

Hoping to hear from you again soon, I am your Affct Son. Daniel Chisholm.

May 4th, 1865 — *Ward 7, McClellan U.S.A. Genl Hospital, Philada Pa.*
Dear Father,

I received yours of April 28th several days ago, and thought that I would not answer it until I heard from Bro Alex. I received a letter from Alex yesterday dated April 29th. He was well. I seen a Capt out of the Reg't in the City yesterday. He told me that Capt Weltner was home on leave of absence. I think the greater portion of the Army will be discharged in the course of a month or so, and I guess they will begin to discharge all soldiers in the hospitals that don't require any more medical treatment as soon as possible. It will be some time before they can get the description lists &c. We were mustered for two months pay on last sabbath, and signed the pay rolls on Monday. I visited the Fairmont water works yesterday. They supply about one half of the City with water.

It is said that they have captured all of Booths accomplices excepting two. There is offered by the Government One Hundred Thousand Dollars for the arrest of Jefferson Davis. I believe he will be captured yet as our Cavalry was in hot pursuit from last accounts.

I do not know what Hospital Serg't Jolliffe is in as I have not seen or heard from him since he left City Point. I expect Capt Weltner would know where he is. I suppose you have heard of the plot to burn Philadelphia and all the Hospitals around it.

We have very fine weather here, it rained all day on Monday. Where is Tom Williams now. I have written to him twice addressing my letters to Pittsburgh Hospital. As the war is now over I think Mother and Aunt Martha had better come to Peaceable terms.

How is the oil business progressing about town. When did you hear from Uncle Tom's. I must bring my scribbled Letter to a close.

From Your Son, Daniel Chisholm.

May 7th, 1865 — *McClellan U.S.A. Gen'l Hospt'l Philada Pa. Ward 7.*
Dear Father,

I received your letter of May 2nd several days ago, and was glad to hear that you all were well. My health is good but my leg does not appear to heal.

My name has been taken for discharge, and I would be mustered out on Monday or Tuesday if my description list was here. But it is not and no telling when it will be, for the Serg't being wounded it has fell into very poor hands for to attend to such business. It may be a month before I get it.

I am glad that you have got the house and that it is paid for, because I think you got a good bargain.

If I could get home now, I would not mind going to school some this summer. Alex and I each have four months pay coming to us. I expect that I will not get any pay now until I am mustered out.

I don't expect to get the money due me for Rations while on a Furlough. If Alex gets home it is very likely that he will go to work on the Rail Road, and if he wants to it is the best plan to let him, for I dont think he would ever went a soldiering if he had got to have done as he wished.

It rained all day here yesterday, but the sun is out, and it is very pleasant this morning. I believe I have nothing more of importance to write of at present. Hoping to hear from you soon I bring my letter to a close.

from Your Son, Daniel Chisholm.

May 11th, 1865 — Ward 7, McClellan U.S.A. Gen'l Hospital, Philada Pa.
Dear Father,

I received your letter of May 7th yesterday morning, and was glad to hear that you were all well. My health is all right, have a good appetite for Uncle Sam's grub. I wrote a letter to you three or four days ago. There is some talk of the Pennsylvania Soldiers that are here in the Hospital being mustered out to day. I see there is an order in the paper this morning from the war department to discharge all Volunteer Soldiers that are in the Hospitals immediately. Also for all Brigade Commanders to see that all men in Hospitals be furnished with their Description Rolls. Mine is not here yet. I dont expect to be discharged before the 1st of June. The second and Fifth Corps are marching to Washington. There will be two Corps of Negroes, Hancocks Veteran Corps and One Corps of Regulars kept in the service.

I think Jefferson Davis is pretty well surrounded by this time and will be captured soon. There is a large sum of money on his head, besides the hundred Thousand Dollars that the president offers for him. The Cavalry General offers one hundred thousand in Gold, making it equal to a quarter of a Million in Greenbacks. It rained here day before yesterday, and was cold and cloudy yesterday. I expect a letter from Brother Alex every day. My leg looks tolerably well. I received the ten dollars you sent me all right, and would like to have another one in your answer to this.

I have something over Eighty dollars coming to me. Some say they are paying the balance of the three hundred dollars government bounty, but I doubt it, but if it is so I will have two Hundred dollars bounty coming to me beside the monthly pay.

This is a very poorly written letter, and full of all kinds of mistakes which I will not undertake to correct for fear I make it so bad you cannot read it at all. Write soon and don't forget the ten dollars, for after getting what I wanted with the other one it left me pretty bare. Goods are high here. I do not know whether to buy a suit of Clothes here or wait until I get to Pittsburgh or home. The last letter I got from Alex was dated April 29th.

From Your son, Daniel Chisholm.

May 14th, 1865
Extract from Bro Alex's Letter.

Spoke of our march from Burkesville to Washington City by way of Richmond, a-past Old Libby Prison, camped near the City over night. We were 11 days on the tramp. James Collins was lucky in getting his furlough when he did as it saved him a long march. Wm Sembower and Lt Zadoc Springer is well. We lay near Washington in Camp.

May 15th, 1865 — Ward 7, McClellan U.S.A. Gen'l Hosptl.
Dear Father,

I received yours of May 10th several days ago, and would have answered it sooner had I not been expecting a letter daily from Brother Alex. The last one I received from him was dated April 29th and I have written twice to him since then.

I wrote to T. B. Williams the other day, and told him to see that my Descriptive List was sent. I think it will come some time this week.

The Mustering Officer is here to day and is mustering out Pennsylvanians. Joseph Renshaw is here, and I expect that he will be discharged to day. If mine was ready I could have company home with him. I was surprised to hear that Tom had got back to the Regt.

This mornings Inquirer has the news of the capture of Jeff Davis, Wife and Company with their plunder. The paper does not say anything about his specie. I received the Ten dollars all right that you sent me and wrote for another in my last letter and expect that I will get it in a day or two. Jospeh Renshaw says that we get the balance of the bounty which is not due by installments, he asked the paymaster. If I get it I will have about two hundred and fifty dollars to come home with. Have you heard anything from James Jolliffe or the others boys that was wounded. I suppose James Cope will not return to the Company. Enclosed is a Photograph of a Zouave friend of mine who was discharged the other day, he was wounded above the left eye. This is a very fine day, and I would not mind being at home instead of being in the hospital here. But I guess the best way is to take it coolly, for that is the way Uncle Sam does, and he is sure to always come out all right. If I receive a letter from Bro Alex soon, I will write to you again. No more at present.

Your Son, Daniel Chisholm.

May 17th, 1865 — Near Washington City
Extract from Bro Alex's Letter

Thos Williams, Dick McClean, William Nycum has come up to the company. Lt Cope is here and looks well. Dan's descriptive list was sent to him day before yesterday. I expect he is tired of Hospital Life. We are having easy times now, and we think we will be home by July 4th.

May 23rd, 1898 — Ward 7, McClellan U.S.A. Gen'l Hospl, Philadelphia.
Dear Father,

I received yours of May 18th several days ago, and was glad to hear that you all are enjoying your usual good health. My health is good although I have had to stay in the house for several days on account of having a poisoned face, but it is pretty near well now. My leg is still about the same way, but it looks a good deal better than when I was at home last winter. I think with a little good care it can be cured in a short time. When I get home I shall have something different used from what has been used in the hospitals. I am glad you sent me the advertisement of the One Hundred Dollars for discharged wounded soldiers. I shall go to the office and see what I can do, but I dont think I can get it, for I think it is only for wounded Soldiers discharged on Account of Disability. I will be mustered out just the same as if I was with the Regiment.

To day the Army of the Potomac is to be Reviewed and tomorrow Shermans Army. If I had got my discharge I think I would have went to Washington. My descriptive List came yesterday, and I got to see it, and I believe it is all right, and I intend to have the Doctor take my name again for Discharge in the morning. If the Regiment comes here to be mustered out, it is very likely that I will go to their Camp and be mustered out with them. I have not had any word from the Regiment for about a month, although I have written to Alex four or five times. If you have received a letter from him lately please let me know in your next.

We have had a good deal of rainy weather here lately. Well I must bring my letter to a close, hoping to be able soon to quit writing home.

Your Son, Daniel Chisholm.

May 24th, 1865
Extract from Bro Alex's Letter

We had a big time in Washington yesterday. Genls Grant, Sherman and Sheridan and all was on hand to see us pass in review. The 5th Corps first, ours the 2nd next, then others and the Cavalry, making a grand show. One of Dans Hospital friends was to see me concerning his descriptive list. He had not got it yet. We sent it 7 days ago. We hear nothing from Thos Thorndell, he must be dead.

I saw Tim McInnerny, Jacob Prettyman and some others that was in the Hospitals. They did not see or hear of him anywhere.

May 27th, 1865
Extract from Bro Alex's Letter

Near Washington D.C. yet, was over to Fort Ethan Allen. Stayed all night with Joseph Keffer. Seen Capt Jno Bierer, Lieut Henry White, and Buntow. They are very nicely fixed in good quarters. Sergeant Sembower is well and we are bunking together. Lieut Cope is now with us, also Springer. Cope has Command of the Company. Capt Weltner is down in Alexandria. Lt Springer had me promoted to Sergt. I would enlist for 3 years more if necessary to drive the rebs from the land.

Comments by Brother Alex

We were soon forwarded to Harrisburgh, Pa. where we were discharged in July 1865, the war being over. I was with the Co all the time, not getting wounded to hurt me much and being well except for some Rheumatism and at one time had a severe spell of Diarrhoea. Scott Hutchison a mess mate of mine died with it. I doctored myself with Burnt Cheese, Gun powder and Whiskey.

Was in some 24 engagements, John Moore and myself being the only ones who was with the Company at all times. And just before the war closed I was recommended for promotion to first Lt of Co by Col McGraw and Lt springer (who by the way was well liked). Also by Brevet Brigadier St Clair A. Mulholland. Lt Springer to be first Lt acting as quarter master independent of the Company. James Collins was recommended for 2nd Lieutenant. Capt Weltner intended to leave the service on acct of his health. We seen hard service. From the Wilderness to the James River we did not have our accoutrements off except for a very short time during a period of 40 days. Battles Wilderness 3 days, Spottsylvania, Cold Harbor and all those fights were hard and losses great on both sides. We were in the Second Corps, ("Hancocks"), 1st Division, 2nd Brigade called Irish Brigade. After our numbers were reduced we were consolidated into the 4th Brigade under Genl Ramsey, Genl Humphrey commanding the Corps. Hancock resigned on acct of wounds, took charge of the Invalid Corps.

May 31st, 1865 — McClelland Hospital, Philada Pa.
Dear Father,

I received your letter of May 27th this morning, and was glad to hear from you, that you was all well &c. You have commenced to look for me too soon. I have idea [*sic*] when I shall get away from here. There was about one hundred men mustered out yesterday, but they were a week getting their papers ready, the regiment will be here the last of this week or the first of next. They will go into Camp here until they are paid off. They will be mustered out of the service at Washington City. As for waiting for Alex I think he will be at home before I do, though if they come here I shall go and see him. When I get to Pittsburgh, I will go to Days office and see whether I can get the one hundred Dollars for my wound or not, but I dont think that I can. If the government does pay that money I think they are very foolish, for there is not many soldiers but what can sport a wound, and it would be only increasing their enormous debt. I think and almost know that it only has reference to those that are discharged on account of disability, and are entitled to it. My leg is a great deal better now, than what it has been since it was done. I can only account for it being so much better by my having to stay in the house all day until after supper. They do not give us any passes until after supper for fear our names might be called for discharge and we would not be in. I only gave twenty five cents to Joseph Renshaw but I suppose he thought it was fifty. I received a letter some days ago from Alex dated May 19th. There has been three or four Penna Regiments mustered out of the service and arrived here. I dont think there is much danger of me getting my discharge this week nor before the last of next. If you write, write soon.

Your Son Daniel Chisholm.

N.B. I copied The list of Battles in which Alex and I have been in from the Philadelphia Inquirer, which gives a short history of the Regt. The Regt has been engaged in twenty-six battles. Alex has been in twenty of them and me in nine. Alex was in as follows. Wilderness, May 5th & 6th

1864. Todds Tavern, May 8th. Po River, May 10th. Spottsylvania, May 12th. Spottsylvania C.H., May 18th. North Anna, May 24th. Pamunkey, May 27th. Tolopotomy, May 31st. Cold Harbor, June 3rd. Petersburgh, June 16th, 17th & 18th. Williams Farm, June 22nd. Strawberry Plains, Deep Bottom, July 27th and August 14th & 21st. Dabneys Mills, Feb'y 5th 1865. On the line in front of Petersburgh from June 25th 1864 until March 28th, 1865. South Side Rail Road, April 2nd 1865. Hatchers Run, Dec 9th 1864. High Bridge, April 6th 1865. Farmsville, April 7th 1865. I was in Wilderness, Todds Tavern, Po River, Spottsylvania, North Anna River, Pamunkey, Tolopotomy, Cold Harbor, Petersburgh.

June 3rd, 1865 — McClellan U.S.A. Genl Hospital, Philada Pa
My last letter

Dear Father,

I seat myself to address you a few lines this pleasant afternoon. My health is good. And I feel pretty good all over, for I think I shall get my discharge the first part of the week. I was called to the room of the surgeon in charge this forenoon and seen him sign my Bird, as the boys call it, and expect to be mustered out the forepart of the week if everything goes right. I have not seen any account of our regiment having arrived here yet, although there has been quite a number of Penna Regts paid off here and at Harrisburgh. If the Regiment comes the forepart of the week it is quite likely that I shall come home with the company. If you have not written an answer to my last letter it will not be worth while to write here any more without further instructions.

Your Son, Daniel Chisholm

Appendix

Listing of Men, Their Rank and Vital Statistics

JOHN R. WELTNER, Captain

> Discharged by special order June 22, 1865.
> Born 1830. Died April 6, 1867, aged 33 yrs, 6 months, 22 days.
> The above is according to his tombstone inscription in the Church
>   Hill Cemetary near McClellandtown, Fayette Co, Pa.
> Date mustered into service April 7, 1864.

JAMES D. COPE, 1st Lieutenant

> Was taken prisoner at William's Farm, Va, June 22nd 1864.
> Was in command of Company at different times on account of the
>   absence of Captain Weltner, sick.
> Commissioned Captain June 22, 1865 — not mustered.
> Mustered out with Company July 14, 1865.
> Date Mustered into service March 17, 1864.

ZADOC B. SPRINGER, 2nd Lieutenant

> Was taken prisoner at Reams Station, Va, August 25, 1864.
> Commissioned Quarter Master, June 3, 1865 — not mustered.
> Mustered out with Company July 14, 1865.
> Born October 12, 1835. Died at noon October 24, 1905.
> Date mustered into service April 7, 1864.

JAMES E. JOLLIFFE, 1st Sergeant

> Wounded at Five Forks, Va, March 31, 1865.
> Absent, in hospital, at muster out.
> Died July 7, 1884.
> Date mustered into service March 31, 1864.

SAMUEL A. CLEAR, 1st Sergeant

> Promoted from Corporal May 29, 1864.
> Wounded at Spottsylvania May 18, 1864.
> Mustered out with Company July 14, 1865.
> Born February 18, 1836.
> Date mustered into service February 29, 1864.

WARREN S. KILGORE, Sergeant

Veteran, served in 85th Regt Penn Vols.
Killed at battle of Spottsylvania, Va, May 12, 1864.
Date mustered into service March 1, 1864.

EDWARD PENCE, Sergeant

Wounded June 16, 1864, near Petersburgh, Va.
Died at Annapolis, Md, in hospital, June 24, 1864.
Date mustered into service February 29, 1864.

WILLIAM H. SEMBOWER, Sergeant

Promoted to Sergeant April 16, 1864.
Mustered out with Company July 14, 1865.
Born August 9, 1829. Died at midnight Wednesday, August 12, 1908.
Date mustered into service February 29, 1864.

JAMES COLLINS, Sergeant

Promoted to Corporal April 16, 1864. To Sergeant December 26, 1864.
Commissioned as 2nd Lieutenant, sent in, not mustered on account of close of war.
Mustered out with Company July 14, 1865.
Born June 6, 1845.
Date mustered into service February 29, 1864.

ALEXANDER CHISHOLM, Sergeant

Promoted from Corporal June 1, 1864.
Commissioned as 1st Lieutenant, sent in, not mustered on account of close of war.
Voluntarily acted as sharpshooter at Cold Harbor and Petersburgh, Va.
Mustered out with Company July 14, 1865.
Born August 26, 1846. [Died June 27, 1927.]
Date mustered into service February 29, 1864.

ROBERT J. BROWNFIELD, Corporal

Wounded near Spottsylvania Court House, Va, May 18, 1864.

Died in hospital June 12, 1864, at Washington, D.C. Buried in National Cemetery, at Arlington.

Date mustered into service February 29, 1864.

RICHARD A. McCLEAN, Corporal

Wounded May 18, 1864, near Spottsylvania Court House, Va. Arm amputated.

Discharged by General Order June 13, 1865.

Born September 15, 1844.

LLOYD PATTERSON, Corporal

Promoted to Corporal, June 4, 1864.

Mustered out with Company July 14, 1865.

Born October 21, 1837. Died October 19, 1904.

Date mustered into service March 30, 1864.

ANDREW J. SEESE, Corporal

Promoted to Corporal March 16, 1865.

Mustered out with Company July 14, 1865.

Date mustered into service March 3, 1864.

GEORGE W. GANOE, Corporal

Promoted to Corporal June 2, 1865.

Mustered out with Company July 14, 1865.

Date mustered into service April 1, 1864.

WILLIAM H. NYCUM, Corporal

Taken prisoner at Williams Farm near Petersburgh, Va, June 22, 1864.

Promoted to Corporal June 2, 1865.

Wounded at Wilderness May 18, 1864.

Mustered out with Company July 14, 1865.

Date mustered into service February 29, 1864.

TIMOTHY McINERNY, Corporal

Promoted to Corporal August 24, 1864. Promoted to Color Bearer.

Wounded at Five Forks, Va, March 31, 1865.

Absent, in hospital, at muster out July 14, 1865.
Served in 11th Penna Reserve Corps.
Date mustered into service March 13, 1864.

DANIEL CHISHOLM, Corporal

Promoted to Corporal March 16, 1864.
Wounded at Petersburgh, Va, June 16, 1864.
Discharged by General Order June 9, 1865.
Date mustered into service February 29, 1864.
Born February 26, 1845. [Died February 9, 1914.]

JACOB ALLAMON, Private

Wounded on Picket May 6, 1864, at Wilderness, Va.
Mustered out with Company July 14, 1865.
Born January 29, 1849.
Date mustered into service February 29, 1864.

JOHN H. BAGSHAW

Wounded at Wilderness, Va, May 5, 1864.
Wounded at Reams Station, Va, August 25, 1864.
Wounded at Five Forks, Va, March 31, 1865.
Absent, in hospital, at muster out July 14, 1865.
Born April 16, 1845. Died May 6, 1895.
Date mustered into service February 15, 1864.

ALFRED J. BAILES

Wounded at Petersburgh, Va, June 16, 1864.
Transferred to Veterans Rescue Corps (Company I 6th Regt
    V.R.C.) January 7, 1865.
Date mustered into service February 29, 1864.

HENRY J. BELL, Veteran

Veteran, served in the 85th Penna Vols.
Killed at Spottsylvania, Court House, Va, May 12, 1864.
Date mustered into service March 23, 1864.

ALFRED W. BOLEN

Veteran, served in the 16th Penna Calvary.

Wounded near Spottsylvania, May 12, 1864.
Mustered into service March 23, 1864.

PARKS A. BOYD

Killed at the Battle of the Wilderness, Va, May 5, 1864.
He was the first man killed in the Company.

WILLIAM P. BRICKER

Veteran, served in the 168th Regt Penna Vols.
Wounded at Wilderness, Va, May 5, 1864.
Transferred to Vet Res Corps 1864.
Died March 23, 1901.
Date mustered into service March 31, 1864.

CHRISTIAN BURKHOLDER

Wounded at Cold Harbor June 3, 1864.
Died at 1st Division, 2nd A.C. Hospital of wounds.
Date mustered into service March 31, 1864.

JOHN CAMPBELL

Wounded at Cold Harbor, Va, June 3, 1864.
Mustered out with Company July 14, 1865.
Date mustered into service March 31, 1864.

JOHN W. CHALFANT

Discharged by General Order June 5, 1865.
Date mustered into service March 22, 1864.

MICHAEL CLEMMER

Killed at Cold Harbor, Va, June 3, 1864.
Date mustered into service March 31, 1864.

WILLIAM N. CONN

Killed near Spottsylvania, Court House, Va, May 18, 1864.
Date mustered into service March 31, 1864.

HEZEKIAH DEAN

> Wounded at Petersburgh, Va, June 17, 1864.
> Mustered out with Company July 14, 1865.
> Date mustered into service February 29, 1864.

STEPHEN H. DEAN

> Wounded and captured at Reams Station, Va, August 25, 1864.
> Died at Salisbury, N.C., December 3, 1864. Burial Record, December 13, 1864.
> Date mustered into service March 30, 1864.

WILLIAM H. DITMORE

> Discharged by General Order June 28, 1865.
> Date mustered into service March 3, 1864.

MICHAEL FISHER

> Wounded at Cold Harbor, Va, June 3, 1864.
> Discharged on Surgeon's Certificate May 18, 1865.
> Died March 4, 1900.
> Date mustered into service March 30, 1864.

ALBERT FRAZIER

> Wounded May 18, 1864.
> Discharged by General Order June 10, 1865.
> Died February 11, 1899, at Granville, West Va.
> Date mustered into service March 24, 1864.

LEVI GILMORE

> Wounded at Cold Harbor, Va, June 3, 1864.
> Died of wounds at Alexandria, Va, Grave #243, June 17, 1864.
>   (Grave #2413 according to Bates History)
>   (Grave #2423 according to John W. Hanan, June 1908)
>   (National Cemetery at Alexandria, Va.)
> Date mustered into service March 31, 1864.

ROBERT GLENDENNING

> Wounded and captured at Williams Farm, Va, June 22, 1864.

Died at Salisbury, N.C. Prison July, 1864.
Date mustered into service March 31, 1864.

WILLIAM HAGER

Mustered out with Company July 14, 1865.
Date mustered into service March 30, 1864.

HENRY HALL

Mustered out with Company July 14, 1865.
Born September, 15, 1844.
Date mustered into service March 23, 1864.

WILLIAM HALL

Died of smallpox, in field Hospital, near Brandy Station, Va.
Date mustered into service March 23, 1864.

GEORGE W. HANAN

Killed at the Battle of the Wilderness, Va, May 6, 1864.
Born February 1814.
Date mustered into service February 29, 1864.

JOSEPH J. HANAN (correct name Thomas J. Hanan)

Died March 27, 1864, Burial Record, Thomas Hayman, at Alexandria, Va, March 29, 1864. Grave #1692. First man (or boy
rather) to die in Corps.
Born April 25, 1849.
Date mustered into service February 29, 1864.

JOHN HAUS

Captured at Williams Farm near Petersburgh, Va, June 22, 1864.
Died in prison at Andersonville, Ga, August 1, 1864. Grave # 4474.
Date mustered into service March 30, 1864.

JOHN R. HAYDEN

Wounded at Po River May 10, 1864.
Mustered out with Company July 14, 1865.
Date mustered into service March 23, 1864.

ABRAHAM HULL

Died at 1st Division, 2nd A.C. Hospital June 23, 1864.
Served in 168th Penna Vols. (Grave #2972 according to John W.
Hanan, June 7, 1904, at National Cemetery, Alexandria, Va)
Date mustered into service March 23, 1864.

JOHN J. HULL, Veteran

Died 1865 at U.S. General Hospital.
Date mustered into service March 23, 1864.

SCOTT HUTCHESON

Died in U.S. General Hospital, Alexandria, Va, July 1864.
Date mustered into service February 29, 1814.

JOHN H. INKS

Wounded at Tolopotomy, Va, May 31, 1864.
Died June 15, 1864. Buried in National Cemetery, Arlington, Va.
Date mustered into service February 24, 1864.

JOSEPH A. JORDAN

Transferred to Company A, 10th Regt Vet Res Corps.
Discharged by General Order July 29, 1865.
Born January 10, 1824. Died January 2, 1901.
Date mustered into service February 29, 1864.

ELIAS LEHMAN

Absent, sick at muster out, July 14, 1865.
Date mustered into service March 31, 1864.

JOHN W. LUCKEY

Taken prisoner while on Picket near Deep Bottom, Va, August 19,
1864.
Exchanged March 13, 1865.
Discharged by General Order June 20, 1865.
Date mustered into service March 29, 1864.

JOSHUA LUCKEY

Died of disease at Alexandria, Va, April 8, 1864. Grave #1724, National Cemetery at Alexandria, Va (according to John W. Hanan, June 7, 1904).
Date mustered into service February 29, 1864.

JOHN McCUEN

Drummer boy, discharged by General Order May 2, 1865.
Disabled by a fall.
Died November 5, 1912.
Date mustered into service February 29, 1864.

JOHN D. MALLORY

Mustered out with Company July 14, 1865.
Taken prisoner while on Picket in front of Petersburgh, Va, October 1, 1864.
Parolled about March 1, 1865.
Born June 3, 1842.
Date mustered into service March 31, 1864.

JACOB MAUST

Died of disease March 28, 1864, at Alexandria, Va. Burial Record, March 29, 1864. Grave #1689 (according to John W. Hanan, June 7, 1904). National Cemetery Alexandria, Va.
Date mustered into service March 3, 1864.

JOHN MOORE

Mustered out with Company July 14, 1865.
Date mustered into service March 29, 1864.

ROSS MORRISON

Wounded at Po River, Va, May 10, 1864.
Discharged by General Order June 7, 1865.
Died June 15, 1910.
Date mustered into service March 30, 1864.

HENRY O. NEAL, Veteran

Served in 85th Regt Penna Vols.
Wounded at Spottsylvania, Va, May 12, 1864.
Mustered out with Company July 14, 1865.
Born December 23, 1834. Died April 15, 1906.
Date mustered into service March 31, 1864.

JACOB PRETTYMAN, Veteran

Served in 11th Penna Vols. Transferred to Vet Res Corps.
Absent, sick, at muster out July 14, 1865.
Date mustered into service February 29, 1864.
Wounded at Battle Wilderness, Va, (according to Bates History).

MILTON RATHBURN

Killed at Spottsylvania, Court House, Va, May 12, 1864.
Date mustered into service February 29, 1864.

DAVID J. RIFFLE

Killed at Williams Farm, Va, June 22, 1864.
Date mustered into service February 29, 1864.

SIMON SAMPSELL

Absent, sick, at muster out July 14, 1865.
Date mustered into service March 28, 1864.

EDMOND SAVAGE

Wounded at Spottsylvania, Court House, Va, May 18, 1864.
Absent at muster out July 14, 1865.
Date mustered into service March 23, 1864.

JOHNATHAN SHEETS

Transferred to Vet Res Corps.
Date mustered into service February 29, 1864.

WILLIAM D. SHIPLEY

Discharged by General Order, June 2, 1865.
Date mustered into service March 31, 1864.

DANIEL SICKLES

Wounded and captured at Spottsylvania C.H., Va, May 12, 1864.
Died at Andersonville, Ga, July 19, 1864. Burial Record, July 19,
1864. Grave #3586.

JAMES SMITH

Wounded at Wilderness, Va, May 6, 1864.
Died at U.S. General Hospital, Annapolis, Md, August 24, 1864
(Burial Record).
Date mustered into service March 31, 1864.

JOHN W. SMITH

Wounded at Cold Harbor, Va, June 3, 1864.
Died June 14, 1864. Buried in National Cemetery at Arlington, Va.
Date mustered into service February 29, 1864.

JOSEPH J. SMITH

Killed at Battle of Spottsylvania, Va, May 12, 1864.
Date mustered into service February 29, 1864.

BENJAMIN TAYLOR

Died May 5, 1864. Buried in Military Asylum Cemetery, D.C.
Died in U.S. General Hospital, Alexandria, Va.
Date mustered into service March 23, 1864.

THOMAS T. THORNDELL

Fifer, killed at Five Forks, Va, March 31, 1865 (last man killed in
action, in the Company).
Born April 4, 1839, in North Leech, Gloucestershire, England.

JOHN TIERNAN, JR.

Killed at Battle of Wilderness, Va, May 6, 1864.
Date mustered into service February 29, 1864.

NEWTON UMBLE

Captured at Reams Station, Va, August 25, 1864.
Died at Salisbury, N.C., October 19, 1864, of pleurisy.
Date mustered into service April 1, 1864.

AARON S. WATSON

Transferred to Veteran Reserve Corps January 24, 1865.
Date mustered into service February 29, 1864.

WILLIAM WHOOLERY

Mustered out with Company July 14, 1865.
Date mustered into service February 29, 1864.

THOMAS B. WILLIAMS

Wounded at Po River, May 10, 1864.
Discharged by General Order June 13, 1865.
Born March 26, 1845.
Date mustered into service February 29, 1864.

JOHN W. WOOD

Honorably discharged on account of eyesight.
Born March 14, 1843. Died at 2 O'clock Saturday, February 5, 1910.
Date mustered into service February 29, 1864.

CHARLES YAUGER

Served in 85th Regt Penna Vols.
Wounded at Cold Harbor, Va, June 13, 1864.
Mustered out with Company July 14, 1865.
Date mustered into service March 23, 1864.

★

Total No of men in Co "K" 116th Regt Penna Vols as recruited to fill up the Company in the months of February and March 1864, 81 including officers and men.

COMMISSIONED OFFICERS

1 wounded but recovered, also prisoner
    Second Lieutenant Zadoc B. Springer, wounded, captured at Reams
        Station, Va, August 25th 1864.
2 taken prisoner and exchanged

First Lieutenant James D. Cope captured at Williams Farm, Va, June 22nd 1864.

Second Lieutenant Zadoc B. Springer captured at Reams Station, Va, August 25th 1864.

1 Escaped from Bullets, Death by disease, or without being captured
Captain John R. Weltner

NON COMMISSIONED OFFICERS

2 killed

Sergeant Warren S. Killgore, Veteran, killed at battle of Spottsylvania, May 12th 1864.

Corporal Daniel Crawford, killed at battle of Spottsylvania, May 18th 1864.

2 died of wounds received in battle

Sergeant Edward Pence, wounded June 16th 1864 at Petersburgh, Va., died at Annapolis, Md, in Hospital, June 24th 1864.

Corporal Robert J. Brownfield, wounded at Spottsylvania, May 18th 1864, died at Washington D.C. in Hospital June 12th 1864.

9 wounded but recovered

First Sergeant James E. Jolliffe at Five Forks, Va, March 31st 1865.

Sergeant Samuel A. Clear at Spottsylvania, Va, May 18th 1864.

Sergeant Alexander Chisholm at Petersburgh, Va.

Corporal Stephen S. Beckett at Petersburgh, Va, June 16th 1864.

Corporal Daniel Chisholm at Petersburgh, Va, June 16th 1864.

Corporal George I. Cruse at Tolopotomy May 31st 1864, and Five Forks, Va, March 31st 1865.

Corporal Richard A. McClean at Spottsylvania, Va, May 18th 1864.

Corporal Timothy McInerny at Five Forks, Va, March 31st 1865.

Corporal William H. Nycum at Spottsylvania, Va, May 18th 1864.

1 taken prisoner and exchanged

Corporal Wm. H. Nycum captured at Williams Ferry, Va, June 22nd 1864.

1 transferred to Vet Res Corps

Corporal George I. Cruse transferred to Vet Res Corps, Co G, 18th Regt.

5 escaped from wounds, death by disease, or without being captured
Sergeant William H. Sembower
Sergeant James Collins
Corporal Lloyd Patterson
Corporal Andrew J. Seese
Corporal George W. Ganoe

PRIVATES

10 killed

Parks A. Boyd, May 5th 1864, at Battle of the Wilderness, Va, 1st man killed.

Henry J. Bell, May 12th 1864, at Battle of Spottsylvania C. House, Va.

William N. Conn, May 18th 1864, at Battle of Spottsylvania C. House, Va.

Michael Clemmer, June 3rd 1864, at Battle of Cold Harbor, Va.

George W. Hanan, May 6th 1864, at Battle of the Wilderness, Va.

David J. Riffle, June 22nd 1864, at Battle of Williams Farm, Va.

Milton Rathburn, May 12th 1864, at Battle of Spottsylvania, Va.

Joseph J. Smith, May 12th 1864, at Battle of Spottsylvania, Va.

John Tiernan, May 6th 1864, at Battle of Wilderness, Va.

Thomas T. Thorndell, March 31st 1864, at Battle of Five Forks, Va.

8 died of wounds received in battle

Christian Burkholder, groin, died at 1st Division 2nd A Corps, Hospital.

Levi Gilmore, foot, died July 17th 1864, at Alexandria, Va. Grave No. 2413.

John H. Inks, leg, died June 15th 1864, buried in National Cemetery, Arlington, Va.

John W. Smith, side & arm, died June 14th 1864, buried in National Cemetery, Arlington, Va.

James Smith, neck, died Aug 24th 1864, at USA Gen'l Hospital, Annapolis, Md.

Daniel Sickles, foot, died July 9th 1864, at Andersonville, Ga. Grave No 3586.

Stephen H. Dean, died Dec 3rd 1864, at Salisbury, N.C.

Robert Glendenning, head, died July 1864, at Salisbury, N.C.

15 wounded but recovered

Jacob Allamon, wounded on Picket, May 6th 1864, at Wilderness, Va.

John H. Bagshaw, wounded at Wilderness, Va, May 5th 1864, also Reams Station, Va, August 25th 1864, Five Forks, Va, March 31st 1865.

Alfred J. Bailes, wounded at Petersburgh, Va, June 16th 1864.

Albert W. Bolen, wounded at Spottsylvania, Va, May 12th 1864

William P. Bricker, wounded at Wilderness, Va, May 5th 1864.

John Campbell, wounded at Cold Harbor, Va, June 3rd 1864.

Hezekiah Dean, wounded at Petersburgh, Va, June 17th 1864.
Michael Fisher, wounded at Cold Harbor, Va, June 3rd 1864.
John R. Hayden, wounded at Po River, Va, May 10th 1864.
Ross Morrison, wounded at Po River, Va, May 19th 1864
Henry O. Neal, wounded at Spottsylvania, Va, May 12th 1864.
Edmund Savage, wounded at Spottsylvania, Va, May 18th 1864.
Thomas B. Williams, wounded at Po River, Va, May 10th 1864.
Charles Yauger, wounded at Cold Harbor, Va, June 3rd 1864.
Albert Frasier, wounded at Spottsylvania, Va, May 18th 1864.

5 taken prisoners and died in prison
    Stephen H. Dean, wounded, captured at Reams Station, Va, August
        25th 1864. Died at Salisbury, North Carolina, Dec 3rd 1864, burial
        record Dec 13th 1864.
    Robert Glendenning, wounded, captured at Williams Farm, Va, June
        22nd 1864. Died at Salisbury, North Carolina, July 1864.
    John Haus, captured at Williams Farm, Va, June 22nd 1864. Died in
        prison at Andersonville, Georgia, August 1st 1864. Grave 4474.
    Daniel Sickles, wounded, captured at Spottsylvania Court House, Va,
        May 12th 1864. Died in prison at Andersonville, Georgia, July 9th
        1864, burial record July 19th 1864. Grave 3586.
    Newton Umble, captured at Reams Station, Va, Aug 25th 1864. Died
        in prison, at Salisbury, North Carolina, October 19th 1864.

1 paroled prisoner, and died shortly afterwards in Hospital
    James Smith

1 exchanged prisoner
    John W. Luckey

6 transferred to Veteran Reserve Corps
    Alfred J. Bailes, transferred to Vet Res Corps June 7th 1865, on acct
        of wound.
    William P. Bricker, transferred to Vet Res Corps 1864, on acct of
        wound.
    Joseph J. Jordan, transferred to Vet Res Corps, Co A, 10th Regt, dis-
        ease.
    Jacob Prettyman, transferred to Vet Res Corps on acct of disease.
    Johnathan Sheets, transferred to Vet Res Corps on acct of disease.
    Aaron Watson, transferred to Vet Res Corps Jany 24th 1865, on acct
        of disease.

4 escaped from wounds, death by disease, or without being captured
William Hager
Henry Hall
John Moore
William Whoolery

6 died of disease

William Hall
Joseph J. Hanan
Scott Hutcheson
Abraham Hull
Joshua Luckey
Jacob Maust

1 discharged on acct of wounds
Michael Fisher

★

Total number of men killed of the Company 1 K 116th Regt P.V.12. Died of wounds received in battle 10, and of being confined in Southern Prisons 5, and of Disease 6. Making total number of Deaths in the Company while in service 33, being in service about 16 months. Wounded 26. Taken prisoners and exchanged 4. Transferred to Veteran Reserve Corps 7. Escaped from Death by Bullet, Disease or without being captured 11. Making the total number of the strength of the Company 81 men. Of these, [12] never did any active duty, leaving [69] that started in on the campaign in camp near Brandy Station on the night of May 3, 1864 at 10 O'clock, and going into battle in the evening of May 5 between the hours of three and four O'clock. At this time, Feby 18, 1899, So far as we know, there has been since the war 22 deaths among the survivors and they are now living and accounted for 25 survivors, and one unaccounted for.

★

When General George A. Stewart, formerly of Baltimore was captured and brought to General Hancock, on the 12th of May at Spottsylvania, the latter proffered his hand to his prisoner. Stewart, with a ridiculous assumption of dignity, refused the civility and replied that under the circumstances his feelings did not permit him to shake hands. Hancocks response, keen but courteous, was — "It is only under the circumstances of your being a prisoner that I offered my hand."

Sherman's March to the Sea

by S.H.M. Byers.

Our camp fires shone bright on the mountains
That formed on the river below,
While we stood by our guns in the morning
And eagerly watched for the foe —
When a rider came out from the darkness
That hung over mountain and tree
And shouted "Boys up and be ready
For Sherman will march to the sea."

Then cheer upon cheer for bold Sherman
Went up from each Valley and Glen
And the bugles re-echoed the music
That came from the lips of the men,
For we knew that the stars in our banner
More bright in their splendor would be,
And that blessings from Northland would greet us
When Sherman marched down to the sea.

Then forward boys forward to battle
We marched on our dangerous way,
And we stormed the wild hills of Resaca
God bless those who fell on that day,
Then Kenesaw dark in its glory
Frowned down on the flag of the free,
But the East and the West bore our Standards,
And Sherman marched on to the sea.

Still onward we pressed till our banners
Swept out from Atlanta's grim walls
And the blood of the patriot dampens
The sail where the traitor flag falls;
But we paused not to weep for the fallen
Who slept by each river and tree
Yet we twined them a wreath of the laurel
As Sherman marched down to the sea.

Oh! proud was our army that morning
That stood where the pine darkly towers,
When Sherman said "Boys, you are weary,

This day fair Savannah is ours."
Then sang we a song for our chieftain
That echoed o'er river and lea
And the stars in our banner shone brighter,
When Sherman marched down to the sea.

(Copied by Saml Holey for D. Chisholm, March 18th, 1898.
— Recopied by D. Chisholm.)

The Veterans Reunion

We met at Chickamanga. I hadn't seen
   him since
We looked across the trenches, and his
   bullet made me wince;
But we both shook hands in friendship,
   as hearty as could be.
Though he had marched with Sherman,
   and I had marched with Lee.

We walked across the battlefield, where
   once the bullets flew,
And the green and bending grasses felt
   The fall of crimson dew;
And we talked the whole thing over,
   where the flag was waving free —
How he had marched with Sherman, and
   I had served with Lee.

The drums had ceased their beating, we
   saw no sabres shine;
The hair about his forehead fell as snowy
   white as mine,
And voices seemed to call us o'er the far,
   eternal sea,
Where the men who marched with Sherman
   are in camp with those of Lee.

We parted; eyes grew misty, for we knew
   that nevermore
We'd meet until the roll-call on the other
   peaceful shore;
But both shook hands in friendship, as
   hearty as could be,
Though he had marched with Sherman,
   and I had fought with Lee.

— Frank L. Stanton

Jacob Prettyman's Obituary Page

Jacob Prettyman, died at his late home on West Berkely St. Uniontown, Penna, Wednesday, June 29, 1898, at 11 O'Clock P.M. of General Debility in the 74th year of his age. Deceased had been in poor health and a crippled condition for years and his death was not unexpected. He was born in Delaware on December 4, 1824, and came to Uniontown when a young man. Being a blacksmith by trade, he secured a position with the Stockton Stage Company and worked in their yards at this place till near the breaking out of the rebellion, when he enlisted in the 11th Penna Volunteers "Reserves" and went to the front, serving the full time that famous regiment was in the field. While employed in stage yard he became widely known to all the teamsters and others who had to do with the famous road. After coming home from the rebellion, he secured work in the Miller Foundry at this place and was there employed for a number of years. He leaves a wife and two sons John and Thomas by his first wife, having been married the second time. Funeral at 2 O'clock Friday afternoon, June 1, 1898, interment in Oak Grove Cemetery.

The above was printed in the "Daily News Standard", and is only partially correct. Mr. Prettyman did not serve the full time that the 11th penna Vol Reserves were in the field. He having been unwell, was discharged from that regiment and in February enlisted in Co "K" 116 Regt Pa Vols, was in several battles and was transferred to the Veteran Reserve Corps. Also in regard to his working at the Stockton Stage Company's yards until the beginning or near it of the rebellion is not correct. Before the war for some time he had been working at Millers foundry. Stockton's yards were not being operated for some time before the war.

John R. Weltner
Obituary
Died April 6th, 1867

At the residence of Charles S. Seaton, Esqr in Uniontown, of Consumption, Capt John R. Weltner, son of John and Elizabeth Weltner, of German Township, in the 37th year of his age.

At the breaking out of the rebellion Capt Weltner was among the first to rally at the call of his country. In the summer and fall of 1861, he recruited company "I" of the 85th Pa Regt, and was commissioned Captain by Gov Curtin. He served faithfully with the regiment up till after the disastrous campaign on the Peninsula, participating in the battles of Yorktown, Williamsburg, Fair Oaks, and the seven days battle before Richmond. In consequence of exposure and hardships in the Swamps of the Peninsula during this Campaign, he contracted the disease of which he finally died, and which compelled him to resign. He came home and after regaining his health, raised another Company — "K" 116th Regt P.V. and was again commissioned Captain by the same Governor. With his Company he was sent right to the front, and in a few days, with the Army under Genl Grant, went into the fight at the "Wilderness" and participated with his brave company in nearly every fight on up to Petersburgh.

When Grant made his final blow, Capt Weltner was in command of the 116th Regt, all the field officers having been before that time killed or disabled, so hard had been the service of the regiment. Captain Weltner handled the regiment with great skill and bravery, and was handsomely complimented by his superiors for it. He continued in command of the regiment and participated in the several battles immediately preceding Lee's surrender and had the proud satisfaction of being present with the army that compelled it, and of having done his full share as a patriot and brave man in the great struggle. He was mustered out of the service in the summer of 1865 and returned home.

His constitution however was shattered, and it was only periodically that he could attend to business. At last, his disease assumed a stronger hold upon him, and he was confined to his room for nine weeks, when death came to relieve him from earthly sufferings and another of our countries young heroes was carried to an honored grave.

"How sleep the brave who sink to rest,
By all their country's wishes blest!"

Copied from John Cope's Diary

The following is copied by myself (Daniel Chisholm) from a book loaned me by Mr John Cope that belonged to and was kept by his brother Lt James D. Cope of Company "K" 116 Regiment P.V., of which Company I was a member. The book that was used as a memorandum or diary was found on the battlefield near Petersburgh, Va, June 22, 1864 — near the place Lt Cope was taken prisoner. At the same time and place William H. Nycum, John Haus and Robert Glendenning died in prison in July 1864. Also the Serg and Major of our Regiment was captured at the same time; his name was William J. Burk. There was also confined in the confederate Military Prison at Macon, Georgia at the same time that Lt Cope was there Capt and A.A.G. Anderson Stewart; also Capt John Hayden, Company "F" 11 Penna R Corps; and as cook at same time, Lt Chas D. Livingstone 1st Va Pav.

DARK DAYS

At the same time Lt Cope was taken prisoner there was a number of other officers taken, Sixty seven (67) in all. They were taken to Richmond, Virginia and confined in Libby Prison on June 24, 1864 and received on that day rations of corn bread, on the 25th received rations of corn bread, meat and bean soup. Sunday, June 26 still at Libby, had preaching by Rev Hudson who is a prisoner. 27th still in Libby. Blankets issued to 115 officers. Health good. Was visited by a surgeon from Rebel service, and hospital steward from U.S. Army drew rations, corn bread, pork, bean soup, vinegar, salt and soap — small rations. Monday, 28th still in Libby. Washed my pants. Drew the usual rations. Day past off with a rumor that we were to go in the morning to Georgia. Tuesday, June 29, got up early and had breakfast early to go some place, do not know where, all packed up ready. We start and are now on the cars on the south side of the river and are hungry for something to eat. Rode all day and all night, and waked up after a small and tiresome sleep on the bottom of the car. June 30 at Lynchburg, Va. Start and march a short distance from Lynchburgh and camp for the night. Drew rations at Lynchburgh for four days. Said to be going to Danville, Va. July 1, start about sun up on the march, feel rather bad after being sick all night with pain in the right side. Stopped for breakfast in a flat meadow, take breakfast consisting of water and hard tack made of coarse rye meal — 65 to 70 miles to Danville. Stopped for the night on a little river called Stanton River and remained there until morning. July 2, waked up with the word pack up. So I got up — all hands ready to go. The morning is pleasant but I feel stiff. 25 miles to go to day, 50 miles to Danville. Stopped for breakfast after a short march — start — stopped at a stream called Stink River. Watered. Started anew and stopped for the night at a creek or river called Georgia River. July 3rd, broke camp and start with a large squad of citizens to guard us, went four (4) miles towards Pittsylvania Court House and stopped for breakfast, start and pass Pittsylvania Court House, a nice little place. It was Sunday and the negroes were out en masse to see the Yankees pass, thinking it must be all of Grants army. Stopped for the night on a small stream by the name of Dannestan. July 4, started on the march, said we have eleven miles to go without water — we are at the water and resting, 5 miles to Danville. This morning, Citizens gave the officers some bread and last night Major Scaggs of Pittsylvania Court house came and gave us some bread and meat. Arrived at Danville about noon and was placed in a house with a guard marching backward and forward, orders to move in half an hour. Received two days rations, one of corn and one of hard tack and bacon. Start for the cars — arrive and now are sitting on the ground waiting to get on the train. Get on and start — arrive at Greenboro, North Carolina. Forty-Eight (48) miles from Danville, Va. July 5, 1864, drew rations at Greenboro Va., consisting of hard tack and bacon and start for South again. Arrived at Charlotte, South Carolina and got off to camp for the night. July 6, 1864, wake up alive and get something to eat, move to the other side of the railroad to get in the shade, lay all day and now evening, ordered to go to the other side of town to camp until morning. And then I suppose we will go on our journey — did not start until morning, July 7, 1864. Started and moved up to the Junction and stayed a short time — started again and got along slow, stopped at Columbia, South Carolina all night July 8th. Left Columbia for Augusta, Georgia, arrived at Augusta about 11 O'clock a.m. at night. Layed all night near the railroad, and left in the morning, July 9, 1864. Moved a piece from our old place and found it no better. Arrived at Macon, July 10, went into camp when we found sixteen hundred and thirty officers of the U.S. Army and Navy. Met Capt Andrew J. Stewart and Capt James Hayden of Uniontown. How long we will stay here I cannot say. July 11, 1864 still in Camp at Macon, Ga. Also 12—13 and on up to July 27. On this day 600 started for Charleston, South Carolina. 28th — 600 more started. July 29th got up and commanded to bake corn bread, to move off at about 4 O'clock P.M. Commenced to count off the prisoners, counted out and stayed between the stockade and dead line until O'clock [sic]. Started for the cars, arrived about 3 O'clock in the morning on the cars. News came

that our raiders was close to us, and we were taken back to camp about daylight, July 30. July 31 in the same old prison. Monday morning, August 1, 1864 at Confederate Military Prison at Macon, Ga. Stonemans raiders are not about as we can learn. Report says they are captured, evening dark. Gen Stoneman and about 30 of his officers came into prison, it caused quite a sad feeling among the officers to hear of the captures of Stoneman. Well I never was so hungry as I was this day, as our rations ran out yesterday. August 2, 3, 4, 5, 6, great news of exchange of 50 general and field officers that was sent to Charleston are reported to be exchanged — God grant an exchange in effected rations rather smaller than usual. Excitement this morning on exchange. Spirits of the camp good at this time. August 7, 1864. Exchange news rather dull at this time, but still a prospect. Report says we go tomorrow Tuesday, August 8 to Charleston, and another report says we go by squad of 300. August 8, 9, 10 and 11. 300 officers started for Charleston this morning, leaving the 1st and 2nd lots to go tomorrow. They are staying at the old camp. August 12, 1864, did not go but to go tomorrow, August 13, 1864. All packed ready to go and the bell has rung for us to fall into start. Start — get on the cars — cars leave the depot for Augusta. Arrive at Augusta August 14, 64 change cars and guard for Charleston, South Carolina. Arrive at Charleston about dusk, get off the cars for the purpose of being conveyed to prison, so off we go for the workhouse — Arrive there and find it a nice looking building outside, but a hell hole inside, go in and take quarters out in the yard for the night. August 15, 1864, moved up in the third story in a cell and a damned dirty one it is. Drew rations of hard tack and bacon. August 16, 1864, drew rations of flour, meal, rice, soap, salt and molasses, hard stuff.
August 17 to August 22 still at the same place. Shells commenced coming near us from our guns in the afternoon and continued that day and night.
August 23, 1864 still on hands in the same yard, and the shells still fly as usual.
Wednesday, August 24, 25, 26, 27, 28, and 29, 1864. Firing still goes on and the shells burst a short distance from us. Refused our or a portion of our rations today, and may not get any more today. There goes a shell now.
August 30, 1864. Still in the old place, the jail yard. Rations slim.
August 31, 1864. We have not received any rations of any account for several days.
September 1, 1864. Morning clear and cool, prospect of a nice day. No rations on hand for breakfast, still in hopes of exchange.

September 2. Day nice, but night cool. Shells continue to come.

September 3. Nice and warm. 4th still the same. 5th moved from jail yard to workhouse. 6th drew rations of rice for four days. 7th nothing to eat but rice and beef. 8th and 9th the same.

September 10. Drew rations for 10 days and tolerably good.

September 11. Drew rations today, not very much. 21st drew more beans and molasses.

September 22, 1864. Three (3) months since I was captured. Did nothing but eat today.

September 23, 1864. Flag of truce today (Early defeated). 24th morning nice. A lot of Sherman's men to go off. 25th Sunday, all quiet, headache bad.

September 26, 1864, Monday. Shells last night came close to house.

September 27, 1864, Tuesday. Nice day. Genl Stoneman exchanged.

September 28, 1864, Wednesday. Nice Day. Received rations of beef.

September 29, 1864, Thursday. Shelling still goes on.

September 30, 1864, Friday. Gun boat officers gone for exchange.

October 1, 1864, Saturday, 2, 3, 4. All nice days, and the shells continue to fly. 5th ordered to be moved to Columbia. 6th leave for Columbia at 5 O'Clock a.m.

October 7 arrive at Columbia about 3 O'clock a.m.

October 8 to camp about 2½ miles out.

October 9 in camp. No tents and no meat. From the 10th to November 1, 1864 at camp Sorghum, S.C. 1st Lieut James D. Cope, William H. Nycum and Robert Glendenning and John Haus were all captured on Williams Farm near Petersburgh, Va., by Mahoners Brigade of A.P. Hills Corps. Nycum, Glendenning, and Haus were taken to prison at Andersonville, Georgia, and Lieut Cope to Macon, Ga., and from there to Charleston, South Carolina.

Prices of articles in 1864 in Southern Confederacy in money as quoted by Lt Cope. Greenback $1, $10 and upwards. Flour for $300, bread pr loaf from $1 to $2. Eggs pr dozen $4 to $7. Tin cup $5 to $8. Tin plate $5, 1 gallon stone jug $5. 1 gallon tin bucket $10. Matches pr block $1. Tomatoes pr doz $2, shoes $75, boots $200 to $300 per pair. Small bar of soap $10. Canteens $15. Tooth brush $6. Deck of cards $12, bullets for $6 to $10. Molasses pr gal $6, Irish potatoes $30 to $40 pr bus. Black berries pr qt $1, watermelons from 5 to $10 each, black pepper can ground $20, apples pr doz 2 to $3. Baking soda per tablespoonful $1, peaches pr doz $3, knife and fork $8.50, beans pr qt $1, beef steak pr lb $4 to $6. Green corn pr doz $3.50 to $4.00. Corn meal pr qt $1, chickens pr pair $30. Sweet potatoes $80 pr bus, cabbage per head $5 to $7.

★ OBITUARY ★

The following is Daniel Chisholm's obituary as it appeared in the
Uniontown, Pennsylvania, *Morning Herald* on February 10, 1914.

DANIEL CHISHOLM DIES FOLLOWING LENGTHY ILLNESS

VETERAN LAYS DOWN HIS ARMS IN UNEQUAL BATTLE

Pioneer Uniontown Merchant Battles Valiantly, but Loses Uneven Struggle With Grim Reaper

Suffered a Stroke Over a Year Ago

Complications Later Developed, but Turning Point Came Last Month When Aged Resident Gradually Declined — Funeral Arrangements Not Completed

Daniel Chisholm, Uniontown's oldest merchant and a lifelong resident of Fayette county, died at his home, 150 Morgantown street, at 6:15 o'clock last evening. He was approaching his sixty-ninth birthday. Death came after an illness of 18 months. On August 3, 1912, he suffered a stroke of paralysis. Complications later set in, and during the last month he had been seriously ill. The turning point in his sickness came on last January 10. Since that time he fought gamely, his rugged vitality keeping him up.

Funeral arrangements have not yet been completed, but will be announced some time today. Surviving are his widow, Mrs. Sarah A. Chisholm; two sons, Alexander Chisholm, Jr., and Clarke McQ. Chisholm; a brother Alexander Chisholm, Sr.; a sister, Miss Jennie Chisholm, and one granddaughter, Miss Sarah Eleanor Chisholm, all of Uniontown.

A pioneer merchant in Uniontown, Daniel Chisholm was one of the best known men in Fayette county, and had a wide circle of friends throughout the state. He was born in German township, February 26, 1845. He was a son of the late Alexander and Mary Ann Williams Chisholm, the former a native of Halifax, Nova Scotia. His father was of Scotch blood, the clan of Chisholm having a prominent place in the chronicles of the history of Scotland about the year 1315. The plaid worn by the famous Chisholm clan in the Highlands is still worn in the mountains of Scotland. In the reign of King David Bruce, Sir Robert Chisholm was a powerful northern baron. In Strathglass, Inverness, among the rugged crags of the Highland country was Erchless castle, the Chisholm stronghold. Near this place, William Chisholm, the great-great-grandfather of Daniel Chisholm, was born.

His son, William Chisholm, emigrated to the United States in 1822, and died near Goff's Mills, Preston county, Va. This William Chisholm's son, Alexander, was born in Scotland and came to America, settling in Halifax, Nova Scotia. He afterward moved to Oakland, Md. In 1837 his son Alexander moved to Fayette county, near Uniontown, where he spent his life. He was married on May 26, 1841, to Mary Ann Williams, daughter of Daniel and Jemima Williams. He died December 22, 1891. Her death came February 7, of the same year.

Their son, Daniel Chisholm, married Sarah Ann Clarke on May 16, 1878. To this union were born two sons, Alexander, born January 19, 1879, and Clarke McQueen, born March 25, 1884.

Daniel Chisholm attended school in German township, and after completing the course there, came to Uniontown where he studied for one term. He worked with an uncle at the manufacture of brick, and later obtained a position in the dry goods store of the late Ewing Brownfield, remaining there until in February, 1864.

It was at this time that he patriotically answered the call of his country and enlisted in Company K, One Hundred and Sixteenth Pennsylvania Volunteer Infantry. His regiment was a part of the army corps which fought through the severe campaign of 1864. Daniel Chisholm fought for his country with that same pride that his ancestors had driven back the foe in the historic battles in the Scottish highlands. It was just a few days before his death that Mr. Chisholm received a bronze medal, an award from the United States Congress to the veterans of the Civil war. He was the first veteran in Fayette county to receive this honor.

Returning to Uniontown at the close of the war, Mr. Chisholm was employed by W. H. Baily and by J. A. Modisette, druggists. In 1878 he established a millinery and dry goods store in Pittsburgh street. He was unusually successful. In 1893, he moved his store to 27 West Main street, its present location. Up until the time of his illness he was actively connected with the management of the store, enjoying a large business.

Daniel Chisholm was a member of the William F. Stewart Post No. 180, Grand Army of the Republic. He was also a member of the First Presbyterian Church of Uniontown.

★ AFTERWORD ★

As a little boy I enjoyed passing endless hours playing soldier, imagining that I was a conqueror, and a hero of my nation. My grandmother gave me a book that contained the remembrances of a real soldier, one who fought for his country—my great-great-grandfather, Daniel Chisholm. Incredible pride and honor rushed through me with every new passage, imagining that I too was that soldier. *What was it like? How did he feel?* I wondered.

While in college I wondered no longer. A friend and I decided to join the Marine Corps, and some of that wonderment became a quick reality. Military indoctrination abruptly began when we were introduced to our drill instructor. Parris Island, South Carolina, is one of the best places to teach a youngster the art of war, especially with its muggy summer days and surplus of sand fleas. Still, we survived—but only because we were trained to survive. We soon believed that anywhere on the planet would be a far better place to go to war than this dreaded island surrounded by swamps.

Romantic visions of the military attract men into the service. I'm sure that idea had something to do with my decision to enter the Marines, as I'm sure it also had something to do with my ancestors' decisions. Along with Daniel and Alex Chisholm on my grandmother's side of the family, my grandfather's great uncle, Zadoc B. Springer, was a lieutenant in the same company that left Uniontown, Pennsylvania. Side by side these men fought, unbeknownst to them that two generations later their offspring would unite their two families in marriage.

The name *Chisholm* is of Anglo-Norman origin; soon after the Norman conquest the family founded a small but independent Highland clan and established itself in Roxburghshire and later in Inverness-shire, Scotland. Their principal seat was Erchless Castle and their chief was known as "the Chisholm." There was a familiar saying in Scotland that there were four "the's" in the Highlands: "the Chisholm, the MacIntosh, the Devil, and the Pope." *Chisholm* itself signifies "gravelly island."

The first mention of the name was in 1296, when Richard de Chisholm swore allegiance to Edward III, and signed the Ragman's roll. His son Sir John de Chisholms, knight, fought with Robert Bruce at the famous battle of Banuockburn in 1314.

Chisholms first appeared in America in New England in 1653, represented by Thomas Chisholm. Later, in 1717, Alexander Chisholm (the first of many Alexanders) emigrated to the province of Carolina and settled near Charlestown (now Charleston). The Chisholm plantation, called "The Retreat," was headquarters for Sir Richard Lee during the Revolutionary War.

On October 9, 1838, Alexander Chisholm, son of the Alexander who settled in Carolina, became a United States citizen, and was sworn in under the Alleghany County Court, state of Maryland. This Alexander was the father of the Daniel and Alexander who fought in the Civil War.

My grandmother's father, Alex Chisholm (Daniel's son), attended Redstone Academy in Uniontown, Pennsylvania, where he met a fellow named George Marshall. From there the two went on to further their military education. Alex attended Cheltenham Military Academy and Marshall attended Virginia Military Institute. Upon graduation Alex went on to Penn State University and Marshall joined the U.S. Army, becoming a general and later chief of staff. He and Alex remained close friends. Alex often visited Washington, D.C., to join George for horseback rides and was present for many of his decorations at the capital during World War II.

The Chisholms were known as good writers. Catherine Chisholm, cousin of my great-grandfather Alex, wrote plays, one of which was *Topsy and Eva* for the Duncan sisters, which opened on Broadway in 1924. Bell Z. Chisholm wrote novels and children's stories, which I read when I was young. Not one to miss out on the act, my great-grandfather Alex was the editor of the Uniontwon *Daily News Standard.* Later he came out with his own newspaper, *The Independent.*

My mother's family remained in Uniontown and my grandfather, William Fulton Springer, became a prominent dentist. He graduated from the University of Pittsburgh in 1925. As an undergraduate he worked as a soda jerk in a local pub. My grandmother graduated from Chatham College in 1925, and married my grandfather on August 3, 1929. She was a teacher in the Uniontown public school system.

Uniontown, Pennsylvania, known for its coal mining and its coke ovens for the early steel mills, has seen its share of American history, especially during the French and Indian Wars and the American Revolution. Fort Necessity is where young George Washington and his men made winter quarters while fighting the French and Indians. Near Fort Necessity is the grave of the famous British general Edward Braddock. I remember my grandparents taking me on picnics to the fort and surrounding battlefields. I remember standing on the same ground where George Washington had stood, looking into the fields and tree lines for Indian scouts.

For my eighth birthday my grandparents took me to Gettysburg, to see its battlefield and monuments. I was in awe of the entire setting, its battlefields lined with cannon and grassy knolls marked with historic artifacts. I still find it hard to believe that such a bloody battle could have happened in such a beautiful, peaceful place.

The days of the American Civil War are gone, yet the memory of the men who fought and served our country, men like Daniel and Alex Chisholm, will live on. They were "regular guys" who, when called upon, were happy they weren't as scared in the first battle as they thought they would be. If ever I may be called to serve my country in war, I hope I serve as well and as honorably as they. May we all touch elbows someday.

William Springer Menge

Index